Cognition, Education, and Communication Technology

Edited by

Peter Gärdenfors
Petter Johansson
Lund University

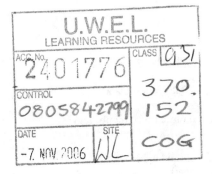

2005

LAWRENCE ERLBAUM ASSOCIATES, PUBLISHERS
Mahwah, New Jersey   London

Lawrence Erlbaum Associates, Inc., Publishers
10 Industrial Avenue
Mahwah, New Jersey 07430
www.erlbaum.com

Cover design by Kathryn Houghtaling Lacey

Library of Congress Cataloging-in-Publication Data

Cognition, education, and communication technology / Peter
  Gärdenfors, Petter Johansson.
    p. cm.
  Includes bibliographical references and index.
  ISBN 0-8058-4279-9 (cloth : alk. paper)
  ISBN 0-8058-4280-2 (pbk. : alk. paper)
  1. Cognitive learning. 2. Education—Effect of technological in-
  novations on. 3. Information technology. I. Gärdenfors, Peter.
  II. Johansson, Petter.
LB1062.C643   2005
370.15'2—dc22
                                           2004053338
                                                CIP

Books published by Lawrence Erlbaum Associates are printed on acid-
free paper, and their bindings are chosen for strength and durability.

Printed in the United States of America
10 9 8 7 6 5 4 3 2 1

In memory of Mike Scaife,
1948–2001

Contents

Preface

Information and communication technology (ICT) is seen as having great potential for revolutionizing education. Large investments in terms of computers and political commitments are made. Often times these commitments of resources do not include an equally strong understanding of how ICT will or should be implemented. The expectation is that students will show immediate improvements in terms of their motivation to learn and their learning achievements. The reality is different. It is not simply the number of computers in the classrooms that is the bottleneck of the progress of ICT in education. Above all, it is our lack of understanding of the complex processes contributing to human learning and how they interact with new technologies.

What is missing in much of the current debate is a theoretical perspective on the learning processes that can be used as a foundation for creative recommendations of how to construct pedagogically valuable tools based on ICT. Such a perspective will also result in grounded recommendations on how learning processes, with or without the support of ICT, should be evaluated. In particular, theories concerning how learning can be mediated by ICT ought to build on what is known about human cognitive processes.

Our purpose in this book is to present some of the recent theoretical developments in the cognitive and educational sciences and the implications for the use of ICT in the organization of school and university education. This book is a collection of articles by internationally renowned researchers who combine a theoretical perspective with proposals for and evaluations of educational practices. What is special about the book is its combination of the results from cognitive science and pedagogy with more practically oriented suggestions for how ICT can or should be used in various forms of education. This combination makes the book suitable for researchers and

ix

students in the cognitive and educational sciences as well as for practitioners and planners of education.

The articles in this book connect central questions in cognitive science with educational practices, some with an emphasis on the relation between theory and educational practice, some with an emphasis on practice. In the articles, different aspects of the use of ICT in education are discussed such as the role of perceptual processes in learning, external cognition as support for interactive learning, the role of metacognition, simulation learning environments as cognitive tools, the role of science controversy for knowledge integration, the use of ICT in the development of educators, and the role of narratives in education.

The editors' introductory chapter (Johansson & Gärdenfors, chap. 1, this volume) begins with a discussion of what a theory of learning should look like. We contrast three objectives: (a) a descriptive theory of the processes of learning, (b) a prescriptive theory of instruction derived from or anchored at the descriptive level, and (c) a theory of instructional design with recommendations for the use of ICT. The main part of the chapter is a survey and comparison of some of the more influential theories of learning: behaviorism, classical cognitivism, constructivism (Piaget), the sociocultural perspective (Vygotsky), and situated cognition. Chapter 1 (this volume) also relates the articles in the volume to these theories. The theoretical overview in the introduction together with the general accessibility of the chapters will make the volume suitable to use as a textbook.

Chapter 2 (this volume) by Dan Schwartz, Taylor Martin, and Na'ilah Nasir begins by noting that in cognitive psychology, the general methodological strategy has been to identify distinct cognitive mechanisms by studying each mechanism in isolation from the rest of the system. However, this does not give much guidance when trying to model how one learns more complex ideas or abilities in educational situations in which multiple cognitive mechanisms work in concert. Schwartz et al. (chap. 2, this volume) advocate an alternative approach called "design for knowledge evolution." The main idea is to expose the knowledge of the student to a process of "natural selection" in which ideas can mutate, grow, and adapt by "surviving" in different environments. As an application, Schwartz et al. describe a study that taught children descriptive statistics. The study not only measured the students' abilities to apply what they had learned, but it also examined their abilities to evolve new knowledge when placed in new contexts.

In chapter 3 (this volume), Lydia Plowman points out the importance of a narrative structure for understanding in educational settings. Plowman emphasizes the dialogic process of narrative guidance and narrative construction. One of the main functions of the teacher is to provide a coherent structure in the learning material despite its fragmented nature. Plowman examines under what circumstances interactive educational multimedia can provide a narrative structure, trying to find a balance between freedom and linearity for the students' interaction with the material. Plowman describes an empirical study in which she investigated the link between narrative structures on a CD-ROM and support for learning.

The starting point for Lauren Resnick, Alan Lesgold, and Megan Hall in chapter 4 (this volume) is that the goal of producing active learners will require that teachers and school leaders are provided with opportunities to reflect on the educational needs. To achieve this, Resnick et al. propose a hierarchical educational system in which the teacher acts as a facilitator or guide in the classroom. On the next level, Resnick et al. put the teacher in the role of the apprentice in a group consisting of other teachers, with the principal as facilitator. The principals of a district form yet another study group, and so on. The aim of this layered organizational setup is to promote continuous learning for all participants in the educational system. However, it also provides an ideal environment for spreading theoretical insights about teaching and learning. Resnick et al. developed new software designed to further teachers' understanding of learning processes that gives them a common framework to evaluate their teaching practice.

William Clancey (chap. 5, this volume) takes as a starting point that the educational system launching into widespread use of ICT without an adequate theory to relate perceptual processes to conceptual learning. Clancey reviews the symbolic approach to perceptual processing and shows its limitations for explaining the difficulties children encounter in interpreting a graphic display. In Clancey's alternative analysis, perceptual categorization is coupled to behavior sequences in which gesturing and emotional changes are essential for resolving impasses. To illustrate this approach, Clancey analyzes a log of two students trying to solve a math problem. Clancey shows that the symbolic model cannot account for all the intricacies of human perceptual understanding and that we are far from having a complete theory of how this understanding is accomplished. Clancey also rules out the construction of a tutoring-like computer program that understands what the student is doing or thinking, as one does not know how to model the cognitive processes of the student in the first place.

Chapter 6 (this volume) by David Kirsh explores the metalevels of learning. Kirsh's concerns are how to use external cognition as a tool in metacognition and how to teach students to structure their own learning. The design of electronic-learning systems can be improved by structuring the visual display of learning contexts to facilitate metacognition. Typically, page layout, navigational appearance, and visual and interactivity design are not viewed as significant factors in metacognition. To the contrary, Kirsh argues that the way visual cues are structured can make a difference. Documents that make effective use of markers such as headings, callouts, and italics can improve students' ability to comprehend documents. Kirsh concludes that once metacognition has been incorporated in the situated and distributed perspective, a better understanding of how to create good visual design in learning will be achieved.

In chapter 7 (this volume), Mike Scaife and Yvonne Rogers argue that situated cognition is an ideal research paradigm for the new field of educational technology. Scaife and Rogers' focus is on the ways that technologies can allow new forms of representations and how these might be exploited for learning. In Scaife and Rogers' empirical work, the focus lies on how to use virtual worlds and avatars to improve children's capacity to change perspectives. The strategy implemented in the software is to make the students actively explore multiple representations of a concept at different levels of abstraction. Scaife and Rogers emphasize the study of the cognitive benefits that particular representational formats and technologies may provide what he calls an analysis of "cognitive interactivity."

Like Clancey, Jonas Ivarsson and Roger Säljö also present, in chapter 8 (this volume), a nonstandard theory of visual perception and explore what consequences it may have on an understanding of conceptual development and learning. From a Vygotskyan perspective, the use of artifacts and tools is an integrated aspect of the human cognitive abilities—the authors think with our things. This holds not only for physical objects but for symbolic artifacts as well, such as words, numbers, charts, diagrams, maps, and so forth. So how can we understand the relation between cultural artifacts and the cognitive development of children? Ivarsson and Säljö argue that there is no such thing as how things really look, but our perceptions are always filtered by our interpretations of the world. In their empirical work, Ivarsson and Säljö study to what extent children understand the theory of gravity in relation to the spherical shape of the earth. This is an exploratory case study of how young children growing up in the digital age handle a certain kind of digital representation. Ivarsson and Säljö primarily analyze the nature of reasoning the children engage in and how it is coordinated with the technology at hand.

Marcia Linn explores the notion of scientific controversy in chapter 9 (this volume). This is used as means to teach the essence of science— construction of arguments, interpretation of data, the ongoing debate between opposing opinions, and so forth. To extend the impact of science instruction, Linn studies "pivotal cases" and offers criteria to help designers create new pivotal cases. Comparisons of courses with and without pivotal cases show how examples can take advantage of the interpretive, cultural, and deliberate character of the learner. Using the Web-based Inquiry Science Environment learning environment that was developed by Linn, the students are introduced to a contemporary controversy in science, such as how to fight malaria, and in this way, the students get a grasp of how science is conducted.

Chapter 10 (this volume) by Ton de Jong et al. is an illustration of the use of computer simulations in education that can be used to give students a sense of the complexity of interconnected dynamical systems. In simulation environments, learners can change values of input variables and observe the consequences for output variables. De Jong et al. start with the notion of discovery learning, a process in which the learner uses inductive reasoning to generate hypotheses that can be tested and evaluated by evidence. The discovery learning is carried out in a simulation environment set in the context of the properties of optics. There, the students can match their predictions against different representations of the simulated optical process. The actual discovery processes of learners are determined by factors that are partly outside the learner and partly internal to the learner. As internal determinants of discovery learning, de Jong et al. distinguish prior domain knowledge, general model knowledge, discovery skills, intelligence, and general metacognitive skills.

The chapters in this volume are based on a symposium on Cognition, Education and Communication Technology that was held in Stockholm, March 30 to April 1, 2000. The conference was initiated and financed by the Bank of Sweden Tercentenary Foundation. The organizers were Peter Gärdenfors, Petter Johansson, both from Cognitive Science, Lund University, and Ulla Riis, Department of Education, Uppsala University. We thank Dan Brändström at the Bank of Sweden Tercentenary Foundation for his generous support for the conference and during the extended work with this book. The work of Peter Gärdenfors has also partly been supported by the Swedish Foundation for Strategic Research. We want to thank Dan Schwartz for his help with the project, Lars Hall for his encyclopedic knowledge, Yvonne Rogers for taking care of Mike Scaife's work after his untimely death, and Lori Hawver Kelly at Lawrence Erlbaum Associates for her patience with this project.

LIST OF CONTRIBUTORS

Petter Johansson
Lund University Cognitive Science, Sweden
Peter Gärdenfors
Lund University Cognitive Science, Sweden
Daniel L. Schwartz
School of Education, Stanford University, USA
Taylor Martin
School of Education, Stanford University, USA
Na'ilah Nasir
School of Education, Stanford University, USA

Lydia Plowman
Institute of Education, University of Stirling, UK
Lauren B. Resnick
Research and Development Center, University of Pittsburgh, USA
Alan Lesgold
Research and Development Center, University of Pittsburgh, USA
Megan W. Hall
Research and Development Center, University of Pittsburgh, USA
William J. Clancey
Institute for Human and Machine Cognition and NASA-Ames Research Center
David Kirsh
Department of Cognitive Science, University of San Diego, USA
Mike Scaife
School of Cognitive and Computing Sciences, University of Sussex, UK
Jonas Ivarsson
Department of Education, Gothenburg University, Sweden
Roger Säljö
Department of Education, Gothenburg University, Sweden
Marcia C. Linn
Graduate School of Education, University of California at Berkeley, USA
Ton de Jong
University of Twente, The Netherlands
Casper Hulshof
University of Twente, The Netherlands
Jos Beishuizen
Leiden University, The Netherlands
Frans Prins
Leiden University, The Netherlands
Marcel Veenman
Leiden University, The Netherlands
Pascal Wilhelm
Leiden University, The Netherlands
Hedderik van Rijn
University of Amsterdam, The Netherlands
Maarten van Someren
University of Amsterdam, The Netherlands

1

Introduction to Cognition, Education, and Communication Technology

Petter Johansson
Peter Gärdenfors
Lund University, Sweden

Computers are quickly becoming natural components in many educational settings. Some years ago, there was a tendency to believe that if one could only install enough computers in the school, many educational problems would be solved. However, students as well as teachers are to an increasing extent questioning the value of information technology in education. Even if computers are frequently used for word processing, information search, e-mail, and chatting, the worry is whether these tools really improve how students learn.

The fundamental problem seems to be that one does not know enough about the interplay between learning and tools for learning. In particular, the potential of modern information and communication technology (ICT) seems far from fully exploited in education. Educators clearly need more developed and more encompassing theories of learning that can help educators choosing the right kind of technical support and how it should be used in education.

What would such theory of learning look like? There have been more than 100 years of research on learning, memory, attention, and problem solving in psychology and brain sciences. If this research is worth anything, it should be possible to derive an encompassing theory for how learning works. The seemingly obvious answer is that one should be able to construct the following three cornerstones:

1. A descriptive theory of the processes of learning.
2. A prescriptive theory of instruction derived from or anchored at the descriptive level.
3. A theory of instructional design including implementational recommendations for the use of ICT.

In the construction of these three parts of a unified theory of learning, one should also be able to benefit from the insights derived from the accumulated body of educational practice. These insights should serve as the empirical foundation for theories that could support their validity.

If this answer is so obvious, why have these three components not been developed? For comparison, in physics and in medicine, theoretical gains have led to immensely powerful practical applications. Why have psychology and the brain sciences not had the same effect on education?

An analogy with the development of medicine may be helpful here. Before modern medicine was developed, there was a large body of folk medicine—practices to treat illnesses that were based on a mixture of traditional knowledge of the effects of various herbs and treatments with myths and superstition. These practices did not have any backing in the form of controlled experimental testing. They often resulted in conflicting recommendations and, in retrospect, many of them were directly harmful. Gradually, this epistemologically chaotic state has been replaced by modern medicine that is based on an increased knowledge about the functioning of various bodily systems together with strictly controlled experimentation before new drugs are introduced. Science is now reaching the state in which new drugs can be chemically designed rather than found by laborious trial-and-error testing on laboratory animals.

The analogy we hold out is that the knowledge of how education should be practiced is still on the level of folk medicine; pedagogy has not yet found its Pasteur. Most instructional practices are motivated by a combination of folk psychology and a reference to tradition that leads to inconsistencies and potentially harmful recommendations.

The reason folk psychology still functions as a foundation is that the sciences of learning are not as mature as could be hoped. What one finds is not one unified theory of learning but a multitude of theories on different levels of explanation—from learning in neurons to learning in groups of individuals. The theories are often fragmented and far from complete, and they cover scattered application areas. In most cases, it is difficult to see how the theories can be made to work together for more general explanations and recommendations. As a matter of fact, different theories sometimes result in conflicting recommendations. There are a lot of conflicts among researchers in the fields of learning, and they seem to have widely diverging visions of what learning really is.

If now the sciences of learning and instruction are in a state analogous to the pioneering wild West, it would be premature to attempt a unification of existing theories. To be sure, there have been attempts at such unification. For example, Skinner (1954) presented a theory of instruction based on the behaviorist theory of learning. However, later developments have found the behaviorist attempts rather limited.

Furthermore, regardless of the validity of the theories, it could be questioned whether all aspects of the descriptive enterprise are actually relevant for theories of instruction and implementation. For example, what are the potential benefits to be gained by understanding the mechanisms of neural encoding of memory from an instructional perspective? If one aims for instructional design, does one really need to be informed of all levels?

On the other hand, who is to identify one level of description as the most fruitful and promising? For the time being, one must accept that there is no limited set of universal laws covering all aspects of learning. Therefore, one must still accept a plurality of theoretical positions in the educational sciences. It could even be the case that learning is not one unified phenomenon but must be described in terms of many mechanisms operating on a multitude of levels. After all, what is common in the learning of pottery, navigation, grammar, mathematics, and so forth?

It is also important to note the fundamental tension between the descriptive and prescriptive aspects of learning as regards their aims. The main aim of a descriptive theory is to explain various aspects of learning processes. On the other hand, the prescriptive aims essentially involve developing an optimal theory of instruction in relation to a set of educational goals. In the attempts to develop a descriptive theory, that is, an explanatory theory of how learning occurs, the learning process is observed and manipulated but not guided. The problem when trying to utilize existing models from a descriptive level in education is that it is not at all certain that they convey the most efficient approach. In other words, they try to capture how humans learn things, not necessarily how we best learn things.

Another difference between descriptive and prescriptive theories is that they are based on different methodologies. In chapter 2 (this volume), Schwartz, Martin, and Nasir describe the difference in methodology as follows: In cognitive psychology and other descriptive theories, one tries to isolate variables that are relevant for learning to experimentally investigate their effects. In contrast, in a real-life instructional setting, all variables are active at the same time and cannot be treated in isolation, so a holistic solution to the educational framework must be sought.

Even if the relation between descriptive and prescriptive theories is somewhat problematic, many descriptive models of learning can be useful when dealing with educational issues. As we show in the next section, many more or less successful attempts have been made to ground new educational initiatives in existing theories from psychology and cognitive science.

The third cornerstone of a theory of instruction is the role of ICT tools. Because they have only recently been introduced in educational practices, one cannot hope that these practices will tell us what the optimal use of ICT in education is. The space of possibilities is not sufficiently explored. Ideally, one should be able to derive what is the best use of these tools from the available theories. However, the fragmentation of the theoretical field makes it very difficult to formulate any generally applicable recommendations at the level of implementation.

The upshot is that one cannot hope to find a unifying theory of learning from which one can derive a generally applicable theory of instruction. In spite of the fragmented nature of the sciences of learning, we believe that nevertheless there is much to gain from the different theories that have been formulated and the experience that has been collected in different educational settings. The strategy should therefore not be to search for Utopia but to be more eclectic: Take what is available today and use it as a basis for recommendation on instructional practices, in particular, practices involving ICT. In the following, apart from providing a brief historical description of a few of the major theories of learning and education, we outline some consequences of these and other theories that we find important for the design of educational practices. In this, we also show where in the theoretical landscape the chapters of this book can be placed.

FROM A HISTORICAL PERSPECTIVE

Behaviorism

Even if few copies would be sold if a new educational software were promoted as being developed in strict accordance with the principles of behaviorism, it is nevertheless true that much of what is being produced today is still guided by the basic tenets of Skinner (1967, 1968).

From having been the dominating theoretical approach in regular psychology as well as educational psychology and instructional design, behaviorism is now often treated primarily as a contrasting case, something that it is important to not be associated with (Jonassen & Land, 2000). Behaviorism is portrayed as representing learning without understanding, teacher-centered lectures with scant opportunities for curiosity and individuality, passive students, reductionistic, and conforming, that is, everything one wants to avoid in the modern school. Interestingly enough, much of Skinners (1954) ideas on education were aimed at resolving these very issues.

In a simplified summary of Skinners (1968) position, the phenomenon of learning is explained by a limited set of basic conditioning mechanisms. Positive reinforcement and negative reinforcement (i.e., avoidance of an expected negative outcome) increase the probability that a response will be repeated in the future, whereas nonreinforcement and punishment decrease the likelihood of future occurrences of a response. The learning effect is further regulated by the reinforcement schedule, that is, at what ratio or interval a response is reinforced, and by the timing of the reinforcement, that is, at what time the reinforcement is delivered in relation to the response.

Having constructed what aspired to be a universal theory of learning covering all species as well as all instances of learning, the obvious next step was to apply these ideas to human society in general and education in particular (Skinner, 1948, 1954, 1968). The traditional educational method with a teacher up front holding a lecture and passive students listening and trying to absorb did not fit well with behavioristic ideas of learning. In Skinner's (1954) highly influential article, "The Science of Learning and the Art of Teaching," he argued for a more individualistic approach in which the student should be the active part. Given Skinner's (1954) concept of learning, this is not very surprising. It is only by strengthening responses that learning can occur, and in a passive learning situation, there is no behavior to reinforce. Skinner (1954) also emphasized the importance of immediate reinforcement. There is no point in taking an exam and then having to wait 2 or 3 weeks for the result; the reinforcement needs to be delivered immediately or the learning effect will be diminished dramatically. According to Skinner (1954), instruction and learning should also proceed in an incremental fashion, with small and manageable steps toward a preset and well-defined learning goal, that is, a method similar to shaping of behavior in animal training. These three steps, (a) an active learner, (b) immediate reinforcement, and (c) successive approximations toward a well-defined learning goal, form the core of what is known as programmed instruction.

To suitably direct and govern the individual students' learning trajectory, each learning task must be examined and its components described in detail. This means that for each learning task, a detailed, step-by-step, instructional sequence should be produced as well as a description of the corresponding sequence of desired behaviors. For this to be of any value, there must of course also be a reliable procedure to measure and compare the students' learning behavior with the original plan. This focus on task analyses and behavioral objectives came to be one of the most influential aspects of the behaviorists' educational project.

In his critique of traditional educational methods, Skinner (1954) also pointed out that a single teacher cannot individually and appropriately reinforce an entire class of students. In his 1954 article, Skinner introduced the notion of a teaching machine to solve this problem. A machine could implement the instructional method of programmed instruction: present information or instruction, measure every response and reinforce appropriately, branch to the next level of difficulty depending on the individual's performance, and so forth. This would not only increase the efficiency of schooling, it would solve a number of additional problems. It would give the teacher more time for emotional, artistic, and intellectual issues; to help those students that really need it; and so forth. It would also make it possible to individually tailor instruction and let each student work at her or his own level and pace. The machine would never get bored or impatient no matter how many times the student failed.

Skinner (1968) held great hopes for the use of technology in education: "There is no reason why the schoolroom should be any less mechanized than, for example, the kitchen" (p. 27). A number of different machines and accompanying instructional programs were built, increasingly more technically advanced (Glover & Ronning, 1987). However, after a few years of initial interest, the use of teaching machines in education started to decline. One reason for this was that even though the machine never got bored, the students often did. The step-by-step, incremental nature of the material became tedious and repetitive. This was before the advent of cheap personal computers, and the interface of levers, knobs, and slides did not make the task more appealing. The downfall of behaviorism as the dominant paradigm in psychology also lead to a decreased interest in the behaviorists' recommendations for education.

Many of the first computer programs that reached the classrooms were of the drill and practice type, and this general approach is still quite common in certain domains such as foreign language vocabulary, geography, mathematics, and so forth. One example is "Jurassic Spelling," which is a spelling practice program that provides a verbal reward every time a word is correctly spelled, and after gaining a certain number of points, the student is rewarded with a picture and information about a dinosaur. Present day tutorials, often accompanying software such as Microsoft® Word or PowerPoint®, are also examples of reinforced step-by-step learning, with progress to the next "level" only when initial stages has been mastered completely.

Additional criticism that can be leveled against behaviorism is of course its shortcomings as a general theory of psychology. By rejecting the use of internal mechanisms in its theoretical constructions, many aspects of human behavior were left unexplained. One of the important and much debated topics was language learning in which the reinforcement model did not seem to be a satisfactory answer (Chomsky, 1959; Skinner, 1957). When it comes to education, programmed instruction and teaching machines focus solely on the individual learner. There is no room for collaborative efforts; it is only the individual's own progress that is taken into consideration. The use of excessive reinforcement is also somewhat problematic, as external reinforcement has a tendency to decrease intrinsic motivation (Deci, Koestner, & Ryan, 1999; but see Eisenberger, Pierce, & Cameron, 1999).

Cognitivism

Whereas behaviorism treated the mind as a black box not to be examined or included in its explanatory scheme of stimuli and response relations, the mechanisms of the mind is at center stage in the cognitivist tradition. The mind (and brain) is seen as an information processing device, with the computer as the basic metaphor. The information being processed is represented by symbols, and it is these symbols that are the carriers of the cognition taking place between perceptual stimuli and motor responses. Following the computer metaphor, cognition is executed by serially manipulating symbols in working memory in accordance with rules stored in long-term memory, thus mimicking the central processing unit of a computer (Johnson-Laird, 1988).

In the early days of cognitive science, much effort was devoted to memory research, both with respect to content, structure, and capacity, and much of that research came to influence theories of instruction as well. For example, the limited capacity of the working memory gave rise to a concern for cognitive load in learning situations, and it was discovered that learning was improved if the learning material was presented in a form that did not tax working memory (Atkinson & Shiffrin, 1968; Miller, 1956). This was accomplished by automating secondary tasks, not introducing too many variables at the same time, and not using conflicting or noncoherent modes of representation concurrently (Chandler & Sweller, 1991).

Expert studies was another field that received a lot of attention, especially with regard to problem solving and learning or memory tasks. The underlying assumption was that expert performance could serve as an approximation of "ideal" or optimal functionality and thus serve as a model for instructional theory. One conclusion that could be drawn from this research was that experts were superior to the novice in recalling new material related to their field of expertise. This was explained as being due to their both vast and well-organized prior knowledge about the field in question, which gave them lot of opportunities to "connect" the new material to previously stored material. The implication for instructional theory was of course that if you know a lot about a subject, it is easier to learn more but also that you needed to assess the students' prior knowledge before you introduce new material.

Even if he has received more attention in the United States than in Europe, one of the most influential contributors to instructional theory is Gagné. Gagné has been described as an eclectic behaviorist (Smith & Ragan, 2000), and although he undoubtedly started out as a behaviorist, his gradual incorporation of cognitivism can be traced in each new edition of his major book, *The Conditions of Learning* (Gagné, 1965, 1970, 1977, 1985). In his work, Gagné (1985) developed a general theory of instruction, and the components that have been most influential and well known is his taxonomy of learning outcomes and conditions of learning. Based on the information processing view of human cognition and learning, Gagné (1985) also defined nine events of instruction, each associated with a corresponding cognitive mechanism. Even if he allowed for exceptions, Gagné (1985) believed that most lectures or instructional situations should follow this form. The first step is gaining the students attention and informing the student of the objectives of the lesson to create an appropriate expectancy; next, asking the student of previously learned material related to the subject to activate the appropriate schema; presenting the content with distinctive encoding and retrieval cues; providing a meaningful and coherent organization of the material to enhance semantic encoding; inducing the student to respond to the presented material and provide feedback and reinforcement; and finally giving opportunities to rehearse and practice the new material. Without recapitulating the entire list in detail, for our purposes, it is interesting to note that Gagné has constructed a domain general and theory-driven tool for how an instructional event should best be conducted.

Going back to the study of experts and problem solving, another important strand of this research was so called expert systems. Within computer science and classical artificial intelligence (AI), much effort was devoted to modeling the structure of how one believed that an expert functioned. The general idea was to construct systems with a large domain-specific knowledge base together with an appropriate set of rules for how this knowledge should be applied and accessed. The expert systems can be seen as the equivalent of the behaviorists' programmed instruction and teaching machines, as it is a fairly direct implementation of the basic ideas inherent in the theory.

Apart from being an empirical test of the feasibility of the architectural assumptions with regards to problem solving and expert performance, the function of these systems was often to provide job assistance or decision support in specific domains. The most cited example of this approach is the MYCIN program, which is a knowledge-based system providing expert advice on the diagnoses and treatment of certain kinds of infections. Closely aligned to the expert systems approach was that of intelligent computer-assisted instruction, which extended the approach of expert systems to include intelligent learning environments and tutoring systems. In the case of

MYCIN, additional modules allowing simulation, teaching, tutoring, and student monitoring were built around the core in an attempt to convert the original expert system into an educational software (Clancey, 1987). This new program called GUIDON (Clancey, 1987), uses a simulation method in which the student is presented with a medical case and then acts as a diagnostician. The program can interrupt the student and ask for motivations if suboptimal decisions are detected, and the student can likewise ask GUIDON for clarifications or elaboration. For educational purposes, the aim of this approach was thus to build a model of expert performance and then transfer both the knowledge and cognitive strategies used by the expert to the student.

However, the attempts to ground computer simulations of intelligence in the symbolic processing model of cognition was in general not very successful, and for example, Clancey came to abandon the approach altogether (see chap. 5, this volume, and following). Others have tried to more directly implement the instructional implications stemming from information processing theory or Gagné's theory of instruction. One example is Guidance for Understanding Instructional Design Expertise (McNelly, Arthur, Bennett, & Gettman, 1996), which is a software designed to introduce Gagné's nine instructional events to teachers, but it also functions as an authoring tool for teachers to develop computer-based instructions in this tradition (McNelly, Arthur, Bennett, & Gettman, 1996).

Plowman (chap. 3, this volume) emphasizes the importance of a narrative structure for cognition and understanding in educational settings. One of the main functions of the teacher is to provide a coherent structure in the learning material despite its sometimes fragmented nature and despite moving between different modes of presentation and learning activities. This is being achieved by continuously interacting with the students, monitoring their level of understanding, asking and answering questions, steering discussions in useful directions, and so forth. However, much of this teacher–student interaction is lost when students work with educational multimedia. Plowman examines to what extent and under what circumstances interactive educational multimedia can provide a narrative structure, trying to find a balance between freedom and linearity for the students' interaction with the material. Plowman is not a traditional cognitivist, but her emphasis on understanding and meaning puts her in line with the original ambitions of the cognitive movement, namely, to reintroduce the creation of meaning as an essential part of the learning process (Bruner, 1990; Gardner, 1985).

In chapter 2 (this volume), Schwartz et al. point out one particularly problematic aspect of using cognitive psychology as the foundation for a prescriptive theory of learning. In cognitive psychology, the general methodological strategy has been to identify distinct cognitive mechanisms by trying to separate and study each mechanism in isolation from the rest of the system. This has lead to an increased understanding of the capacity of each subsystem such as the short-term or working memory. However, this does not give much guidance when trying to model how we learn more complex ideas or abilities, that is, situations in which multiple cognitive mechanisms work in concert. Schwartz et al. advocate an alternative approach: to examine how people integrate processes and resources to support learning. Schwartz et al. use their ICT learning platform called Evolutionary Design is put forward as an example of this strategy. The main idea is to expose the knowledge of the student for a process of "natural selection" in which the ideas can mutate, grow, and adapt by "surviving" in different contrasting environments.

The "cognitive revolution" began as a reaction to behaviorism and its neglect of the internal mechanisms of the mind, but during the last 15 years, the pendulum has swung back again. In the attempt to explain all aspects of human psychology in terms of information processing, too much focus came to lie on the workings of the individual mind. Social interaction and the use of artifacts were to a large extent ignored. The human mind (or brain) came to be studied almost as if isolated from the external world. In a sense, the information-processing paradigm reversed the problems of behaviorism and instead omitted the social and physical context from their explanatory scheme. As a reaction to classical cognitivism, a number of different views emerged and gained influence, all with the common notion of cognition as being essentially situated.

Sociocultural and Situated Cognition

The most important feature of the sociocultural tradition is the focus on interaction between individuals. It is argued that individual development cannot be understood independently of the social context in which the person is placed and brought up. This holds for all aspects of learning as well as for the development of cognitive abilities such as reasoning and problem solving. Vygotsky (1960/1981), the originator of this approach, stated in an often-quoted passage that "any higher mental function necessarily goes through an external stage in its development because it is initially a social function" (p. 162). This means that cognition and cognitive development is in fact constituted by the internalization of the social processes and communicative acts humans share with other individuals. On this view, communication and language is of course of primary importance. Another central notion is the idea of tools as mediators of thought, with a very wide definition of tools including ordinary physical tools as well as signs, symbol systems, arguments, and theories. Because of the focus of the sociocultural tradition on interaction and social context, qualitative and ethnographic methods are often preferred. This puts them in contrast to previous theories, not only in terminology but in their methodological approach as well.

In learning and education, the most well-known contribution of Vygotsky (1960/1981) is probably the zone of proximal development (ZPD). The idea is basically that in collaboration with other students and the teacher, the student can reach further in understanding and problem solving than could be done on her or his own. The teacher functions as a form of scaffolding, supporting the students to solve tasks that are above their current level of understanding and thus guiding the students through their individual ZPD. The motivation for this procedure is that working on and solving problems slightly ahead of their present capabilities increases the pace of the student's development (Wells, 1999). The concept of scaffolding, that is, to build and use external structures in cognition, is a notion that is favored by most researchers adhering to sociocultural or situated theories.

A related tradition is the one we here call situated cognition (Brown, Collins, & Duguid, 1989). It is also known as external cognition (Clark, 1998), distributed cognition (Hutchins, 1995), situated action (Clancey, 1993), situated learning (Lave & Wenger, 1991), and so forth. Within this set of more or less similar approaches, two different strands can be discerned. One is the anthropological, represented by researchers such as Lave (1988) and Suchman (1987), which focuses on cultural construction of meaning and learning by apprenticeship. This group is similar in spirit to the sociocultural tradition and has a considerable overlap in terms of theory construction and methodology. The other strand can be seen as a reaction to cognitivism coming from within cognitive science, with such names as Clark (1998), Clancey (1997), Hutchins (1995), and Kirsh and Maglio (1994). What unites this group of researchers is the belief that the process of cognition cannot be captured solely by a focus on the mechanisms of the mind and brain, by the internal computation on mental representations. What is missing in this picture is the agent's interaction with the external world. Cognition is embedded in action, in the manipulation of objects, and in the interaction with others, that is, we think as much in the world as in the head. One source of inspiration for this group is the work on autonomous robots, which started as a reaction to classical AI and its failure to produce intelligent behavior in knowledge-based systems (Brooks, 1991).

To many practitioners in the field, sociocultural studies and situated cognition are two entirely separate enterprises not to be lumped together under the same heading. However, we have chosen to do so for two reasons. First of all, they share the same unit of analyses. Both when it comes to learning and psychology in general, it is the agent and the context that are in focus. Second, they share, if not a common epistemology, at least a conviction that the traditional "conduit" metaphor is not the right one.

This touches on a fundamental divergence in the theories of learning, namely, what is regarded as the object of learning. One can distinguish between two main traditions, one that focuses on the contents of what is learned and one that focuses on the practices involved. Within classical cognitivism, the contents of what is learned is transferred to the learner. This view is tightly connected to the conduit metaphor of learning. However, also in constructivist theories of learning (see following), what is learned is seen as a construction—an object that is built up by the learner. Both these traditions thus focus on the contents of what is learned. Within sociocultural and situated cognition, the focus is on what the learners do—their activities, the (social) practices they result in, and so forth. Lave (1988), for example, described learning as "participation in practice" and would have rather not included the notion of knowledge in her analyses at all. Behaviorism falls somewhat outside this classification—what is learned, a disposition to behave, can either be seen as a behavioral pattern (a form of practice) or as a conditioning that has been transferred to the learner.

Before the invention of a public school system, most formal knowledge was transmitted through apprenticeships. Cognitive apprenticeship can be seen as a continuation of this tradition, but in the domain of cognition, the student is initiated in an authentic practice of experts, learning the craftsmanship of experts (Collins, Brown, & Newman, 1989). The teacher acts as a coach or guide rather than instructor, making the previously mentioned ZPD a useful concept for this approach. If one considers the essence of learning to be "participation in practice," using apprenticeship as a template for education comes in hand.

In chapter 4 (this volume), Resnick, Lesgold, and Hall take the idea of apprenticeship one step further. Resnick et al. propose a hierarchical educational system in which the teacher acts as a facilitator or guide in the classroom. However, Resnick et al. put the teacher in the role of the apprentice in a group consisting of other teachers, with the principal or a team leader as facilitator. The principals of a district form yet another study group with a district leader as guide, and so on. The primary aim of this layered organizational setup is to promote continuous learning for all participants in the educational system. However, it also provides an ideal environment for spreading new theoretical insights about teaching and learning, which is a problem facing everyone that attempts to introduce new ideas in school. Resnick et al. also developed new software designed to further teachers' understanding of learning processes to give them a common framework and vocabulary to analyze and evaluate their teaching practice. Even if the principles of learning being advocated in this program are taken from many fields in cognitive and instructional science, it is still firmly rooted in the sociocultural tradition, both with respect to content and the method of delivering the message.

Clancey (chap. 5, this volume), who has published many books and articles on both situated cognition in general (Clancey, 1997) and its implications for education (Clancey, 1992; Roschelle & Clancey, 1992), takes as a starting point the heated debate concerning the nature of visual representation and the possibilities of mimicking these processes in a computer simulation. On one side, one finds Vera and Simon (1993) defending the language of thought hypothesis of cognitivism and classical AI; on the other side, one finds Clancey (chap. 5, this volume) himself advocating his notion of visual categorization as a nonsymbolic embodied activity in which perception is coupled to behavior sequences, emotional changes, and so forth. In the end, Clancey (chap. 5, this volume) concedes that the only way to solve this issue, that is, whether all stages of perception and categorization can be reduced to symbolic descriptions, is to examine what people actually do when they visually examine, struggle with, and ultimately come to understand a given problem. To illustrate this approach, Clancey (chap. 5, this volume) sets out to analyze a log of two students trying to solve a math problem. In this arduous endeavor, Clancey (chap. 5, this volume) convincingly shows that the symbolic model cannot account for all the intricacies of human perceptual understanding but also that one is far from having a complete theory of how this understanding is accomplished. With this conclusion, Clancey (chap. 5, this volume) also rules out the construction of a tutoring-like computer program that in any real sense understands what the student is doing or thinking, as one does not really know how to model the cognitive processes of the student in the first place.

Kirsh (chap. 6, this volume), who also has had a longstanding interest in the relation between internal and external processes (Kirsh, 1991; Kirsh & Maglio, 1994), explores the metalevels of learning, that is, how we can teach students to learn. Kirsh's (chap. 6, this volume) primary concern is how to use external cognition as a tool in metacognition, to teach students how to structure their own learning environments, and to use and create external representations to enhance performance. For some reason, metacognition has not been scrutinized and reinterpreted from a situated perspective in the same manner as most other aspects of cognition have been. Most often, it is still regarded as an exclusively internal process—thoughts about thoughts. Kirsh (chap. 6, this volume) argues that metacognition is just as interactive as other forms of cognition and that it is part of a continuum in which no sharp boundaries can be drawn between metacognition and planning, problemsolving, and so forth. Once metacognition has been reconceptualized and incorporated in the situated and distributed perspective, one's ideas of what counts as good visual design in learning environments will be altered as well.

In a similar vein, Scaife and Rogers (chap. 7, this volume) argues that external cognition is an ideal research paradigm for the new field of educational technology, as the relation between internal and external representations, the integration of multiple and multimodal representations, and the capacity for novel forms of external representations are all important questions that can be approached within the situational framework. In Scaife and Rogers' (chap. 7, this volume) empirical work, the primary focus lies on how to use virtual worlds and avatars to improve children's capacity to change perspectives and understand other people's points of view. The strategy implemented in the software is to give the students the opportunity to actively explore multiple representations of a concept at different levels of abstraction.

Like Clancey in chapter 5 (this volume), Ivarsson and Säljö in chapter 8 (this volume) also present a nonstandard theory of visual perception and explore what consequences it may have on our understanding of concep-tual development and learning. From a Vygotskyan perspective, the use of artifacts and tools is an integrated aspect of humans' cognitive abilities— we think with our things. This holds not only for concrete physical objects but for symbolic artifacts as well such as words, numbers, charts, diagrams, maps, and so forth. A natural continuation of this idea is that humans' tools and practices not only affect how we think and act but also how we perceive the world surrounding us. Ivarsson and Säljö use Wartofsky's (1983) theory of historic epistemology as a starting point in their analyses, a theory according to which humans' perceptual representations are deter-mined by previously encountered and internalized theories of what we see. There is no such thing as visual realism, that is, how things really look, but as humans, our perceptions are always filtered and fostered by our inter-pretations of the world. In their work, Ivarsson and Säljö study to what ex-tent and in what form children understand the theory of gravity in relation to the spherical shape of the earth. This is done by analyzing how children interact with novel forms of dynamic representations in a computer sup-ported learning environment and how they develop and negotiate the meaning of these representations by scientific reasoning centered around fragmented and often incompatible theories of how the world works.

One issue that has been subject to much discussion is whether the sociocultural and situated perspective can account for the concept of learning transfer, that is, the ability to apply previously acquired knowl-edge in novel situations. The problem stems from the definition of learning as being the ability to participate in practice, which can be read as being a very context-specific capacity. If knowledge is not an object people obtain and use at will, it is a bit unclear what it is you carry with you when you en-ter into a new discourse or practice. If this is definitional nitpicking or a fundamental flaw in the theory, it is yet to be decided. Another concern raised is if the apprenticeship model really is the most efficient form of learning and if all subjects could be learned in this fashion (Sfard, 1998). It seems that for some areas, such as physics, mathematics, or medicine, "brute force" studying or at least a long preparatory phase before entering apprenticeship is an essential part of mastering the discipline. On the other hand, it could be argued that these objections only arise because of a stereotypical picture of what apprenticeship could be based on traditional apprenticeship situations such as trade or craftsmanship and that any elements necessary could be incorporated without losing the apprentice-like nature of learning.

Constructivism

Constructivism is an amalgam of many different theories and traditions. First and foremost comes the influence from Piaget (1969, 1970) whose epigenetic epistemology, schema theory, and views on development are at the core of most forms of constructivism. The sociocultural tradition, originating with Vygotsky, is another major factor in its emphasis on the cultural and social aspects of learning. Additional influences are the ecological psychology of Gibson (1979), the radical constructivism of von Glasersfeld (1995), and the work of Bruner (1973). It is also important to note that there is no single constructivist theory; there are a number of people calling themselves constructivists with more or less overlapping theoretical perspectives.

Constructivism differs in many ways from the previously mentioned theories. First of all, it is not and does not aspire to be a general theory of psychology as is arguably the case with behaviorism and cognitivism. Constructivism as such has never been a major force in mainstream psychology, even though it is currently the dominating paradigm in education. Learning and instruction is the main focus of the theory, and prescriptive elements and implications for education form a natural part of the tradition.

The one idea that brings all strands together is that knowledge is not received, it is constructed. Through exploration and discovery, through their actions in the world, people create their own understanding. This notion has far-reaching implications for many aspects of instruction and education. Comparing with behaviorism and cognitivism, it results in quite different learning goals, conditions of learning, and implications for the construction of educational technology.

The general learning goals of constructivism are for the learner to develop problem solving and reasoning skills, critical thinking, and self-regulated learning, that is, the ability to engage in independent thought. It is of course not impossible for a teacher with behavioristic or cognitivistic inclinations to set up and strive for overall goals like these, but the road to get there would probably differ markedly.

Driscoll (2000) identified five conditions of learning in the constructivist tradition related to the general learning goals presented previously.

1. Embed learning in complex, realistic, and relevant environments. The world is complex, therefore, the students should engage in complex and realistic learning tasks. This includes both possible tools and principles to use as well as the learning environment itself. Spiro, Feltovich, Jacobson, and Coulson (1992) further recommended the use of so called "ill-structured domains," which are problem scenarios that do not have a correct solution or at least not a solution that can easily be proven to be the right one.

2. Provide for social negotiation as an integral part of learning. Collaboration is important in itself, for example, to learn to function and solve problems in a social group, to understand other peoples perspectives, and to defend your own views. Furthermore, as constructivism adheres to the sociocultural perspective in viewing communication and social exchange as a prerequisite for the development of higher mental functions, social interaction is a vital component in all educational settings.

3. Support multiple perspectives and the use of multiple modes of representations. When facing a problem, the student should not rely on just one model, principle, or metaphor. It is by viewing a problem from many different and sometimes incompatible perspectives and by constructing and comparing different interpretations and alternative models that the student can come to fully understand and endorse the solution.

4. Encourage ownership in learning. It is important that the student actively participates in the construction of the learning task. By being responsible for one's own learning goals and also for the realization of these goals, a higher sense of involvement is achieved.

5. Nurture self-awareness of the knowledge construction process. The student should be aware both of how to best learn something, that is, how their own cognition and learning processes works, and how much knowledge he or she has in the domain under study. In constructivism, metacognitive awareness also entails a sensitivity to the fact that one's own point of view is as constructed as everybody else's, and therefore, it needs to be examined and compared to other perspectives.

Many recent educational initiatives, both with and without the support of ICT, work in agreement with these principles. One influential trend that fits neatly with all the conditions of learning stated previously is problem based learning (PBL). In this approach, the students are supposed to address a real and relevant problem of their own choosing, work in groups, make a decision regarding how much background material needs to be reviewed, present and account for multiple perspectives and solutions to the problem under study, and finally, construct and argue for their own solution.

Linn, in chapter 9 (this volume), a well-known proponent of constructivism, explores the notion of controversy. The focus on controversy is primarily used as means to teach the essence of science—construction of arguments, interpretation of data, the ongoing debate between opposing opinions, and so forth. Using the Web-Based Inquiry Science Environment the students are introduced to a contemporary controversy in science, such as how to fight malaria, and this way, the students get a good picture of how science is conducted. However, controversy as such is also an approach that fits well with the constructivist assumptions in that it encourages the student to form an opinion of her or his own, to take side in an ongoing scientific controversy and evaluate the strengths and weaknesses of a position.

Computer-supported collaborative learning (CSCL) is an umbrella term for various approaches that explore new ways of interaction in the realm of computer-mediated communication. They are not meant to replace face-to-face communication but to facilitate collaboration by enabling common access to documents, chat boards, mind maps, and so forth. Many of the people working with CSCL refer to constructivism as their theoretical foundation and emphasize the importance of social interaction for cognitive growth.

Another new field aligned with the constructivist agenda is computer simulations in education, which is often used to give students a sense of the complexity of interconnected dynamical systems as well as an opportunity to find out for themselves which causal links and connections govern the systems under study. De Jong et al. (chap. 10, this volume) is a good illustration of this approach set in the context of optics. De Jong et al. start with the notion of discovery learning, a process in which the learner uses inductive reasoning to generate hypotheses that can be tested and evaluated by evidence. The discovery learning is carried out in a computer simulation environment, and there, the students can match their predictions against different representations of the simulated optical process. Both Linn (chap. 9, this volume) and de Jong et al. (chap. 10, this volume) fulfill the central constructivist dictum, as the students are responsible for the construction of their own knowledge and understanding.

An epistemological problem inherent in constructivism is how one knows that the constructions are useful: What is it really that students construct? It is of no value to construct knowledge that is not correct or is too limited to be of any use. A general problem for constructivist versions of learning is how deep theoretical knowledge can be achieved. For example, there are certain versions of PBL in which the students are supposed to formulate the problems to work on their own. However, if the students do not know anything about the theoretical background for the area of their studies, it is futile to expect that they will, on their own, discover the variables that are most relevant for the problems they are trying to solve. One cannot hope that every student or group of students will rediscover the achievements of hundreds of years of science.

In traditional education, the theoretical background to a study area is presented by a teacher or in a textbook. The question for an orthodox constructivist is how this can be achieved by a student or a group of students. Maybe a mixture of constructivism and more traditional methods will yield better learning results. An interesting example of such a mixed strategy has been employed by Schwartz et al. (chap. 2, this volume) in a study of how high school students best learn statistical concepts. When confronting the notion of statistical variance, the students were first given a series of examples of sets of numbers with the same mean but with different variance. The assignment was to formulate, in mathematical terms, what characterizes the variance of the sets. After struggling with this task, they were then given a lecture in which the formula for the variance of a set was introduced. Their understanding of the concept was then tested with the aid of new, more difficult test cases. It turned out that the students who had first been given the opportunity to formulate the formula for variance on the basis of the first examples performed much better than control groups of students who had only been given a theoretical introduction to the concept and students who had only worked with the examples but had not been given the theoretical lecture.

CONCLUSION

Our presentation of descriptive and prescriptive theories has admittedly been eclectic and summaric. However, as we argued in the first part of the chapter, there is so far no unifying theory of learning that we could use as a foundation. As a consequence, we need to find inspiration from all kinds of theories and successful implementations.

At this stage of theoretical development, the most reasonable thing to do is to build a large corpus of both teaching implementations and theories of learning processes. We hope this will some day lead to somebody being able to formulate a theory that will unify the area.

The present lack of a unifying theory also explains the diversity of this book. As an analogy of its aims, we can compare it to research in AI. In AI, the only real way to know if an idea works is to build a computer or robot that implements the idea and then let the world judge. Similarly, the only way to judge ideas about learning is to test them on individuals that learn. From a metaperspective, one can say that we are recommending to apply Dewey's (1938) principle of "learning by doing" also to learning itself, so that we learn how to learn by doing learning.

REFERENCES

Atkinson, R. C., & Shiffrin, R. M. (1968). Human memory: A proposed system and its control processes. In K. W. Spence (Ed.), *The psychology of learning and motivation: Advances in research and theory* (Vol. 2, pp. 89–195). New York: Academic.

Brooks, R. A. (1991). Intelligence without representation. *Artificial Intelligence Journal,* 47, 139–159.

Brown, J. S., Collins, A., & Duguid, P. (1989). Situated cognition and the culture of learning. *Educational Researcher,* 18(1), 32–41.

Bruner, J. (1973). *Going beyond the information given.* New York: Norton.

Bruner, J. S. (1990). *Acts of meaning.* Cambridge, MA: Harvard University Press.

Chandler, P., & Sweller, J. (1991). Cognitive load theory and the format of instruction. *Cognition and Instruction,* 8, 293–332.

Chomsky, N. (1959). A review of B. F. Skinner's verbal behavior. *Language,* 35, 26–58.

Clancey, W. (1987). *Knowledge-based tutoring: The GUIDON program.* Cambridge, MA: MIT Press.

Clancey, W. J. (1992). Representations of knowing: In defense of cognitive apprenticeship. *Journal of AI Education,* 3, 139–168.

Clancey, W. J. (1993). Situated action: A neuropsychological interpretation (Response to Vera and Simon). *Cognitive Science,* 17, 87–107.

Clancey, W. J. (1997). *Situated cognition.* Cambridge, England: Cambridge University Press.

Clark, A. (1998). *Being there: Putting brain, body, and world together again.* Cambridge, MA: MIT Press.

Collins, A., Brown, J. S., & Newman, S. E. (1989). Cognitive apprenticeship: Teaching the crafts of reading, writing, and mathematics. In L. B. Resnick (Ed.), *Knowing, learning, and instruction: Essays in honor of Robert Glaser* (pp. 453–494). Hillsdale, NJ: Lawrence Erlbaum Associates.

Deci, E. L., Koestner, R., & Ryan, R. M. (1999). A meta-analytic review of experiments examining the effects of extrinsic rewards on intrinsic motivation. *Psychological Bulletin,* 125, 627–668.

Dewey, J. (1938). *Experience and education.* New York: Macmillan.

Driscoll, M. P. (2000). *Psychology of learning for instruction* (2nd ed.). Needham Heights, MA: Allyn & Bacon.

Eisenberger, R., Pierce, W. D., & Cameron, J. (1999). Effects of reward on intrinsic motivation—Negative, neutral, and positive: Comment on Deci, Koestner, and Tyan (1999). *Psychological Bulletin,* 125, 677–691.

Gagné, R. M. (1965). *The conditions of learning* (1st ed.). New York: Holt, Rinehart & Winston.

Gagné, R. M. (1970). *The conditions of learning* (2nd ed.). New York: Holt, Rinehart & Winston.

Gagné, R. M. (1977). *The conditions of learning* (3rd ed.). New York: Holt, Rinehart & Winston.

Gagné, R. M. (1985). *The conditions of learning* (4th ed.). New York: Holt, Rinehart & Winston.

Gardner, H. (1985). *The mind's new science: A history of the cognitive revolution.* New York: Basic Books.

Gibson, J. J. (1979). *The ecological approach to visual perception.* Boston: Houghton Mifflin.

Glover, J. A., & Ronning, R. R. (Eds.). (1987). *Historical foundations of educational psychology.* New York: Plenum.

Hutchins, E. (1995). *Cognition in the wild.* Cambridge, MA: MIT Press.

Johnson-Laird, P. N. (1988). *The computer and the mind: An introduction to cognitive science.* Cambridge, MA: Harvard University Press.

Jonassen, D. H., & Land, S. L. (2000). *Theoretical foundations of learning environments.* Mahwah, NJ: Lawrence Erlbaum Associates.

Kirsh, D. (1991). Today the earwig, tomorrow man? *Artificial Intelligence, 47*, 161–184.

Kirsh, D., & Maglio, P. (1994). On distinguishing epistemic from pragmatic action. *Cognitive Science, 18*, 513–549.

Lave, J. (1988). *Cognition in practice: Mind, mathematics, and culture in everyday life.* Cambridge, England: Cambridge University Press.

Lave, J., & Wenger, E. (1991). *Situated learning: Legitimate peripheral participation.* Cambridge, England: Cambridge University Press.

McNelly, T. L., Arthur, W., Bennett, W., & Gettman, D. J. (1996). *A quantitative evaluation of an instructional design support system: Assessing the structural knowledge and resulting curricula of expert and novice instructional designer.* Retrieved February 18, 2004, from http://www.ijoa.org/imta96/paper75.html

Miller, G. A. (1956). The magical number seven, plus or minus two: Some limits on our capacity for processing information. *Psychological Review, 63*, 81–97.

Piaget, J. (1969). *The mechanisms of perception.* London: Rutledge & Kegan Paul.

Piaget, J. (1970). *The science of education and the psychology of the child.* New York: Grossman.

Roschelle, J., & Clancey, W. J. (1992). Learning as social and neural. *The Educational Psychologist, 27*, 435–453.

Sfard, A. (1998). On two metaphors for learning and the dangers of choosing just one. *Educational Researcher, 27*(2), 4–13.

Skinner, B. F. (1948). *Walden two.* New York: Macmillan.

Skinner, B. F. (1954). The science of learning and the art of teaching. *Harvard Educational Review, 24*, 86–97.

Skinner, B. F. (1957). *Verbal behavior.* New York: Appleton-Century-Crofts.

Skinner, B. F. (1968). *The technology of teaching.* New York: Appleton-Century-Crofts.

Smith, P. L., & Ragan, T. J. (2000). The impact of R. M. Gagné's work on instructional theory. In R. C. Richey (Ed.), The legacy of Robert M. Gagné (pp. 147–181). Syracuse, NY: Syracuse University.

Spiro, R. J., Feltovich, P. J., Jacobson, M. J., & Coulson, R. L. (1992). Cognitive flexibility, constructivism and hypertext: Random access instruction for advanced knowledge acquisition in ill-structured domains. In T. Duffy & D. Jonassen (Eds.), *Constructivism and the technology of instruction* (pp. 57–76). Hillsdale, NJ: Lawrence Erlbaum Associates.

Suchman, L. (1987). *Plans and situated actions: The problem of human/machine communication.* Cambridge, England: Cambridge University Press.

Vera, A., & Simon, H. (1993). Situated action: A symbolic interpretation. *Cognitive Science, 17*, 7–48.

von Glasersfeld, E. (1995). *Radical constructivism: A way of knowing and learning.* London: Falmer.

Vygotsky, L. S. (1981). The genesis of higher mental functions. In J. V. Wertsch (Ed.), *The concept of activity in Soviet psychology* (pp. 144–188). Armonk, NY: Sharpe. (Original work published 1960)

Wartotsky, M. W. (1983). From genetic epistemology to historical epistemology: Kant, Marx, and Piaget. In. L. S. Liben (Ed.) *Piaget and the foundations of knowledge* (pp. 4–17). Hillsdale, NJ: Lawrence Erlbaum Associates.

Wells, G. (1999). *Dialogic inquiry: Towards a sociocultural practice and theory of education.* Cambridge, England: Cambridge University Press.

2

Designs for Knowledge Evolution: Towards a Prescriptive Theory for Integrating First- and Second-Hand Knowledge

Daniel L. Schwartz
Taylor Martin
Na'ilah Nasir
Stanford University

Despite the contention that a better understanding of the mechanisms of thought should lead to better models of instruction, the usefulness of cognitive psychology for the development of productive teaching practices is uncertain. A critical challenge for the field is to develop methods and measures that yield prescriptions, not just descriptions, of learning. An impediment to this challenge is cognitive psychology's common methodology of isolating cognitive mechanisms. The method of work separates the learner from access to nonfocal cognitive resources because exposure might contaminate the isolation of a specific mechanism. Learning complex ideas, however, depends on recruiting multiple cognitive (as well as social and motivational) mechanisms and resources. To make robust prescriptive theories, it is important to consider how people integrate processes and resources to facilitate learning.

Our specific example of an integrative prescriptive theory is called designs for knowledge evolution (DKE). We are unclear whether our prescription constitutes a theory, but it does draw inspiration from biological theory, which has a rich vocabulary for describing change. DKE presupposes that the development of understanding involves the coevolution of different "species" of knowledge in response to environmental demands. For example, the abilities to perceive and communicate coevolve in a particular task environment; each shapes the other. Smith and Sera (1992) provided a nice metaphor of child development that captures our emphasis on the coevolution of cognitive resources. In the context of examining how children learn perceptual words, Smith and Sera (1992) state that development is

> Like the evolution and colonization of an island biotope. Perception and perceptual language can be thought of as two species in this biotope. The adaptations of each species clearly depend on each other and all other species on the island. No adaptations can be understood in isolation. Moreover, it makes no sense to ask whether one species *determines* the adaptation of the other. The outcome of development, the structure of the island biotope as a whole and the adaptations of the individual species, is best understood as a dynamic system of continual interaction and mutual influence. (p. 140)

As we add to this story, the evolution metaphor works even better for human learning if we view the coevolving species of knowledge as moving from environment to environment. Unlike animals on an isolated island, people move, and this movement helps evolve an understanding that can continue to adapt as it moves beyond the original "habitat" of learning.

The chapter comes in three parts. In the first part, we argue that despite its scientific effectiveness, isolating cognitive mechanisms can blind researchers to significant components and indicators of learning. In particular, we highlight that much of the relevant learning research has tended to focus on how people learn from direct experience or how they learn from communicated experience but not how people coevolve the two. We also argue that the outcome measures of learning interventions have not sufficiently looked at people's subsequent abilities to adapt to new environments, and this has led researchers to overlook the value of certain forms of instruction. In the second part, we consider more integrative alternatives, and we turn to the work of developing a method for integrative research. We describe the methods and measures of the DKE framework and defend each empirically. In the third part, we combine the methods and measures of DKE and describe the results of a study that taught children descriptive statistics. The study not only measured the students' abilities to apply what they had learned, it also examined their abilities to evolve new knowledge when placed in new contexts. This latter test of "learning at transfer" is extremely important. The goal of most school-based instruction is not simply to train students to solve a specific class of problem efficiently or to transfer a specific procedure untouched to a new context. We argue instead that the goal of school-based instruction should be to prepare students to adapt and learn in the future (Bransford & Schwartz, 1999).

COGNITIVE PSYCHOLOGY AND "METHODOLOGICAL ISOLATIONISM"

An original catalyst for the growth of cognitive psychology was to handle complex forms of learning that behaviorism could not: for example, perceptual learning (Gibson, 1986), language acquisition (Chomsky, 1966), and hypothesis testing (Levine, 1975). The enterprise has been hugely successful, but it has stalled somewhat at the door of classroom education. Cognitive psychology's successes in designing instruction are swamped by criticisms (Cobb, Yackel, & Wood, 1992; Lave, 1988) and defensive replies (Anderson, Reder, & Simon, 1996; Mayer, 1996). The state of affairs suggests that the complexity of classroom learning may exceed cognitive psychology just as learning with understanding exceeded behaviorism.

We attribute some of cognitive psychology's classroom limitations to its methodological isolationism. We begin our discussion by reviewing two facets of isolationism: the attempt to study cognitive mechanisms in isolation and the attempt to measure learning in settings isolated from resources for continued learning.

Isolating Cognitive Mechanisms

There are many self-acknowledged limitations to cognitive psychology for developing prescriptive classroom learning theories. These include small effect sizes that are not robust to the natural variability of the classroom, the belief that science should avoid prescriptions of what should be, and a limited consideration of contextual sources of information and interpretation that naturally occur in the highly social environment of the classroom. However, we see a more methodological impediment to cognitive psychology's contribution to a prescriptive learning theory. Cognitive psychologists frequently attempt to dissociate and isolate cognitive systems. They distinguish working and long-term memory, implicit and explicit memory, declarative and procedural knowledge, metacognition and problem solving, visual and verbal processing, and many other subsystems. It is a highly analytic endeavor, and the double dissociation is the most prized experimental demonstration. Once psychologists have distinguished a particular cognitive mechanism, they study this mechanism often to the exclusion of others.

The method of dissociation is very effective. It has revealed distinct cognitive mechanisms and is beginning to locate their neurological basis. However, an emphasis on one system, often to the neglect of another, may not be the best way to develop a prescriptive theory. Learning complex topics, such as calculus or car repair, involves many cognitive systems. Isolating one system for study does not explain how that system integrates with others nor how its development depends on other systems. This shortcoming has been noted by the instructional psychologist Glaser (1992) who stated that "Even if we accept that it will be difficult to achieve a unified theory of learning, we should attempt to discover grounds for the integration of key aspects of human competence that are considered separately" (p. 255).

At the risk of oversimplification, we illustrate our point with a high-level division that has run through the research literature for many years. This division separates theories that emphasize the acquisition and application of first-hand knowledge and theories that emphasize the acquisition and application of second-hand knowledge. First-hand theories focus on direct experience, and second-hand theories focus on descriptions of experience (i.e., communicated knowledge).

First-hand theories depend on people directly interacting with the phenomena of interest. Before children develop skills of interpreting and generating descriptions, they engage their world directly. First-hand theories largely focus on perception and action, and they tend to be more individualistic than second-hand theories because they emphasize direct, personal experience. Examples include Shepard and Cooper's (1986) and Kosslyn's (1980) studies of imagery because their emphasis was on how people internally represent perceptual phenomenon. Similarly, Piaget's (1970) first-hand theory examined how children abstracted understanding based on their actions with and perceptions of the immediate world. Although Piaget and other first-hand theorists have acknowledged the significance of second-hand sources of knowledge and interpretation, it has not been the focus of their research and they typically have not contributed to second-hand theorizing and research. For instance, although Piaget studied children's egocentric speech, he did so to make the point that young children are cognitively egocentric rather than exploring the influence of language and description on cognition.

First-hand theories are highly relevant to learning. No amount of reading is sufficient to learn to drive a car. People need a chance to turn the wheel, feel the acceleration, and hit the breaks in real time. Nevertheless, first-hand theories alone are insufficient for prescribing instruction. For example, embodied theories of cognition emphasize the mental simulation and organization of bodily experience (Barsalou, 1999; Glenberg & Kaschak, 2002; Lakoff & Nuñez, 2000). They are a response to the amodal, symbol-processing theories common to early information processing, and they argue that expressions such as "he pushed his way to the top of the company" or "a force applied to an object ..." gain meaning from bodily experiences of pushing. However, they have minimal advice for when external symbols or simply being told something, should offer significant support for learning.

Second-hand theories of knowledge acquisition depend on individuals interpreting descriptions often in the absence of the original referent. The second-hand information comes through symbolic forms like language and mathematics, and more recent research is examining multimedia. Second-hand theories centrally locate communicable symbolic structures. For example, Anderson's (1983) theory of how people convert declarative knowledge or instructions (words) into procedural knowledge (actions) emphasizes the "internalization" or "processing" of second-hand knowledge to permit meaningful action.

Second-hand theories are also highly relevant to learning. An incalculable amount of people's knowledge comes second-hand from books, and understanding how this happens is important. Nevertheless, we doubt that second-hand theories are sufficient for prescribing instruction. Models of text comprehension (e.g., Mannes & Kintsch, 1987), for example, often focus on the relations between the words within a passage. They are an attempt to describe how people use verbal and textual devices (e.g., pronoun position, capitalization, sentence ordering) to integrate sentences to "comprehend" a text. Such theories, however, provide limited guidance for when people should experience a situation instead of just read about it.

The division between first- and second-hand theories has a strong empirical basis; cognition is not uniform. For example, Schwartz and Black (1999) asked people to reason about pouring liquid from glasses. There were two glasses of equal height but different diameters as shown in Fig. 2.1. Each glass had a line drawn the same distance from the rim to indicate the level of water (although there was no actual water in the glasses). In the second-hand condition, participants could only look at the glasses and had to reason by describing what would happen. They had to decide if the two glasses would start to pour at the same angle of tilt or whether one glass would pour sooner than the other. In the first-hand condition, people held a glass (without water), closed their eyes, and tilted the glass until they "saw the water reach the rim of the glass in their imagination." Schwartz and Black (1999) measured the angle of tilt and repeated the process with the second glass. The tasks were administered with three different cup shapes using three different participant pools.

People performed below or at chance in the second-hand condition. Moreover, when people worked in pairs and increased their reliance on communicated descriptions, they were never correct (Schwartz, 1999). The first-hand condition presents a different picture of people's knowledge. Except for one person, everybody who was tested correctly showed that the

FIG. 2.1. Will the glasses pour at the same or different angles?

glass with a wider opening would start to pour sooner than a comparable glass with a narrower opening. Fig. 2.2 shows their average tilts for three shapes of glass. This research indicates a dissociation between the processes referred to by first-hand and second-hand theories, and evidently, the processes do not always coordinate with one another (the same people were accurate when they tilted the glasses but inaccurate when they reasoned verbally). The challenge of this chapter is to acknowledge and take advantage of these different processes.

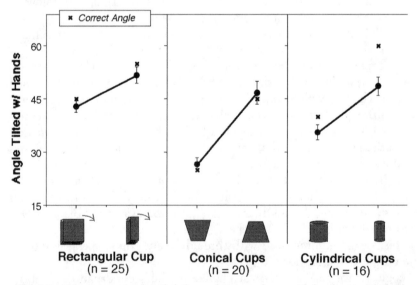

FIG. 2.2. The average angles of tilt for participants who turned the glasses with their eyes closed and imagined they had water. *Note.* From "Inferences Through Imagined Actions: Knowing by Simulated Doing," by D. L. Schwartz and T. Black, 1999, *Journal of Experimental Psychology: Learning, Memory, Cognition, 25*, p. 120. Copyright 1999 by the American Psychological Association. Reprinted with permission.

First-hand and second-hand theories attempt to isolate the cognitive processes that people apply to perceptual-motor content and to symbolic content, respectively. This divide and conquer strategy is a superior way to make scientific progress until researchers exclusively rely on one or the other to explain complex cognition. First- and second-hand theorists often attempt to generalize their favored mechanism to explain complex cognition and learning. In our case, when we began research on people's abilities to imagine complex devices, we were first-hand theorists. We assumed people's perceptual experiences were the wellspring of all understanding. Through a process of abstraction, perception-based knowledge would turn into explicit description. However, we have failed to find evidence of bootstrapping from first-hand knowledge to second-hand knowledge.

For example, Schwartz and Black (1996) asked people to reason about chains of gears: "Imagine a horizontal chain of five gears. If the gear on the far right tries to turn clockwise, what will the gear on the far left do?" Over multiple trials with differing numbers of gears, most people induced a parity rule; for even chains of gears, the first and last gears turn opposite directions. Before people learned the parity rule, they used hand gestures to portray the gears. They depended on their first-hand knowledge. Once they induced the parity rule, they stopped gesturing and relied on second-hand descriptions of the gears, for example, "All the odd gears turn the same direction." At first glance, the results appear to show that people abstracted their first-hand knowledge of object interactions into second-hand descriptions of the larger pattern of gear behavior. Although the gestures seemed to play a necessary role in the rule induction, they were not sufficient. Second-hand representations and processes were critical to the transition from gestural simulations to rule-based descriptions. We examined the differences between people who did and did not induce the rule. People who verbally described the gears' positions with numbers induced the parity rule 100% of the time, whereas people who did not count the gears only induced the rule 26% of the time.

In another study, Schwartz (1995) examined the differences between 10th-grade children working alone or in pairs. The children who tried to solve the gear problems alone only induced the parity rule 14% of the time. In contrast, children who worked in pairs induced the rule 58% of the time. This is well above the probability that any of the pairs would have included at least one individual who might have solved the problem in isolation. Evidently, first-hand experiences were not sufficient to induce the rule—people also needed to integrate descriptions using numbers, often in communication with others.

We have found similar results when looking at the development of proportional reasoning over physical situations. For example, when young children were encouraged to use mathematics to explain problems about a balance scale or involving juice and water, they developed a more complex understanding of torque and concentration than if they just relied on first-hand experience (Schwartz, Martin, & Pfaffman, 2005; Schwartz & Moore, 1998). Although it seems obvious in retrospect, brute induction over first-hand experience is not enough to propel the learning and development of complex ideas. People need the structure provided by communicated cultural forms that have been invented over the years (such as mathematics) to help organize complexity. At the same time, second-hand knowledge, without some grounding in first-hand experience, does not get people very far either. Children who merely memorize math facts can end up knowing that $3 + 4 = 7$ yet not know that 7 is greater than 4. Understanding requires first- and second-hand experience, and it is important to figure out how to effectively combine the two through instruction.

Isolating the Outcomes of Learning

A second manifestation of methodological isolationism involves measures of learning. One problem is that researchers often measure outcomes associated with a single cognitive mechanism. For example, there are measures of memory that distinguish between subsystems ranging from implicit and explicit memory to semantic and episodic memory. The design of precisely targeted measures is an important skill developed by cognitive psychologists, and it leads to significant progress. However, tests of specific memory functions are only proxy measures of deep understanding because deep understanding also includes the ability to perceive, plan, act, and transfer. It is important for education to avoid an overreliance on memory tests unless the goal is to train people to remember specific procedures and facts under narrow retrieval conditions. As we demonstrate following, memory tests can fail to differentiate those who understand from those who do not.

A second (but related) problem with many measures of learning is that they tend to employ sequestered problem solving (Bransford & Schwartz, 1999). After participants in an experiment learn a target concept, they attempt unaided problem solving or retrieval. Like a jury, they are sequestered from contaminating sources of information as they complete tasks that measure their learning. This way the researchers can be sure that any differences between learning conditions are due to the experimental treatments and not some learning that surreptitiously occurred during the assessment.

An important question is whether the goal of education is to prepare people to solve problems without access to resources. For example, typical transfer experiments ask whether participants who have learned a task or concept can apply their learning to a new problem without access to additional resources for learning how to solve the problem. The assumption appears to be that transfer involves the direct application of a confined body knowledge without any adaptation or growth of that knowledge in a new situation. This assumption seems warranted when the goal is efficiency, and the context of application is highly similar to the context of instruction. However, for situations of adaptation, a reliance on tests of sequestered problem solving seems ecologically suspect (Schwartz, Bransford, & Sears, in press). As an everyday example, when students apply the arithmetic they learn at school to go grocery shopping, they need to learn about the particular characteristics of shopping (e.g., best buy comparisons), and they need to adapt their algorithms to work without pencil and paper. If they only transferred their paper and pencil algorithms, they would make very slow shoppers. Hatano and Inagaki (1986) differentiated adaptive experts who continue to learn as the times change from routine experts who apply the same skill over and over. For most school-based instruction, the goal is to prepare people to adapt to new situations, and therefore, it makes sense to assess the quality of the instruction by students' abilities to learn given resources in a new environment.

In addition to questions of ecological validity, tests of sequestered problem solving raise a methodological concern. Tests of unaided problem solving can be obstacles to determining effective strategies for putting learners on a trajectory toward adaptive expertise. They can blind one to the value of activities that prepare students for future learning but do not immediately show benefits on tests of sequestered problem solving. An example of this point comes from a study (Martin & Schwartz, in press) that looked at children learning to add fractions. Over 3 days of guided discovery, fifth-grade students learned fraction addition with physical manipulatives that they could move around to aid in their computations and conceptualization. Half of the students worked with tiles pieces, and half of the students worked with pie wedges (e.g., one-fourth wedges, one-eighth wedges, etc.). Given feedback, students in both conditions learned to do fraction addition problems with their material, and the groups did not exhibit any significant differences. In a transfer phase, students from both conditions tried to solve new fraction addition problems without any feedback. Students tried to solve problems in their heads. When they could not solve the problems in their head, the students received new manipulatives they had not seen before (e.g., fraction bars that indicated fractions by their length, and beans and cups). To successfully solve the problems with the new materials, the children had to adapt to the new environment and figure out how to use the materials to support their reasoning. In this setting, the tile students did much better than the pie students. Over several trials, the tile students learned how to use the new materials, whereas the pie students did not.

The fraction study provides an important lesson. When the students worked with their original learning material or had to solve problems in their head without access to new resources for learning, they looked the same across the groups. However, when Martin and Schwartz (in press) looked at how well they performed in a context with new resources (i.e., new materials), the benefits of the tiles became apparent. Had the knowledge assessments only relied on sequestered problem solving, they would have overlooked the value of the tiles for preparing students to learn during transfer. Tests of sequestered problem solving can be too blunt an instrument for measuring early stages of learning and for evaluating the effectiveness of one instructional treatment over another.

INTEGRATIVE APPROACHES TO COGNITIVE RESEARCH

Although debates about the primacy of first- and second-hand processes can successfully advance psychological theory and evidence, these debates will not explain how people integrate the two processes. At the level of educational experience, learners require both, whatever the ultimate atomic structure of cognition may be. Tests of isolated problem solving without evaluations of participant's abilities to learn in new situations can advance cognitive psychology. However, isolating learners from an environment of learning during a test also misses important aspects of the prior knowledge that prepare people to learn, especially when the goal of instruction should be to prepare people to learn from the resources available in their next classes or once they leave school altogether.

In this section, we consider more integrative approaches to cognitive psychology that we believe can advance both cognitive research and the development of prescriptive learning theories. We review a few integrative approaches, and then we describe and test DKE. Afterward, we describe our efforts to develop dynamic assessments (Feuerstein, 1979) that examine whether students are prepared to evolve their knowledge in new situations and learn.

Some Approaches to Integrative Research

Case and Okamoto (1996) provided an excellent example of an integrative model of learning. Case and Okamoto's work arose from the careful analysis of children's natural patterns of development; their theory describes development as the integration of core conceptual structures rather than as the maturation or enhancement of a single knowledge structure. One example comes from Case and Okamoto's analysis of the development of children's understanding of counting and simple addition. In the early stages of the process, children move their fingers down a line of objects. At the same time, they say a counting word for each action. The interweaving of action, perception, and language permits the child to develop a differentiated understanding, for example, of the cardinal value of five and the ordinal value of the fifth position. Case and Okamoto's model provides important guidelines about developmental readiness for learning in mathematics, the significance of some representations over others, and the importance of games that lead to children's fluency in traversing the many representations and manifestations of quantity.

Another approach to developing an integrative research agenda comes from work on scaffolding. Scaffolding research examines the material situations and the social mediations that lead to successful learning. The method of work is analogous to naturalists who look for native plants that have medicinal properties. Once they discover a naturally occurring medicinal plant, chemists can distill the active ingredients into a potent medicine. Similarly, scaffolding research often builds on everyday instances of material and social supports to seed the development of more precise instructional technologies. The central idea of scaffolding is that with mediation, students can complete mature activities that they cannot complete themselves. A common explanation for the effectiveness of scaffolding is that it permits the learner to complete the activity, and over time, the learner internalizes the context and practices of the scaffold. The cognitive mechanisms responsible for internalization are themselves often treated as black boxes, which seems acceptable for the level at which these theories operate.

Scaffolding can take many forms. In one form, learners complete an authentic activity with additional physical support. Training wheels is a canonical example. In another form, the support comes from the social structure and active mediation of more knowledgeable others. Apprenticeship is a good example, and this approach has been nicely generalized to instruction. In reciprocal teaching (Palinscar & Brown, 1984), for example, teachers provide models for how to ask important questions as the teacher and students work jointly to comprehend a text. Gradually, students take on more of the responsibility for asking questions until such time that they can complete the task without the help of the teacher.

A common ingredient of scaffolding is that learners take on partial roles that allow them to learn the form of the activity even though they may not fully understand its function (Saxe, 1991, 1999). For example, in a study (Nasir, 2005) of learning in the game of dominoes, Nasir found that experts managed to scaffold novices' partial moves while still maintaining an enjoyable game for themselves. The experts and novices cocreated a game structure in which novice players were allowed to choose which tile to play, and on the next move, the expert partner determined where to place the tile. A particularly interesting form of scaffolding involves learner's identity as a social participant (Lave & Wenger, 1991; Nasir, 2002). For example, a young child might wear a carpenter's belt filled with plastic tools.

Although the child cannot use the tools to participate in the activity of building an authentic structure, the plastic tools scaffold the child's identity as a builder and conceivably position him or her to learn carpentry in the future.

Scaffolding research offers a nice instance of studying a preexisting, integrative learning activity to build a prescriptive theory. Scaffolding involves perceiving and acting plus the communication and interpretation of other people's understandings that can lend significance and structure to first-hand experiences. However, the study of scaffolding has some limitations for the development of prescriptive learning theories. One limitation is that it has followed the natural tendency for precise terms to become amorphous when taken up broadly. Scaffolding has become so pervasive that anything that supports learning is labeled a scaffold. Another and more foundational limitation is that scaffolding tends to focus on mature performance so that the measure of successful scaffolding is whether a learner can complete a task unaided. From our perspective, one goal of instruction should be to prepare people to learn in the future. Because of its emphasis on performance, not all scaffolding and apprenticeship models include mechanisms to support future learning and adaptation beyond the performance of the original task.

Final in our survey of integrative methods is work on multiple representations. Research along these lines stems from the belief that the juxtaposition of different representations will lead to a deeper understanding. Kaput (1995), for example, developed yoked computer simulations. Students see the movement of an object like a car on a computer screen while yoked graphs simultaneously show graphs of the car's acceleration, velocity, and distance. A similar method allows children to make the movement themselves while showing the plots on the computer screen (Nemirovsky, Tierney, & Wright, 1998). These types of juxtapositions often build on important intuitions and assumptions. For example, in the yoked simulations, the underlying assumption appears to be that meaning arises by finding the similarities between first-hand experiences of an event and second-hand representations of the same event. Students, for example, learn that their bodily acceleration maps onto a steeper slope in the velocity graph. However, by itself, the mere mapping of the similarities between representations may not be the most effective way to learn and understand. For example, work on analogical mapping proposes that people learn by mapping a known structure into an unknown structure. For this to be effective, people need to have the known structure to begin with. What if they do not? Ideally, research on multiple representations will develop a principled account for how people can best integrate different forms of knowing and representation, especially when that knowledge is immature to begin with.

DKE

DKE is an explicit attempt to join first- and second-hand experiences into a prescription for learning. It begins with well-documented mechanisms that generate specific forms of learning. It then proposes a framework in which the multiple representations and mechanisms can interact to coevolve a well-rounded understanding that supports future learning and adaptation. We first describe a mechanism for developing second-hand knowledge and then a mechanism for developing first-hand knowledge. We then present our method of integration and an initial test in the domain of statistics instruction. Afterward, we return to the question of preparing people for future learning.

A powerful and natural mechanism by which people come to describe the world is through the construction of mental and symbolic models. Vosniadou and Brewer (1992), for example, asked young children to draw pictures of the earth. Vosniadou and Brewer found that children spontaneously constructed coherent, albeit unconventional, models. For example, children combined their first-hand experience of a flat earth with their second-hand knowledge that the world is round and they drew round discs or a flat earth resting in a bowl. These constructions illustrate that people are natural model builders, and it follows that this could be a useful mechanism for enhancing learning.

In the case of the earth, the drawings presumably reflected the internal models the children spontaneously constructed. People are also good at intentionally constructing external models to serve as explicit second-hand descriptions. Schwartz (1993) asked seventh-grade children to construct visual representations of causal pathways such as "X can communicate the disease to Y," "Q can get the disease from R," "F gets infected by Y." Their task was to make representations that could solve problems such as "If X has the disease, what else can get the disease?" The children were quite inventive at building models, and most children represented the many-to-one and one-to-many relations needed to solve the problems. Figure 2.3 shows a representative selection of the visualizations the children developed. Interestingly, the opportunity to construct visual models had a lasting effect. Several weeks later, embedded in a class activity, the children spontaneously transferred the idea of using visual representations for a novel problem, although there were no prompts or cues to do so. Even more impressive, over half of the students also tried to invent new visual representations for problems that did not have the same "causal pathway" structure. Appropriate opportunities to build models can prepare students to adapt new structures in novel settings.

In addition to a mechanism for developing second-hand knowledge, we also need a mechanism for developing first-hand knowledge. A critical form

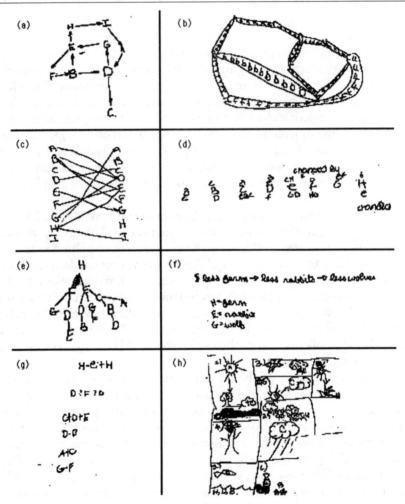

FIG. 2.3. Examples of explicit models students invented to solve problems about chains of causality. *Note.* From "The Construction and Analogical Transfer of Symbolic Visualizations," by D. L. Schwartz, *Journal of Research in Science Teaching, 30,* p. 1313. Copyright © 1993 Wiley Periodicals, Inc. Reprinted with permission.

of first-hand knowledge is the ability to perceive. Contrary to the common assumption that perception is untutored, people learn to perceive. For example, novices cannot taste the subtle flavors that differentiate two wines, whereas experts can. A common "expert trap" is to assume that novices can see what the expert refers to. Students and teachers, for example, can use the same words with very different meanings in mind. For example, in a psychology course, teachers may present an instance of recognition memory, label it for the students, and hear the students use the words "recognition memory." This does not mean the students have noticed what constitutes the phenomenon recognition memory. They may only see the vague phenomenon of "remembering things" and fail to distinguish between recognition memory and free recall, for example.

A significant body of research has described learning to perceive in terms of noticing what differentiates things from one another (Gibson, 1969; Marton & Booth, 1997). Biederman and Shiffrar (1987) demonstrated that people who have to determine the sex of baby chicks learn to differentiate the male and female chicks by discerning the distinctive and often subtle features that uniquely identify each sex. In contrast, novices cannot distinguish between male and female chicks because they do not see the key features. A powerful way to help people notice is to have them examine contrasting cases (Bransford, Franks, Vye, & Sherwood, 1989; Gibson & Gibson, 1955). For example, wine tasting classes ask people to compare one wine against another so that people can isolate what makes each wine distinctive. Gardner (1982) described an art exhibit that juxtaposed original paintings and forgeries. At first people cannot tell the difference, but over time, they begin to notice the features that identify the original. Dibble, as cited in Gibson (1969), even found that opportunities to examine contrasting cases of letters enabled people to subsequently recognize the letters better than copying them.

The goal of DKE is to unite the mechanisms of perceptual learning for developing first-hand knowledge with model building for developing second-hand knowledge. Each mode of understanding has different characteristics and supports different insights and inferences. To bring the two ways of knowing into productive interaction, it is not sufficient to simply juxtapose them. The goal of learning is not to find the correlations or mappings between the two such that they are simply isomorphs in different modalities. Instead, the goal is to find out how the two forms of knowing can complement one another to make a more profound and multifaceted understanding. For example, in the previous example of people learning about gears, the gestured simulations of the gears provided access to primitive physical intuitions of force and movement, whereas the mathematics provided access to highly structured representations. In combination, they generated a generalized symbolic parity rule grounded in physical experience.

Our approach to developing a prescriptive learning theory is to use the unique strengths of each form of knowing to illuminate the other. We design instruction so that the two forms of knowing coevolve as they adapt to new task environments. The key features of DKE draw on some of the concepts found in evolutionary theory:

1. The process begins by students producing a new species of symbolic model that can respond to differences between contrasting situations. This permits students to simultaneously perceive what is significant about the features of the contrasting cases and develop a structured account of what they perceive.

2. Students test their models across contexts of contrasting pairs. As they confront new contexts, some models fail, and students notice properties of the new contexts and attributes of their models that "selected" against survival.

3. Students mutate new models that can survive in the new context. The new models evolve from the understanding developed from previous models, even if the students need to abandon the form of their earlier model and try a new "genetic" line of models.

4. Students juxtapose their respective models to notice their "survival" value. Whereas the contrasting cases introduce environmental variation, the juxtaposed models introduce species level variation. Noticing the varying quality and useful features of different models introduces selective pressures to help students generate useful models.

Across the multiple contexts and opportunities for coevolution, the learner comes to perceive important features of the problem domain while evolving models that can adapt to those and future features. We best illuminate the first three aspects of DKE with a brief study (Moore & Schwartz, 1998) that helped students learn about the statistical concept of variability. Moore and Schwartz presented college students with a sequence of tightly focused contrasting cases. They had to invent formulas to capture what is different about each pair of cases. For example, the first pair of contrasting cases presented the two distributions: {1 3 5 7 9} versus {3 4 5 6 7}. Students knew that the two distributions have something in common, namely, the average. Moore and Schwartz explained that the average is a convenient way to characterize what is common about the distributions. It is much easier to communicate the averages than the complete distributions, especially when the number of items gets very large. Moore and Schwartz then asked the students to notice that there is also a difference between the two sets of numbers called the "spread" and to invent a formula that can capture what is different. The students typically invented a range formula that subtracted the smallest number from the largest. Students then received a new contrasting case: {1 3 3 3 9} versus {1 3 5 7 9}. Students saw that their range formula did not differentiate the two data sets. They came to perceive that spread is not simply measured by the end values; it involves density as well. They had to evolve their original model to handle the new context of contrasting cases. As the process of contrasting cases plus invention continued, students noticed additional features and developed models that were robust to those features. For example, the students received the contrast: {1 3 5} versus {1 1 3 3 5 5}. This helped them notice that distributions also had different sample sizes and that their formulas needed to accommodate this possibility.

Students rarely invented the conventional solution agreed on by experts, namely, the variance formula. However, as we demonstrate following, inventing models over contrasting cases prepares students to understand the statistical formulas at a deep level when they become available. For example, students appreciate that dividing by n elegantly solves the problem of different samples sizes. For now, we simply show that the process of coevolving models and perceptions across contrasting cases helped students become aware of the aspects of context that their representations must handle to be useful. In turn, this awareness provided them with a better understanding of the work that a symbolic model does and the situations to which it refers. Moore and Schwartz (1998) compared the students who completed the DKE activities and never learned a formal solution with two other groups of students. One group of students learned the procedure for computing variance from a worked example and applied it to each of the contrasting data sets in turn. The other group of students had taken a semester of college statistics. A few weeks after the DKE intervention embedded in a regular class, the students from all three groups saw the problem shown in Table 2.1. In this problem, an industrialist has made the claim that blue people are smarter than green people, and therefore, it is better to hire blue people. To support his claim, the industrialist offers the result of an intelligence test that shows that blue people have a higher average IQ than green people. He also points to the work of many other researchers who have found the same result. The students saw an example of the distributions the industrialist had found. The students were asked to write as many arguments as they could think of to disagree with the industrialist.

When Moore and Schwartz (1998) examined the arguments presented by the students, the results were striking. The students from the DKE condition noticed that the averages were misleading. They saw past the symbolic measure (i.e., the average) and perceived the bimodal distribution of the green people. For example, one student stated, "The average is wrong here. Nearly half the green people are smarter than all but the top few blue people." Over 95% of the DKE students noticed that there were green people that were smarter than the blue people. In contrast, less than half of the students in each of the other two groups noticed this. Instead, they tended to accept the interpretation of the average. These students exclusively made arguments such as "IQ tests are not fair," or "IQ tests do not mean they won't be good workers." So, even though the DKE students had worked with fairly limited and abstract sets of data, they were prepared to think deeply about the meaning and applicability of the average and to perceive the quantita-

TABLE 2.1
A Test Item Used to Measure Students' Abilities to Perceive and Evaluate Measures of Central Tendency

A wealthy industrialist wrote a book describing how to make a business work. He said the single most important task was to hire the smartest people possible. In particular, he suggested hiring BLUE people. To back up his suggestion, he reported the results of a study in which he compared the intelligence of BLUE and GREEN people. In the study, he randomly selected 40 BLUE people and 40 GREEN people. He gave each individual in each group an IQ test. Here are the individual scores and the group averages:

GREEN People Scores
82, 83, 84, 86, 87, 88, 88, 88, 89, 89, 89, 89, 89, 90, 90, 90, 90, 91, 91, 92, 95, 95, 97, 101, 106, 108, 108, 109, 109, 109, 110, 110, 110, 110, 111, 111, 111, 112, 113, 115
GREEN average IQ = 98

BLUE People Scores
85, 93, 96, 97, 97, 98, 98, 99, 99, 99, 99, 100, 100, 100, 100, 100, 100, 101, 101, 101, 101, 101, 102, 102, 102, 102, 102, 102, 103, 103, 103, 103, 104, 104, 104, 105, 106, 106, 107, 111
BLUE average IQ = 101

Based on this data, the industrialist claimed that BLUE people are smarter than GREEN people. One hundred activists across the country were outraged and claimed that the industrialist's results were a fluke. They each conducted their own studies by giving IQ tests to BLUE and GREEN people. To their surprise, the activists came up with results that were nearly identical to the industrialist's—the industrialist's results were reliable. The industrialist published an article in the New York Times reporting the results. He repeated his suggestion, "If you want the smartest people to work for you, hire BLUE people."

How would you argue that the industrialist's conclusions are wrong?
Write as many arguments as you can think of in the next 5 minutes.

Note. From "Inventing to Prepare for Future Learning: The Hidden Efficiency of Original Student Production in Statistics Instruction," by D. L. Schwartz and T. Martin, 2004, *Cognition and Instruction,* 22, p. 182. Copyright 2004 by Lawrence Erlbaum Associates, Inc. Reprinted with permission.

tive phenomenon to which the average referred. In contrast, the students that had been directly taught statistics accepted the average at face value and did not consider whether it was a fair summarization of the data.

Measures of Preparation for Future Learning

We now return to our second concern with methodological isolationism. We argued that much of cognitive psychology uses a sequestered problem-solving paradigm that measures the effects of learning with tests of unaided problem solving or memory. We argued that the subsequent ability to learn with resources could be a more important and sensitive indicator of the effectiveness of instruction. We suggested that an alternative to sequestered problem solving is a dynamic assessment that measures preparation for future learning. In this section, we demonstrate one measure of preparation for future learning. Schwartz and Bransford (1998) used it to compare two methods of instruction. Students completed one of two instructional treatments. Afterward, they were measured by how well they subsequently learned from a new information resource. The students who learned more from the resource indicated which treatment better prepared students for future learning.

Schwartz and Bransford's (1998) studies examined whether assessments of preparation for future learning would reveal important information missed by assessments of sequestered problem solving. The studies occurred in the context of teaching college students about memory phenomena including false recognition, primacy, recency, ordered recall, and so on. In one study, some of the students analyzed simplified data sets from classic memory experiments. By design, experiments generate contrasting data sets that help illuminate the consequences of different treatments. Table 2.2 provides a sample of the data sets the students analyzed. A careful examination of the data reveals multiple contrasts that can help students perceive what is significant in the results. The students' task was to analyze the data sets and graph the important patterns they found. Schwartz and Bransford did not tell the students the purpose of the experimental designs; they had to discern and decide which patterns in the data they thought were important. The other students did not work with the contrasting cases. Instead, they read a modified book chapter that described the same studies, showed the graphed results, and explained their theoretical significance. Their task was to write a two-page summary of the important ideas in the chapter. A few days later, the students in both groups heard a common lecture that explained the experiments, the results, and the theories that were designed to accommodate the results. The question is whether both groups of students had been equally prepared to learn from the lecture. The study also included a third group that did not hear the lecture. This group also completed the contrasting cases activity, but instead of hearing the lecture, they analyzed the data sets a second time looking for any patterns they may have missed. All told, there were three conditions: contrasting cases + lecture, summarize chapter + lecture, and double contrasting cases.

TABLE 2.2
Examples of the Simplified and Contrasting Data Sets That Students Analyze to Prepare Them to Learn from a Lecture

Study 1

In this study, psychological researchers brought together five subjects. The researchers read the subjects the following list of 20 words at a rate of one word per three seconds. Here are the words the researchers read to the subjects in the order in which they read them:

car, sky, apple, book, cup, lock, coat, light, bush, iron,
water, house, tape, file, glass, dog, cloud, hand, chair, bag

After the researchers read these words they said: "Recall." When the researchers said "Recall" the subjects wrote down as many of the 20 words as they could remember.

Here are the words the five subjects in the study recalled and the order in which they recalled them:

Sbj #1: bag, hand, chair, dog, car, sky, apple, book, tape, file, house, list, bush
Sbj #2: bag, chair, hand, cloud, sky, car, book, apple, cup, lock, iron, glass
Sbj #3: bag, hand, chair, cloud, sky, car, apple, book, file, bush, coat, iron, tape
Sbj #4: bag, hand, chair, dog, car, sky, apple, water, cup, glass, house, bush, dog, book
Sbj #5: bag, chair, hand, cloud, sky, car, book, coat, water, light, lock, house

Study 2

This study is the same as Study 1, except that the researchers did not tell the subjects to recall the words immediately after reading the list of words. Instead, the researchers asked the subjects to do another task first (i.e., a division problem). This task took 30 seconds. Immediately after this task they were told to recall as many of the words as they could, again in any order they liked.

Here are the words the five new subjects recalled and the order in which they recalled them:

Sbj #6: car, sky, book, apple, bush, house, glass, chair
Sbj #7: car, sky, lock, iron, water, cloud, bag
Sbj #8: car, apple, coat, bag, hand, file
Sbj #9: car, sky, light, cup, tape, dog
Sbj #10: car, apple, cup, water, glass, house

To assess whether the students learned from the lecture, Schwartz and Bransford (1998) employed two measures about a week later. One measure used a recognition test that included claims repeated in the book chapter and the lecture, for example, "When people understand something they have read, they tend to remember it verbatim. True or false?" The second measure was a prediction task that used the description of a novel experiment. The students' task was to predict as many of the outcomes from the experiment as possible. There were eight distinct predictions that could be applied from the materials they had worked with beforehand.

On the recognition test (Schwartz & Bransford, 1998), the two conditions that heard the lecture looked about the same, but the double contrast condition did poorly. By this assessment, the contrasting cases activity appears useless. However, the results on the prediction task reveal a different story. Figure 2.4 shows that the double contrast students again did badly. However, the summarize + lecture students did equally badly. The contrasting cases + lecture students did quite well, producing over twice as many correct predictions as students in the other conditions. By this result, the contrasting cases were very important for learning from the lecture. Students who had read about the descriptions of the experiments instead of analyzing them first-hand did not learn very well from the lecture. In contrast, students who had analyzed the contrasting cases learned a great deal from the lecture. We know they learned from the lecture because the double contrast group that did not hear the lecture did badly.

One important lesson from the Schwartz and Bransford (1998) study is that the activity of analyzing contrasting cases would have looked useless if the researchers had not measured its effects on students' subsequent abilities to learn. Assessments of preparation for future learning can reveal levels of knowing that are imperceptible to sequestered forms of assessments. A second lesson is that assessments of memory, particularly recognition memory, can be misleading. On the test of recognition memory, students who

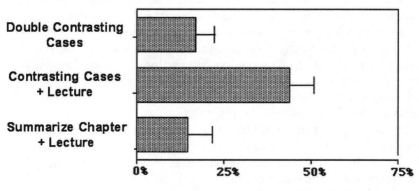

**Percentage of Correct Predictions
Students Made for a Novel Experiment**

FIG. 2.4. Students who studied contrasting data sets were more prepared to learn from a lecture than students who read and summarized a book chapter. *Note.* From "A Time for Telling," by D. L. Schwartz and J. D. Bransford, 1998, *Cognition and Instruction, 16,* p. 502. Copyright 1998 by Lawrence Erlbaum Associates, Inc. Adapted with permission.

summarized the chapter performed the same as students who analyzed the contrasting cases and heard the lecture. The benefits of the contrasting cases appeared when students had to transfer to evaluate a new situation and perceive its significant features.

A final lesson is that lectures can be an effective method of instruction if people are prepared to understand the significance of what the lecture describes. We have met researchers who believe that "telling" is inconsistent with theories of constructivist pedagogy. We have also seen instructors who refuse to tell students an answer for fear of violating effective principles of constructivist instruction. Constructivism, however, is a theory of knowledge growth and not a prescriptive theory of instruction. According to constructivism, all knowledge is constructed whether the building blocks of knowledge come from first- or second-hand experience. Given appropriate experiences, people can be very effective at constructing knowledge (or as we prefer to say it, "effective at evolving knowledge") even if they are sitting quietly listening to a lecture. The question is what activities prepare students to continue to evolve their knowledge.

INTEGRATING METHODS AND MEASURES
TO TEACH DESCRIPTIVE STATISTICS

In the preceding sections, we offered two alternatives to methodological isolationism. One alternative was the development of studies that examine the integration of different forms of knowing rather than their isolation, and we outlined DKE as a promising instance. Our second alternative was to measure students' preparedness for future learning rather than relying solely on measures of isolated performance. We provided an instance of a dynamic assessment in the context of teaching theories of memory that uncovered important indicators of learning that were obscured by measures of unaided performance. We now bring these two proposals together in a single study that involved ninth-grade students learning descriptive statistics.

Statistics is a notorious instance in which people have trouble learning the formulas and the phenomena to which they refer. A large body of cognitive research on statistical understanding has documented misconceptions about probability and statistical inference. Tversky and Kahneman (1973), in particular, showed that people borrow nonprobabilisitic reasoning methods to solve probability problems, and this leads to faulty inferences and misconceptions. The research on "judgment under uncertainty" has powerful implications for policy and practice, but it has not provided much insight into instruction (but see Nisbett, Krantz, Jepson, & Kunda, 1983). This may be because it is very difficult to remediate people's faulty heuristics, or it may be because the design of the research was not learning focused. In either case, Moore and Cobb (1997) proposed that it is better to avoid statistical inference in the early phases of instruction and focus on descriptive statistics. We have adopted this wisdom.

The Coevolution Activities

To examine the value of DKE, especially as a preparation for future learning, Schwartz and Martin (2004) conducted a 2-week study involving eight classrooms of 160 public school students. The instruction consisted of two 3-day cycles. In Cycle 1, students learned about graphing and central tendency. In Cycle 2, they learned about formulas and variance. The study also included a third abbreviated cycle that implemented an experimental manipulation to evaluate whether DKE prepared students to learn. We provide examples of each cycle, which all students completed, and then we develop a description of the experimental treatment in Cycle 3.

In the first cycle (Schwartz & Martin, 2004), students worked with contrasting data sets that highlighted how the value of a central tendency measure depends on the context of application. For example, students decided which of two climbing ropes should get the higher rating. They received data from "load tests" that indicated the weights at which BlueStar and RedGrip ropes broke over multiple trials. Students typically graphed the mean load of each rope, but eventually they began to realize that for a climbing rope, the minimum load at which it will break is a safer measure than the mean. After the rope activity, students further evolved their knowledge by working with contrasts in which the spread of grades differed in two chemistry classes. To provide a concrete instance of the materials, Table 2.3 shows the data and assignment for this activity. Finally, for the third problem set, students had to decide if a drug was more effective than a placebo. In this case, the drug led to bimodal effects such that a simple comparison of the means would be misleading.

Students worked on each activity in small groups for about 30 min. Their task was to invent a graphical representation that would help justify their decisions. They were told that their graphs had to be obvious enough that another student would be able to understand what the graphs represented and what decision the group had made. Students drew their finished graphs on the blackboard. Other students were chosen at random to come to the board and explain a graph and its implied conclusion as if they had been part of the group. The need to make graphs that could "stand independently" of the person who made the graph encouraged the students to develop a more precise and complete second-hand description and alerted them to the importance of communicable knowledge. In addition, just as the contrasting data sets helped students perceive important properties of distributions, the contrasting graphs that filled the board helped students notice important aspects of second-hand representations.

Table 2.3

**An Example of a Contrasting Case the Students Analyzed
to Learn About Central Tendency and Graphing**

MAKING THE GRADE

Imagine your friend Julie is very worried about getting a good grade in Chemistry. She can take the class from Mrs. Oxygen or from Mr. Carbon. Here are the grades each teacher gave out last year.

Mrs. Oxygen: D+, D+, C–, C–, C–, C, C, B–, B–, B–, B–, B, B, B, B, B+
Mr. Carbon: D+, C–, C–, C–, C, C, C+, C+, C+ A–, A+, A+

Which teacher would you suggest? *Create a visual representation of the data to support your position. If your visualization from before does not work, try something new.*

Note. From "Inventing to Prepare for Future Learning: The Hidden Efficiency of Original Student Production in Statistics Instruction," by D. L. Schwartz and T. Martin, 2004, *Cognition and Instruction,* 22, p. 179. Copyright 2004 by Lawrence Erlbaum Associates, Inc. Reprinted with permission.

The cycle (Schwartz & Martin, 2004) on graphing and central tendency introduced the students to the idea of creating their own procedures and representations. This was important because these students had typically received procedures rather than evolved them. Throughout, the instructor merely facilitated and clarified student work and presentation. It was only after completing the three activities that the instructor gave a brief lecture on conventional graphing solutions (e.g., a histogram and box plot), and students practiced for about 15 min. When presented with conventional graphical representations, the representations were offered as solutions that experts had invented over the years to capture important aspects of distributions. So, rather than creating a rhetorical "guided discovery" task, the students were in the position of evaluating how successful they thought the expert's solutions were. (Many preferred their own solutions.)

The second cycle (Schwartz & Martin, 2004), which targeted variance, began with the problem of inventing a "reliability index" for baseball pitching machines. The students worked with the grids shown in Fig. 2.5. Each grid represents a different pitching machine. The X in the center is the target. Each of the black dots represents the location of one pitch from the respective machine. The grids hold many contrasts that helped students notice the distribution characteristics that their formula index would need to capture. Students presented their solutions on the board as before. Many students drew a box around the dots and either found the area or perimeter of the box. Other students used the Pythagorean theorem to measure the distance from a randomly chosen dot to all the other dots. Of all the groups

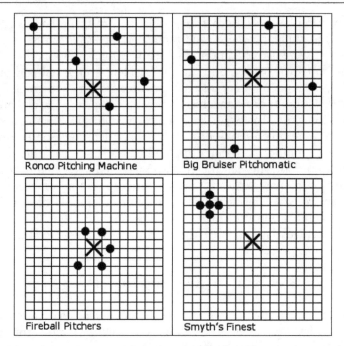

FIG. 2.5. An example of an activity in which students coevolved their perception and symbolic characterization of variance. Each grid represents a pitching machine. The "X" is the target, and the black dots indicate where each ball landed. Students had to invent a "reliability index" to characterize each pitching machine. *Note.* From "Inventing to Prepare for Future Learning: The Hidden Efficiency of Original Student Production in Statistics Instruction," by D. L. Schwartz and T. Martin, 2004, *Cognition and Instruction, 22,* p. 135. Copyright 2004 by Lawrence Erlbaum Associates, Inc. Reprinted with permission.

across all the classes, only one group came up with a general and consistent solution; they measured the distance from each dot to every other dot and summed the distances. Even though no students generated a general solution, this activity plus another using more focused contrasting cases prepared the students to learn from the subsequent lecture. The instructor presented the mean deviation formula in a 5-min lecture. Students practiced the formula with a new set of data for about 15 min.

The final day of instruction implemented the experimental design. All the classes received a scenario in which they had to compare high scores from two distributions, for example, comparing test scores from two different tests. They had to decide which score was higher even though the two test distributions had different means and variances. The appropriate solution to this type of problem is to use standardized scores, which measure how many deviations a score is from the mean. In lay terms, they had to "grade on a curve" and compare where each high score appeared on its respective curve. There were two conditions. In the invention condition, the students had to invent their own solution to the problem. In the tell-and-practice condition, the students were told how to solve the problem graphically by marking deviation regions on a histogram and comparing the deviations of the high scores (i.e., the normalized score). Students worked for about 25 min. There were no presentations, and the instructor never presented the conventional solution for computing and comparing standardized scores. The question was whether the invention or tell-and-practice students would be more prepared to learn the conventional solution when embedded as a learning resource during the posttest. Schwartz and Martin's prediction was that the Invention students would be better prepared to learn because they had grappled first-hand with the contrasting data sets, and they had invented possible models.

Assessments of Performance and Readiness to Learn

In Schwartz and Martin's (2004) study, the students took a 40-min test on a broad array of measures before and after the instructional intervention. The test included several different types of measures to capture the benefits of the first two instructional cycles on graphing and measures of variability. For example, there were computation items, graphing problems, word problems, and symbolic insight problems (e.g., "Why does the variance formula divide by 'n'?"). Students performed quite well at posttest, and when measured a year later, they still outperformed college students who had taken a semester of statistics (for more details, see Schwartz & Martin, 2004). Evidently, the DKE curriculum had prepared the students to learn from the brief lectures. For example, the majority of students knew that dividing by n solves the problem of comparing different sample sizes; it finds the average of how far each data point deviates from the mean. This information was only presented once as one of many points in the brief lecture. Schwartz and Martin (2004) also included an "adaptation" problem. Students had to find a way to estimate variability in bivariate data shown in a scatter plot, although they had only learned about univariate data. This is a difficult adaptation of the mean deviation, and the frequency of students who gave adequate responses only improved from 10% on the pretest to 34% on the posttest. On the other hand, college students who had a full semester of college statistics were only able to solve the problem 12% of the time. Compared to the college students, the DKE students had developed an adaptive base of knowledge.

For the experimental comparison (Schwartz & Martin, 2004) of the invention versus tell-and-practice conditions (which only occurred on the last day of instruction), the test evaluated how well students had been prepared to learn. Of particular focus was whether the students could learn how to compute and compare standardized scores, given summary descriptive measures. (Recall that in the class work, the students had worked with raw data, not descriptive statistics.) To examine whether students were prepared to learn from resources, the final test included a dynamic assessment composed of two items. The "resource item" built into the test came in the form of a worked example. It provided step-by-step instructions for computing standardized scores to compare individual data from different distributions (e.g., is Betty better at assists or steals). As part of the test, students had to follow the worked example to complete a second example at the bottom of the same page. The "target transfer problem" appeared a few pages later in the test. The problem included averages, deviations, and scores of an individual in each of two groups (e.g., two biology classes). The average score and variance differed between the groups, and the students had no raw data to work with. The question was whether the students would understand the implications of the procedure that appeared in the worked example resource problem and transfer it to solve the target problem.

To ensure that students were actually learning from the worked example and using it to solve the transfer problem, Schwartz and Martin's (2004) study used a 2×2 between-subject experimental design. One factor was whether students were in the invention or tell-and-practice condition. The second crossed factor was whether the resource worked example appeared in the posttest. Half of the students from each condition received the step-by-step resource item for how to compute and compare standardized scores, and half did not. If students were prepared to learn from the embedded resource, then students who received the resource should do better on the target transfer problem than students who did not receive the embedded resource.

Figure 2.6 shows the students' performance on the target transfer item (Schwartz & Martin, 2004) at posttest broken out by condition and whether the worked example resource appeared in the test. Students received credit if they gave either a quantitatively correct or qualitatively correct answer, including graphs. Students in the invention condition who received the embedded resource for how to compute standardized scores doubled the performance of the other three groups. The invention students must have learned from the embedded resource example because invention students who did not receive the resource performed poorly. In contrast, the tell-and-practice students did not show any benefits from having the resource item. Their lesson, although well designed and highly visual, had not prepared them to learn the significance of the resource item even though 100% of the students correctly followed the worked example on the resource item.

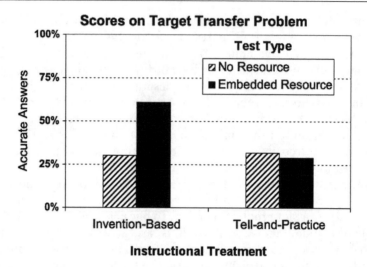

FIG. 2.6.   Students who had evolved their knowledge were more prepared to learn from a resource embedded in the posttest. *Note.* From "Inventing to Prepare for Future Learning: The Hidden Efficiency of Original Student Production in Statistics Instruction," by D. L. Schwartz and T. Martin, 2004, *Cognition and Instruction, 22,* p. 135. Copyright 2004 by Lawrence Erlbaum Associates, Inc. Reprinted with permission.

As fits our overall story, activities that help students perceive important properties of data coupled with activities that encourage the development of models can prepare students for future learning. Had Schwartz and Martin (2004) only measured students' ability to perform without an assessment of their abilities to learn, they would have seen little benefit of DKE over the other method of instruction.

SUMMARY AND PROSPECTS
FOR COMPUTER TECHNOLOGIES

Many cognitive theories are descriptive. They describe how people think, and in many cases, they provide explanations for the mechanisms of those thoughts. Other theories are normative; they describe the behaviors or knowledge of experts, and they often illuminate the limitations of novices. Fewer cognitive theories are prescriptive. They do not convert their descriptive findings into prescriptions for how to achieve particular normative outcomes. We identified two related methodological obstacles to developing prescriptive theories. One obstacle is that cognitive research tends to isolate mechanisms and disregard the multiple levels of knowing and learning relevant to education. As a broad instance, we described a tendency of the field to separate into first-hand theorists who emphasize direct experience with phenomenon and second-hand theorists who emphasize the acquisition of descriptions of experience. We proposed that these types of theorizing do not resolve the problem of how people integrate different ways of knowing. A second obstacle is that cognitive research typically uses assessments that aim to prove psychological theories rather than improve educational goals. We pointed to tests that isolate participants from opportunities to learn during the test. We argued that these types of sequestered assessments of unaided performance can miss an important goal of most education, which is to prepare students to learn once they leave the classroom. We also demonstrated that assessments of sequestered problem solving can overlook important levels of understanding that prepare students to learn.

As an example of research designed to generate prescriptive learning theories, we described our efforts to develop and assess DKE. We borrowed some concepts from evolution to generate activities that help students grow intellectually. Unlike other high level theories such as constructivism, evolutionary theory suggests specific mechanisms of change that can be used prescriptively. In DKE, we encourage students to coevolve first- and second-hand knowledge jointly across a series of different problem contexts. Students generate and revise models to differentiate contrasting cases. Over time, students develop a first-hand understanding of the important features of the domain, and they learn the work that second-hand representations need to accomplish. This prepares students to learn subsequently, for example, when they hear a formal solution in a lecture and when they follow worked examples embedded in a test. By coevolving and adapting their knowledge to different contexts, the students exhibited excellent gains on assessments of preparation for future learning.

This work can translate into instructional technologies. Our goal is a prescriptive learning theory that is easily adapted to current classrooms. For example, we are building technologies that permit students to complete DKE activities as homework before coming to class (instead of the more traditional model in which homework follows a lesson). In this way, they will be more prepared to understand the teacher's lessons. One very simple technological implementation involves putting the problem sets on the Web along with appropriate guidance and access to other people's inventions.

We are also examining solutions that integrate additional cognitive mechanisms into knowledge evolution. One example involves teachable agents (Biswas, Schwartz, Bransford, & The Teachable Agents Group at Vanderbilt, 2001). Teachable agents capitalize on the common wisdom that people "really" learn when they teach. So, rather than have the computer teach the students, we have the students teach the computer. Afterward, students get to see how their agent performs, and they try to learn from its mistakes and improve its performance.

We have built a statistics teachable agent named Orbo.[1] Students "teach by showing." They try to show Orbo how to compute values to differentiate two contrasting distributions. Orbo tries to induce what the students are trying to show and solve subsequent problems generated by other students or teachers who want to test Orbo (e.g., using the Web-based problem sets mentioned previously). At select points, the computer system can introduce new problems that illuminate weaknesses in what Orbo has been taught. This leads the student to evolve new knowledge and reteach Orbo. Finally, Orbo can exhibit misconceptions. Like a good tutor, students need to figure out what Orbo is thinking, and this helps the student's clarify their own understanding. Figure 2.7 describes an example in which a student needs to infer what caused Orbo to misunderstand. Additional information about Orbo and another statistics agent, Milo, may be found at http://aaalab.stanford.edu

Orbo reflects our general methodology of integrating cognitive mechanisms. For Orbo, we are integrating the two previous mechanisms of perceptual learning and modeling with the mechanism of trying to understand another person's thoughts or in this case, another agent's thoughts. Students need to figure out what Orbo understands so they can teach him most successfully. Trying to infer the intentions behind another person's (or agent's) behavior is surely one of the most fundamental and spontaneous of human capacities, and it should be possible to leverage it for educational purposes.

In our view, there is much promise in our approach of explicitly looking for ways to evolve integrated knowledge both for understanding the nature of learning and for developing instructional theories that will be useful to classroom teachers and to students once they leave the classroom. Our hope is that the example of DKE provides one concrete instance that can help the field move in the direction of increasingly integrative models that are directly relevant to building prescriptive cognitive theories.

---

[1] We are deeply indebted to George Chang for developing (and naming) Orbo.

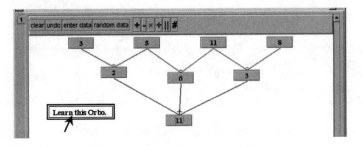

A student shows the Teachable Agent (Orbo) to find variability by summing the differences between adjacent values.

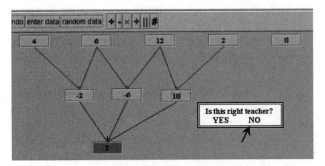

The agent solves a new problem and shows it has induced some misconceptions that the student needs to remediate.

FIG. 2.7. Orbo: A teachable agent for statistics. In the top panel, a students invents a way to find the spread of a data set. The student teaches the method to Orbo by showing the steps for a specific set of values. In the bottom panel, Orbo shows what he learned from the example. Orbo exhibits that he did not understand what the student intended, and the student needs to figure out what Orbo is thinking. In this case, Orbo thought the procedure only takes four numbers as in the original example (instead of all the numbers). This focuses the student on issues of sample size. Orbo also incorrectly learned to subtract the second number from the first. This focuses the student on issues of absolute value.

ACKNOWLEDGMENTS

This material is based on work supported by the National Science Foundation under Grants BCS-0214549, BCS-0214548, REC-0196238, and ROLE-0231946. Any opinions, findings, and conclusions or recommendations expressed in this material are those of the authors and do not necessarily reflect the views of the National Science Foundation.

REFERENCES

Anderson, J. R. (1983). *The architecture of cognition.* Cambridge, England: Cambridge University Press.

Anderson, J. R., Reder, L. M., & Simon, H. (1996). Situated learning and education. *Educational Researcher, 25*(4), 5–11.

Barsalou, L. W. (1999). Perceptual symbol systems. *Behaviour and Brain Sciences, 22,* 577–609.

Biederman, I., & Shiffrar, M. M. (1987). Sexing day-old chicks: A case study and expert systems analysis of a difficult perceptual-learning task. *Journal of Experimental Psychology: Learning, Memory, & Cognition, 13,* 640–645.

Biswas, G., Schwartz, D. L., Bransford, J. D., & The Teachable Agents Group at Vanderbilt. (2001). Technology support for complex problem solving: From SAD Environments to AI. In K. Forbus & P. Feltovich (Eds.), *Smart machines in education* (pp. 71–98). Menlo Park, CA: AAAI/MIT Press.

Bransford, J. D., Franks, J. J., Vye, N. J., & Sherwood, R. D. (1989). New approaches to instruction: Because wisdom can't be told. In S. Vosniadou & A. Ortony (Eds.), *Similarity and analogical reasoning* (pp. 470–497). New York: Cambridge University Press.

Bransford, J. D., & Schwartz, D. L. (1999). Rethinking transfer: A simple proposal with multiple implications. *Review of Research in Education, 24,* 61–101.

Case, R., & Okamoto, Y. (1996). The role of central conceptual structures in the development of children's thought. *Monographs of the Society for Research in Child Development, Serial 246 61*(1-2).

Chomsky, N. (1966). *Cartesian linguistics: A chapter in the history of rationalist thought.* New York: Harper & Row.

Cobb, P., Yackel, E., & Wood, T. (1992). A constructivist alternative to the representational view of mind in mathematics. *Journal of Research in Mathematics Education, 23,* 2–33.

Feuerstein, R. (1979). *The dynamic assessment of retarded performers: The learning potential assessment device, theory, instruments, and techniques.* Baltimore: University Park Press.

Gardner, H. (1982). *Art, mind, and brain: A cognitive approach to creativity.* New York: Basic Books.

Gibson, E. J. (1969). *Principles of perceptual learning and development.* New York: Meredith.

Gibson, J. J. (1986). *The ecological approach to visual perception.* Hillsdale, NJ: Lawrence Erlbaum Associates.

Gibson, J. J., & Gibson, E. J. (1955). Perceptual learning: Differentiation or enrichment. *Psychological Review, 62,* 32–51.

Glaser, R. (1992). *Learning, cognition, and education: Then and now.* In H. L. Pick, Jr., P. Van Den Broek, & D. C. Knill (Eds.), *Cognition: Conceptual and methodological issues* (pp. 239–266). Washington, DC: American Psychological Association.

Glenberg, A. M., & Kaschak, M. P. (2002). Grounding language in action. *Psychonomic Bulletin & Review, 9,* 558–565.

Hatano, G., & Inagaki, K. (1986). Two courses of expertise. In H. Stevenson, J. Azuma, & K. Hakuta (Eds.), *Child development and education in Japan* (pp. 262–272). New York: Freeman.

Kaput, J. J. (1995). Creating cybernetic and psychological ramps from the concrete to the abstract: Examples from multiplicative structures. In D. N. Perkins & J. L. Schwartz (Eds.), *Software goes to school: Teaching for understanding with new technologies* (pp. 130–154). New York: Oxford University Press.

Kosslyn, S. M. (1980). *Image and mind.* Cambridge, MA: Harvard University Press.

Lakoff, G., & Núñez, R. E. (2000). *Where mathematics comes from: How the embodied mind brings mathematics into being.* New York: Basic Books.

Lave, J. (1988). *Cognition in practice: Mind, mathematics and culture in everyday life.* New York: Cambridge University Press.

Lave, J., & Wenger, E. (1991). *Situated learning: Legitimate peripheral participation.* Cambridge, England: Cambridge University Press.

Levine, M. (1975). *A cognitive theory of learning: Research on hypothesis testing.* Hillsdale, NJ: Lawrence Erlbaum Associates.

Mannes, S. M., & Kintsch, W. (1987). Knowledge organization and text organization. *Cognition & Instruction, 4,* 91–115.

Martin, T., & Schwartz, D. L. (in press). Physically distributed learning: Adapting and reinterpreting physical environments in the development of the fraction concept. *Cognitive Science.*

Marton, F., & Booth, S. (1997). *Learning and awareness.* Mahwah, NJ: Lawrence Erlbaum Associates.

Mayer, R. (1996). Learners as information processors: Legacies and limitations of educational psychology's second metaphor. *Educational Psychologist, 31,* 151–161.

Moore, D. S., & Cobb, G. W. (1997). Mathematics, statistics and teaching. *American Mathematics Monthly, 104,* 801–823.

Moore, J. L., & Schwartz, D. L. (1998). On learning the relationship between quantitative properties and symbolic representations. In A. Bruckman, M. Guzdial, J. Kolodner, & A. Ram (Eds.), *Proceedings of the International Conference of the Learning Sciences* (pp. 209–214). Charlottesville, VA: Association for the Advancement of Computing in Education.

Nasir, N. (2005). Individual cognitive structuring and the sociocultural context: Strategy shifts in the game of dominoes. *Journal of the Learning Science, 14,* 5–35.

Nasir, N. (2002). Identity, Goals, and Mathematical Understandings: Learning in Basketball and Dominoes. *Mathematical Thinking and Learning,* v 4 (2 & 3), pp 211–245.

Nemirovsky, R., Tierney, C., & Wright, T. (1998). Body motion and graphing. *Cognition & Instruction, 16,* 119–172.

Nisbett, R. E., Krantz, D., Jepson, C., & Kunda, Z. (1983). The use of statistical heuristics in everyday inductive reasoning. *Psychological Review, 90,* 339–363.

Palinscar, A. S., & Brown, A. L. (1984). Reciprocal teaching of comprehension-fostering and comprehension monitoring activities. *Cognition and Instruction, 1,* 117–175.

Piaget, J. (1970). *Genetic epistemology.* New York: Columbia University Press.

Saxe, G. B. (1991). *Culture & cognitive development: Studies in mathematical understanding.* Hillsdale, NJ: Lawrence Erlbaum Associates.

Saxe, G. B. (1999). Cognition, development, and cultural practices. In E. Turiel (Ed.), *Culture and development: New directions in child psychology* (pp. 19–35). San Francisco: Jossey-Bass.

Schwartz, D. L. (1993). The construction and analogical transfer of symbolic visualizations. *Journal of Research in Science Teaching, 30,* 1309–1325.

Schwartz, D. L. (1995). The emergence of abstract representations in dyad problem solving. *Journal of the Learning Sciences, 4,* 321–354.

Schwartz, D. L. (1999). The productive agency that drives collaborative learning. In P. Dillenbourg (Ed.), *Collaborative learning: Cognitive and computational approaches* (pp. 197–218). New York: Elsevier Science.

Schwartz, D. L., & Black, J. B. (1996). Shuttling between depictive models and abstract rules: Induction and fallback. *Cognitive Science, 20,* 457–497.

Schwartz, D. L., & Black, T. (1999). Inferences through imagined actions: Knowing by simulated doing. *Journal of Experimental Psychology: Learning, Memory, and Cognition, 25,* 116–136.

Schwartz, D. L., & Bransford, J. D. (1998). A time for telling. *Cognition & Instruction, 16,* 475–522.

Schwartz, D. L., Bransford, J. D., & Sears, D. (in press). Efficiency and innovation in transfer. In J. Mestre (Ed.), *Transfer of learning from a modern multidisciplinary perspective.* Greenwich, CT: Information Age Publishing.

Schwartz, D. L., & Martin, T. (2004). Inventing to prepare for future learning: The hidden efficiency of original student production in statistics instruction. *Cognition and Instruction, 22,* 129–184.

Schwartz, D. L., Martin, T., & Pfaffman, J. (2005). How mathematics propels the development of physical knowledge. *Journal of Cognition and Development, 6,* 65–88.

Schwartz, D. L., & Moore, J. (1998). On the role of mathematics in explaining the material world. *Cognitive Science, 22,* 471–516.

Shepard, R. N., & Cooper, L. A. (Eds.). (1986). *Mental images and their transformations.* Cambridge, MA: MIT Press.

Smith, L. B., & Sera, M. D. (1992). A developmental analysis of the polar structure of dimensions. *Cognitive Psychology, 24,* 99–142.

Tversky, A., & Kahneman, D. (1973). Availability: A heuristic for judging frequency and probability. *Cognitive Psychology, 5,* 207–232.

Vosniadou, S., & Brewer, W. F. (1992). Mental models of the earth: A study of conceptual change in childhood. *Cognitive Psychology, 24,* 535–585.

Vygotsky, L. S. (1978). *Mind in society* (M. Cole, V. John-Steiner, S. Scribner, & E. Souberman, Eds.). Cambridge, MA: Harvard University Press.

3

Getting the Story Straight: The Role of Narrative in Teaching and Learning With Interactive Media

Lydia Plowman
University of Stirling

Narrative serves as a formula or framework into which events can be cast to make them comprehensible, memorable, and communicable. That is the primary way in which narrative serves thought.

—Olson (1990, p. 104)

THE PROBLEM

The skills by which teachers mediate and navigate meaning making are at the heart of what it is to be a teacher. Teachers prompt a sense of coherence and understanding in learners by moving between adapting, sequencing, tailoring, and reviewing materials and eliciting, supplementing, and monitoring learners' responses. Teachers use these professional skills to sustain learning discourses and to ensure that classroom activities and processes rarely seem fragmented, although they are manifold and diverse. Ultimately, teachers want to feel assured that learners are getting the story straight.

Teachers lose some of this control over the learning process once interactive media are introduced into teaching. This is often for logistical reasons such as the location of the computers being beyond the classroom in a resource center or a separate computer suite or because the students are using tutorial-type software, and the teacher's role is diminished. Left to their own devices, students can become mired in operational and procedural talk and lose the big picture of what they are trying to achieve and why (Plowman, 1992). If teachers are not on hand to provide guidance, it is even more important that the software provides guidance. The purpose of the research described here was to investigate ways in which the design of software can help to achieve the aim of providing learners with the guidance they need.

It is the structure rather than the content of interactive media that generally causes problems, and much of the low-level operational and procedural talk is concerned with navigation. Learners make sense of interactive media primarily by navigational means, as the sequences of images or text only become activated during the process of interaction. By definition, *interactive* media invoke activity between learners and the computer, and much of this activity involves making decisions about what to do or where to go next; sequencing and navigation. As the potential for discussion and learning tends to occur at the foci of interactivity (Plowman, 1996b), the points at which decisions requiring computer interaction need to be made, navigational issues have a direct impact on group learning.

At these foci of interactivity, learners decide what to do: choose from a multiple choice set of options about where to go next, answer a question, summon up help, repeat the section they have just seen, or exit. Whatever the choice, the narrative flow is disrupted by group discussion and often a change of medium. Although the learners have generally made an explicit decision to choose a particular option, they do not necessarily know the consequences.

These procedures and operations are not a feature of interaction with teachers or traditional linear media, but they can get in the way of understanding and achieving learning goals when activity is computer based. Procedural and operational talk is more seamless in classrooms where teachers are available to direct activities. Although teachers may request everybody to stop what they are doing and listen, accomplished teachers are able to integrate the new instructions or move in a new direction without disrupting the flow of teaching and learning. Such scenarios are based on energetic, reflective, and resourceful teachers; it is acknowledged that some classroom activity falls short of this ideal, and teacher talk is often monologic or variations on a pattern of initiation/response/evaluation (Cazden, 1987; Edwards & Westgate, 1987).

The potentially problematic relation between sequence and navigation can be addressed by considering the role of narrative, universally considered to be one of the most efficient macrostructures. Arnheim (1954/1974) nicely captured this relation in his description of the "path of disclosure" as "the journey that the author prescribes for the spectator or reader" (p. 377).

In complex works, this departs from the actual sequence of events, but in traditional media, the author retains ultimate control over the relation between sequencing and narrative, and so the macrostructure of a linear medium is likely to be coherent and purposeful. The path of disclosure is a useful concept for illuminating a central design problem of interactive media: how to balance authorial (or designer) interest in controlling the navigational path of users, so ensuring a clear narrative, against the freedom afforded by the medium for users to construct their own paths.

Research on other media shows that narrative assists learners' comprehension, and this led the research team to an exploration of the ways in which the design of interactive media could support the learner's construction of narrative. *Design* is restricted here to those elements of the courseware with which learners interact directly, and although the research reported here was based on students using CD-ROMs, the findings vis-à-vis narrative are equally applicable to the Web and other interactive media such as interactive television. The researchers wanted to consider ways in which tasks and activities can be integrated with the narrative so that learning is not constantly fractured as learners work through the materials. Observations of how teachers and students used interactive media in the classroom (Plowman, 1996c) suggested that a narrative structure, whether provided by the design of the CD-ROM or the teacher, can hold everything together at a conceptual level because it provides structure and coherence and underpins understanding.

Although Bruner (2002) claimed that "we are so adept at narrative that it seems almost as natural as language itself" (p. 3), this does not preclude the need to define narrative, especially in the light of the enormous range of theoretical perspectives. For the purposes of this study, *narrative* has been defined as "a process of both discerning and imposing meaning that can be shared and articulated". The focus of this chapter is on narrative guidance and narrative construction as an explanatory framework for the emergence of meaning in educational contexts of using interactive media. In the following discussion, I consider the links between narrative and cognition, how the presence or absence of narrative facilitates or impedes learning, and the dynamic processes involved in producing meaning from presented content. These meaning-making processes cycle between the guidance presented by software, peers, and teachers (along with culturally imparted knowledge) and the activity of constructing new meanings and articulating them to self and others. Much of the chapter is discursive, drawing on the different disciplines of narratology, human–computer interaction, and pedagogy, but it is rooted in many years of observing and using interactive media in classrooms.

In the following sections, I discuss the role of teachers in the mediation of learning, emphasizing the dialogic process of narrative guidance and narrative construction before describing an empirical study in which the research team investigated the link between different narrative structures on a CD-ROM and support for learning. Although the design manipulations and experimental context of the research study in which we explored these issues are summarized here, fuller accounts are available in Laurillard, Stratfold, Luckin, Plowman, and Taylor (2000), Luckin et al. (1998a), Luckin, Plowman, Laurillard, Stratfold, and Taylor (1998b), and Plowman, Luckin, Laurillard, Stratfold, and Taylor (1999). The observations on which the findings are based are of small groups of students aged 11 to 16.

GETTING THE STORY STRAIGHT

"Getting the story straight" is a colloquial expression that usually relates to the process by which people check their understanding of a description of events by another person so that they, in turn, can retell the "story" coherently. This process would usually be prompted by a complex sequence of events, and the implication of the saying is that there is more than one version of the story. It is a collaboration between the teller and the listener intended to create a consistent story, and the phrase itself points to the primacy of narrative in creating understanding.

The word *story* generally relates to a fictional narrative, but in this expression, story is usually an account of reciprocal understanding. Getting the story "straight" refers to a process of mutual adjustment: The teller wants to ensure that the recipient understands a "correct" version. In nefarious situations, this could be a matter of somebody checking that the person who provides an alibi knows what information to pass on to the authorities. In a teaching and learning context, it is a process of co-construction in which both the teacher and the learner check that they have understood the other's intended meaning. (This can just as readily be a learner–learner relationship in which the roles of teacher and learner are typically even more fluid.) It is a tightly coupled relationship that depends on dialogue.

For a learner using interactive media, getting the story straight refers to a reciprocal process in which the purpose is to ensure a degree of consistency between the communication of the educational content (narrative guidance) and how the interactant makes meaning from it (narrative construction).

WHAT IS NARRATIVE?

The term *narrative* is so ubiquitous that it is difficult to capture its meaning or work out which aspects of learning and interaction cannot be accounted for by a narrative approach. Indeed, Barthes (1977) said of narrative that it "is present in every place, in every society … it is simply there, like life itself " (p. 79).

Because the issue of the parameters of narrative remains unresolved I have narrowed the field of enquiry to cognitive processes and how an overall narrative pattern may be discovered, or imposed, in the very act of perceiving (Branigan, 1992). This focus on cognition ignores the equally important relation between narrative and affect, and the vital role of narrative in stimulating motivation, engagement, and enjoyment was not explored as part of this research. (See Mallon & Webb, 2000, for a discussion of narrative and interactive media from this perspective.) Narrative is deeply embedded in human culture, and we are exposed to countless narratives in different media and from different people. A recognition of how this exposure to and participation in other narratives constantly shapes the ways in which one interprets new narratives underlies this study, but the focus here is on the culture of teaching and learning.

Narrative has often been described in two main categories: as a connected sequence of events and as the representation of those events. These categories relate to the distinction between the told (what is told) and the telling (how it is told or the path of disclosure). Narrative theories have different ways of describing this, from the *sjuzet* and *fabula* of the Russian Formalists to the more widespread story (what happens) and discourse (how we are told what happens). Although this can be a useful distinction, the study of narrative has moved from this dissection of the structure of media such as films and books to a less reductive approach that takes account of social and cultural contexts. Narrative does not reside only in the text but must take account of the interactant; it is both a mode of thought and an outcome of interactions.

Whether there is a difference between narrative and story also needs clarification. As McQuillan (2000) commented, people rarely distinguish between the uses of story and narrative in everyday speech and tend to use them as synonyms. For Denzin (2000), they are "nearly equivalent" (p. xi), but he makes a distinction between narrative as a process and story as an account. For Cobley (2001) narrative is a "communicative relation" (pp. 2–3), of story. This is not the place to unpack the contested distinction between narrative and story; for my purposes, stories can be oral, written, or visual texts, but narrative is, in addition, a mode of thought. Within this framework, all stories are narratives but not all narratives are stories.

The distinction is clearer in the educational context in which I discuss narrative here. The focus is not on using stories as a teaching resource as promoted by Pedersen (1995) and McEwan and Egan (1992) but on narrative as a cognitive process or, in the words of Hardy (1977), a "primary act of mind" (p. 12). This is closer to what Lyle (2000) termed "narrative understanding" (p. 45), but I am specifically interested in unraveling understanding or meaning making to identify the closely coupled processes of narrative guidance and narrative construction. Whereas these processes are central to all teaching and learning activities, the focus here is on how they relate to interactive media given the specific problems outlined earlier.

Narrative and Cognition

Narrative shapes our knowledge and experience. Nelson (1996), for instance, described the role of narrative in children's cognitive development from about the age of 2. Some even have claimed (Bruner, 1996; McNeil, 1996) that people have a predisposition to finding and creating narrative and that it determines ways in which we acquire language. Bruner (1996), for instance, referred to narrative as "a mode of thought and an expression of a culture's world view" (p. xiv). Narrative does not therefore simply have an aesthetic function; it is central to human cognition from earliest childhood, as it helps us think, remember, communicate, and make sense of ourselves and the world. (The details of these processes are contested: Bamberg, 1997, outlined six major approaches.) The generation of narrative is an active process of meaning making through which people make sense of their own thoughts and experiences and those of others.

There is a long-established body of research that suggests that texts make excessive demands on human cognitive processes if they do not conform to mental models of narrative because the structure is unfamiliar. Memory and comprehension are more active when the text is clearly structured and navigable. Learners constantly adjust their understanding in accordance with their exposure to conventional narratives, making getting the story straight a central cognitive goal. Narrative can provide a macrostructure that creates global coherence, contributes to local coherence, and aids recall through its network of causal links and signposting. The structure provides a linear dynamic that can accommodate diversions and tangents and performs an essential organizing function for the learner by shaping the creation of meaning. This research has mainly focused on written texts (Hastie, 1981; Kintsch & Greene, 1978; Rumelhart, 1975; Thorndyke, 1977), although Bordwell (1985), Collins (1979), Goldman, Varma, and Sharp (1999), and Salomon (1979/1994) have undertaken work using visual media with similar outcomes.

Meek (1988) described how texts teach what readers learn in terms of the processes by which young children learn to read through the process of interacting with texts and the key role of narrative in offering structure and cues. As narrative depends on and assists memory, so are strategies employed to strengthen the narrative dynamic likely to assist comprehension. One of the problems with interactive media is that it does not offer the guidance within the text identified by Meek in storybooks. The focus of the study I describe here was the use of interactive media for educational purposes and in particular, ways of reducing cognitive processing concerned with navigational and operational problems so that learners can focus on the content rather than the structure. Some form of guided interaction is necessary to avoid the considerable amount of time given over to such problems.

Narrative and Interactive Media

Interactive media superficially appear to combine media with which people are already familiar, such as film, television, and books, but we cannot directly transfer what we have learned about making meaning from such texts. The structure of interactive media differs from that of traditional media because it switches mode between video, text, animation, graphics, sound, and silence; there are combinations of different media on the screen at the same time; users can control pace, sequence, and activity, and there is no fixed running time. These attributes are potentially beneficial, but they are also responsible for the multiplicity of pathways and disruption of the flow of the user's experience, especially as it is sometimes difficult to predict the required user input or system response at the foci of interactivity. The narrative is easily suspended and altered, and this can thwart or confuse the learner's expectation so although concepts of sequence, connection, causality, and linearity are implicit in definitions of narrative, they are not directly applicable to interactive media. Traditional narrative structures are not therefore appropriate (Plowman, 1996a).

These foci of interactivity represent lacunae or gaps in the text where interactivity is invoked, and it is here that there is most pressure on the learners to be interactive. This is both a sensorimotor act, such as selecting an option by clicking on the mouse, and a cognitive response, which involves trying to make sense of these gaps and bridging them in a way that is meaningful. Interactive media thus make explicit the role of learners in determining meaning and constructing narrative. By capitalizing on the learner's role in constructing narrative, it should be possible to improve the design of educational interactive media. However, this needs to be balanced by a perceptible presented narrative. Because learners favor clearly structured and navigable texts, using interactive media generally produces cognitive costs in terms of narrative construction. In these cases, getting the story straight is paramount for the learning process.

Mediating Learning

All learning is mediated by people's cultural and social practices, but additional, more easily identified mediators exist in technology-assisted learning. Silverstone (1999) described mediation as "the circulation of meaning" (p. 13) in the context of cultural artifacts such as newspapers and television. Steiner (1996) referred to the "essence of the full act of reading" (p. 18) as being a process of "dynamic reciprocity." Both definitions refer to the dialogic relationships between authors and audiences that are mediated by texts of various kinds, but they incidentally provide nice descriptions of the teaching and learning process.

A teacher's work is the mediation of learning. This is achieved by the ways in which a teacher presents content (self-generated or through another medium, either talk or text) and then acts on the various ways in which learners respond. The relation between authors, texts, and audiences referred to by Silverstone (1999) and Steiner (1996) are more complex when the mediating text is technologically interactive. The relation between the learner and the text (in this case, interactive media) is less stable and less direct than the relationship is between an author and a reader, and it is in that space that misunderstandings occur. The mediating role of the teacher is therefore critical to getting the story straight whether conceptualized within Laurillard's (1993, 2002) conversational framework, Hoadley and Enyedy's (1999) "middle spaces," or other dialogic models of teaching and learning.

Many teachers are accustomed to a role in which they mediate most classroom learning. In cases in which both the teacher and computers are present, the main resources to help students construct their own narratives are the courseware, their previous knowledge and experience, and the teacher's input. Altering the teacher's role by reducing their mediation of the presented content imposes higher demands on the quality of the courseware because nearly all communication and interaction then takes place between the student and the computer rather than a three-way interaction that includes the teacher. (This is not the case when the teacher uses a data projector or interactive whiteboard for whole-class teaching, as they still mediate the content. In this study, groups of three or four students used computers away from the classroom.)

Narrative is "a solution to the problem of how to translate knowing into telling" (White, 1981, p. 1) and as such is a key means of mediation. Learners generally have no direct access to what it is that teachers teach. They can only access the teacher's chosen representations—talk, writing on a chalkboard, textbooks, or software—through the teacher's mediation. Discovery and active learning approaches still require a teacher's mediation, even if this is less central than it is in other forms of teaching.

Findings from an earlier study (Plowman, 1996c) suggest that the teacher's mediation of content was the main variable in lessons that demonstrated productive work with interactive media. The teacher's active involvement enables checks on students' understanding before moving on. This flexibility in mediating content enables teachers to provide coherence for learners by framing activities and relating them to the students' personal experiences as well as to other parts of the curriculum throughout the lesson. Poorly designed software can be used creatively and with positive learning outcomes in the hands of a competent and confident teacher, but software that is considered to be well designed can fail to deliver if the teacher does not integrate it successfully into teaching and learning activities. Problems are thus distributed between teachers and designers (such as the lack of task structure provided by the teacher, the lack of navigational guidance provided by the software) and exacerbated by other external factors over which the teacher has little direct control. Here, I am concerned with improving design rather than some of the other factors that could contribute to more effective learning such as professional development opportunities for teachers, better resources, or smaller class size.

Narrative Guidance and Narrative Construction

The reciprocity, circulation of meaning, and dialogicality inherent in the mediation of learning are expressed here as the two interdependent processes of narrative guidance and narrative construction. The design challenge is how this interlinked relation of narrative guidance and narrative construction, which can be visualized as something akin to the classic representations of DNA, can be designed into interactive learning environments. *Narrative guidance* comes from the design of interactive media combined with how teachers mediate the text for the classroom context. *Narrative construction* is the active process of meaning making, stimulated by the text and the environment, combined with the vast reservoir of knowledge that each person brings with them to the experience. It is a process of discerning and imposing a structure on the materials and making links and connections in a personally meaningful way.

The design elements presented by the software constitute narrative guidance and can be a combination of features specific to interactive media, such as the need for clear navigational procedures, with features associated with traditional media, such as recognizable narrative and a clear relation between tasks and the macronarrative. I have observed ways in which teachers compensate for its absence by providing their own narrative guidance. They mediate its use for the classroom context by constraining the range of responses, offering interpretative possibilities, and elaborating the task. An example of this is a task in which students aged 11 had to use a CD-ROM to find information relevant to a forthcoming trip to a Roman site. They were going to act out, in costume, a play they had written based on a newspaper account of the discovery of a skeleton at the site; they were able to locate and use information more purposefully than others who did not have this guidance. This example of the teacher providing narrative guidance is unusual because it involves a lot of preparation and familiarity with the materials. More often, students use interactive media in a context in which they do not enjoy such committed teacher input: Narrative guidance therefore needs to be embedded in the software design because there is no guarantee that it will be provided externally.

Manipulating Narrative—An Empirical Study

Although they have been separated for explanatory purposes, narrative guidance and narrative construction are not discrete processes but, in a productive learning experience, a dynamic cycle. The co-construction of narrative is therefore shared between software designers, teachers, and learners with the emphasis on different agents depending on the context. The purpose of this study was to explore ways of enabling learners to supplement their learned sense of narrative so that navigation, comprehension, and accessibility are facilitated. Informed by my observations of students using commercially available interactive media in the classroom, the research team developed three versions of material on a CD-ROM that had the same task and the same content but different structures. These three versions were described as "linear," "resource based," and "guided discovery."

"GALAPAGOS" CD-ROM

The Galapagos CD-ROM was developed for the purposes of the research. It used material produced by the British Broadcasting Corporation for an Open University course and had high production values for the video and the soundtrack. The content used Darwin's experiences in the Galapagos Islands to teach the principles of natural selection. It aimed to stimulate learners to think about how wildlife arrived on the newly formed volcanic islands that were so distant from the nearest land mass and how variation in the islands' bird population had arisen. All learners were given the task of explaining the variation in the wildlife observed by Darwin and constructing their answer to this task using the online notepad. All groups of learners had access to a model answer once some text had been saved in the notepad. At the beginning, the audio track tells learners

> Welcome to the Galapagos Islands, where you can explore for yourself the remarkable wildlife and habitat that was so important to Darwin in developing his theory of evolution.

> Your task, using the resources on this CD, is to explain the variation in the wildlife on the island, particularly the finches which fascinated Darwin so much.

> You can make notes of your observations using the notepad, and when you have prepared a response to the task, you can look at a model answer. You can then resume exploring if you want.

First of all, familiarize yourself with the buttons below and make sure you know what they do.

The functionality of the toolbar buttons (home, search, task, script, notepad, quit) were then described on the audio track. Care was taken to ensure that the interface had the same look and feel in all versions.

All versions had the same content (eight sections, each of which dealt with a different aspect of the Islands such as their formation, location, or the effects of trade winds) and used the same video sequences and audio tracks. It was the structure of the presentation and the associated use of menus that varied. This approach emphasizes the importance of structure rather than other aspects of interaction design, but it was this aspect that my earlier observations had suggested was critical to the learner's construction of narrative. Brief descriptions of the three versions follow, but for more information, readers are directed to Laurillard et al. (2000), as this includes a Quicktime™ movie that provides a visual "walkthrough" and spoken commentary on the three software designs as well as more information on how specific design features afford learning.

The narrative was manipulated three ways. A linear version was designed to present an easily identifiable narrative so that the team could explore the extent to which interactive media should emulate more familiar narrative structures. A resource-based learning (RBL) version was designed to reflect existing commercially available CD-ROMs I had observed in classroom use. A guided discovery learning (GDL) version was designed to combine guidance of the type offered by classroom teachers with the benefits of an interactive medium. Table 3.1 summarizes the main features of each of the three versions.

Linear Version

The linear version is closest to a traditional narrative and was designed in such a way that students are led through the eight sections of the CD-ROM in sequence. There are no search mechanisms, and users cannot change sections except by going backward or forward until they have seen all eight sections once. The educational rationale for this design was that it would be more suitable for novice users, as it limits the need for interaction with the computer. It was also designed to encourage students to view enough resources to be able to answer the set question; my observations had shown that, left to their own devices, learners sometimes missed material they needed to complete the task. There was no explicit external support for narrative construction other than that provided by all versions; narrative guidance was provided by the familiarity of a traditional linear structure.

TABLE 3.1

A Comparison of Features for the Provision of Narrative Guidance
and Support for Narrative Construction on Three Versions
of the Galapagos CD-ROM

	Linear	*Resource Based*	*Guided Discovery*
Narrative Guidance	• Recognizable, linear structure • Easy navigation • Limited need for interaction • Implicit guidance in interface design (order of items)	• No explicit narrative guidance • Implicit guidance in interface design (order of items)	• Three text-based guides offer routes through material and stimulate enquiry • Implicit guidance in interface design (order of items)
Support for Narrative Construction	Same for all versions: Notepad Model answer Easily accessible statement of task Transcript of audio track available		

RBL Version

The RBL version offered no guidance through the CD-ROM sections and left students to define their own route. Its closest equivalent is a multimedia encyclopedia, although this version was on a much smaller scale. The eight sections of the RBL version can be accessed from a main menu or the simple word-search mechanism at the top level. The style is exploratory, and users are free to go where they want; the only constraint is that they cannot access the model answer before they have entered some notes in the notepad as was true for all versions. The interface was more complex than the linear version, as learners had to make selections for control and navigation, but the team endeavored to strike a balance between functionality and simplicity. The educational rationale for this version was to encourage independent learners who are able to search through the resources to research their answers and complete the task. In this design manipulation, learners needed to construct their own questions to break down the task into manageable units. There was no additional support for narrative construction and no explicit narrative guidance.

GDL Version

The GDL version offered guidance in breaking down the task by providing paths through the material, questions to stimulate inquiries, and direction to specific resources. Of the three versions, this was closest to the support given by a teacher. It does not present the narrative as strongly as the linear version but provides more guidance than the RBL version. The eight sections can be accessed from one of three text guides that focus on aspects relevant to completing the task such as formation and location of the Islands, effects of trade winds and ocean currents, and Darwin's exploration of the islands and the bird populations. The guides were not animated or intelligent agents, although this would be an area for future development, but consisted of simple written guidance. After the voice-over welcome and introduction to the package, task, and toolbar buttons, attention was drawn to the "Guides" button. The educational rationale for this version was to encourage and support learners in locating appropriate resources to complete the task. There was explicit support for narrative construction through the provision of this guidance.

Rationale

The team hypothesized that students need some form of presented narrative guidance from the software because the narrative in interactive media is not easily discernible, and there may be multiple narratives depending on the route taken. In tandem, we hypothesized that students also require support for narrative construction, as this increases understanding of the material. The aim was to identify the features that provided narrative guidance as well as those that enabled the learner's construction of narrative.

It was not our intention to measure learning as such because that would require trying to control too many variables in the naturalistic environment used for this study. Our aim was to identify ways in which learning can be supported such as the ease with which students accomplished the task and how they recalled their learning. The CD-ROM was a research tool to analyze the impact of the different narrative versions on learners' behavior. This study therefore involved analysis of the narratives produced by the learners in the process of recall as well as interaction with the presented narrative on the CD-ROM.

The approach learners adopt to complete the given task is determined partly by the version they use. In addition to the narrative guidance manipulations, which are outside the learners' control, other features such as the availability of a model answer and notepad editor scaffold the task (Luckin et al., 1998b) at different points in the narrative construction process. Use of these supports depends on whether students choose to use them, as they are available in all three versions. From earlier observations, we found that if learners are to construct and maintain their own narrative, they have to be supported in the component processes of narrative construction such as goal setting, planning, exploring, investigating, articulating, and revising.

Collecting Data

Twelve groups of three students, mainly aged 15 to 16, were randomly assigned to one version of the material, and none of the groups was aware that different versions were available. Every session had two video-recorded sources: One recorded the group of learners at the computer to capture talk, movement, gesture, and machine interaction; the other was the screen image taken from the computer via a scan converter. The videotapes were mixed in an editing suite, transcribed, and used for detailed analysis of learners' talk and behavior and their path through the material. Design issues cannot adequately be addressed without an overview of student interactions both within their groups and with the courseware, and Luckin et al. (1998a) developed representations of these interactions for analytical purposes. Because the students used Galapagos in groups, their experience was most clearly revealed through their talk. This is particularly useful for illuminating the processes of narrative construction, especially discussion involved in producing a written answer to fulfil the task requirements. This data was supplemented by navigational information from the video recordings, and so the team was able to relate dialogue to screen events and analyze it in terms of narrative guidance.

These methods captured the observable elements of the learning process but not the internal processes of reflection. I illuminated these processes by asking the students to give an oral account of what they had done during the lesson as if to a friend who had been absent. Students were shown how to use a simple tape recorder, and they recorded their accounts individually and without intervention from the researchers. Of course, this was an invitation to narrativize and so has methodological shortcomings, but it enabled Luckin et al., (2001) to compare processes of both written and spoken narrative construction.

All participants completed a questionnaire for self-assessment of confidence and experience of working with computers, and the teacher provided an assessment of each student's oral abilities. The teacher assessed the accounts that were written to complete the task provided within Galapagos.

Findings

For analytical purposes, each group was conceived of as a small case study, and I did not attempt to find quantitatively defined relations between groups and the version used. My focus of interest was in local relations between design features and behavior for the various sources of data I had. Some of these were generated by the group (talk, notepad responses), others were generated by individuals (self-recorded responses to probes). The following discussion is based on detailed analyses of learners' interactions with the software and with each other but has been simplified for illustrative purposes. More detailed analyses are available elsewhere of the ways in which narrative can scaffold learning (Luckin et al., 1998b) and the role of talk, the notepad, and the model answer in constructing narrative (Luckin et al., 2001).

The three versions make explicit the tension described earlier between authorial, or designer, control and learner control. The linear version presented a high degree of narrative guidance and little opportunity for learners to decide their own narrative path, so they had relatively little control. This is more apparent in the early part of a session, as all eight sections were viewed in sequence even though learners were able to move backward and forward. Once they had seen all eight sections, some learners did not look at any of the sections for a second time; others exercised more control but still retained a fairly linear path through the material. Students using this version did not take notes, and they did not interrupt the flow of the narrative or alter the order of the presentation, although this behavior often changed when they reached the end of the sections with its reminder of the task. At this point, they began to behave more like students using the other versions, going back over the material and focusing on the construction of their answer. Not needing to plan their own investigation, as required for the RBL version, reduced learners' understanding of the relation between the presented information and their overall goal.

For the RBL version, the reverse was true. There was very little narrative guidance offered and learners had to construct a narrative by making decisions about sequence, so there was a high degree of learner control and heavy use of the menu to decide the route. In some cases, this meant that they did not access all available sections, but the students needed to interpret the requirements of the task before interacting with the software, and this made learning processes more explicit.

The GDL version offered a balance between narrative guidance and support for narrative construction and this was reflected in a more even balance between designer control and learner control: Learners were able to determine sequence and their course of action but were offered guidance in doing so. The GDL users accessed more sections of the CD-ROM than users of the other versions because the guide had encouraged them to be interactive in their approach and to seek out the material to support their response. This was confirmed by teacher analysis of the completed written responses. The teacher's assessment of the students' response to the written task showed that several groups achieved a high standard. This entailed focusing on the argument that the separate formation of the islands from volcanic eruptions created different environments to which a species of birds migrating from the mainland then adapted to form varieties of subspecies. Table 3.2 summarizes the key findings. Observation of the sessions showed that

- The simple interface design, used for all three versions, elicited a much higher ratio of on-task to procedural talk than the more complex commercial interfaces.
- The provision of a clear, easily accessible task, a notepad, and a model answer were effective in terms of the use all groups made of them and the high proportion of on-task talk they elicited.
- The guide to the component parts of the task of the GDL version tended to focus learners' notes on the essential elements, whereas the more open-ended choices of the RBL version elicited notes on incidental facts that were more difficult for less able learners to build into their response.
- The menu in the RBL version provided free access to all sections of the material and required learners to make an active selection but did not provide guidance on how sections related to each other. This left less confident learners without support for linking the parts together to construct a whole.
- RBL learners were further disadvantaged, as they were more likely to miss key sections of the material, whereas both linear and GDL learners were exposed to all of it.
- The linear version engaged learners in the preconstructed narrative to the extent that they did not disturb the sequence and did not use the notepad until they had seen all sections. This left some learners unable to articulate their own understanding except as recall.
- The continual requirement to decide on the next action in both RBL and GDL versions encouraged learners to take notes as they progressed and began to build their own account. In some cases, this prompted their next action. This was particularly noticeable for the GDL groups but totally absent for the linear groups.
- Learners were much more likely to refer back to other sections as they constructed their answers within the learner-controlled RBL and GDL versions and therefore tended to use quotes from the material in their notes, which linear users did not do.
- Linear users had no menu structure to work through and therefore no overview of the structure of the narrative they were following but appeared to compensate by spending more time on the content selection screen at the end. This end screen prompted a key shift in behavior for the linear groups either to start answer construction or to take control of seeking further information.

TABLE 3.2

A Comparison of Student Responses When Using Three Versions
of the Galapagos CD-ROM

Student Response	Linear	Resource Based	Guided Discovery
Navigation	Access all sections Do not alter sequence	Do not access some sections Information on Darwin accessed first Menu and search used for navigation	Access all sections Information on Darwin mainly accessed first Online guide used for navigation
Task	Access all content before starting to write Do not take notes Construct chunks of text Lack of reference to rest of material	Start written response before viewing all content Low level of text revisions	Start written response before accessing more than half content Text entered in small sections Frequent reference back to content in process of constructing response
Talk	Change in nature of talk at end of initial run—the role of the end selection screen	Talk spread throughout; less relating to answer construction	Text relating to the Guide is focus for talk

The definition of narrative as the process of imposing and discerning meaning emphasizes the fine balance that needs to exist between designer control and that given to the learner. In this study, we highlighted the importance of providing facilities to support personal narrative construction and to guide learners through the narrative within the subject matter. A number of design guidelines emerged from this analysis.

DESIGNING INTERACTIVE LEARNING ENVIRONMENTS

These guidelines are based on *Guidelines: Narrative in Software*, a report produced for the British Educational and Communications Technology Agency curriculum software initiative (MENO, 2001). More detail is provided there and in Plowman et al. (1999). Learners need to be guided to access the information they will use to construct their own narrative. This could include transcripts of audiovisual sequences in which the information presented is complex. As it is the video element that is most closely associated with the narrative, this suggests that when video represents a small proportion of operational time, the narrative dynamic needs to be assisted by other means.

Learners need to be guided to the structure and narrative of the resource. This should include a purposeful overall goal that can be easily accessed whenever required as well as reminders throughout the activities. The relation of subgoals or components of the activities to the overall goal should also be made explicit. This enables learners to relate their investigations to the narrative. Learners need to be guided to construct their own narrative by clear statements of the task, a notepad to help them record their responses, and for some applications, eventual access to a model answer to motivate their own account.

The degree of control over the narrative is central and as with some of the other features likely to vary according to the needs of different students. Full designer control (based on the linear version) provides a default sequence with limited learner control. The surface narrative will be strongest in this mode, but students will not benefit from some interactive features. Full learner control (based on the RBL version) provides most opportunities for sequencing the material, but there is a risk that learners will unknowingly limit their response by missing some sections. Shared control (based on the GDL version) is distributed between the learners and the designer and provides support for both narrative guidance and narrative construction.

CONCLUSIONS

The fragmentation of learning was the key problem investigated in this study. Previous findings from a large-scale investigation of teaching and learning with interactive media (Plowman, 1996a) and the early phase of this study found that learners lacked overall strategies for dealing with a task because they preferred to try out different possibilities fairly arbitrarily at the computer. The lure of interactivity meant that they seemed reluctant to reflect on the task with which they were engaged. Decision making and associated physical interaction with the computer, such as selecting icons or entering keywords, intrude on and militate against coherence of the learning experience, with the result that learning can then become fragmented. The corollary of this is that getting the story straight becomes difficult.

One of the problems is that interactivity as experienced with a CD-ROM is meager compared to human interaction. Human teachers can sense when people are getting lost or need clarification and deal with it. The current state of adaptive systems means that this support is provided at a primitive level, so although students are usually able to follow individual units of content, they are not given the help they need at the foci of interactivity. Neither are they necessarily able to make connections between the units—or there may not be a clear link.

Although both teachers and students are becoming increasingly competent at integrating interactive media into teaching and learning activities, an understanding of the role of narrative continues to be fundamental. Indeed, the increased use of learning objects is likely to lead to increased atomization of learning, that is, its fragmentation into small units that rely on the learner to formulate the connections rather than the teacher or designer. Learning objects are digital units of content with different levels of granularity that operate as "small instructional components that can be reused a number of times in different learning contexts" (Wiley, 2001, p. 3). They can be combined with other learning objects from the same or different sources to produce bespoke educational courses. Learning object metadata standards focus on the "minimal set of attributes needed to allow these learning objects to be managed, located, and evaluated" including "pedagogical attributes such as: teaching or interaction style, grade level, mastery level, and prerequisites" (Learning Technology Standards Committee, 2001, para. 1). If students have problems getting the story straight with CD-ROMs that are designed with some degree of coherence, the potential for problems is likely to be exacerbated by new courseware with no apparent mechanisms for sequencing and macrostructure. The concept of teaching and learning inherent in the use of learning objects is one of "knowledge transfer," an impoverished version of the dialogic processes of teaching and learning described here.

The study described here revealed a cyclical relation in which the learners' experiences of design features affect both group and individual behavior, and this in turn affects their experience of design features. Productive learning experiences benefit from the interplay between the processes of narrative guidance and narrative construction. Learners find narrative coherence that is already there and generate it for themselves: Both processes need to occur simultaneously, and designers need to lay the foundations of narrative and to capitalize on learners actively producing their own sense of a text. Nash (1990) referred to narrative as a way of "getting coherence" and explained that he used getting as a way of leaving open the issue "as to whether the process alluded to is the discovery or production of coherence" (p. xiii).

Teachers provide narrative guidance and support for narrative construction because they are able to assimilate digressions, repeat points, and tie up threads in a highly interactive way that takes account of the individuality of learners, the social context, relevant artifacts, and the environment. They are able to elicit knowledge from students and respond to them, to initiate, confirm, evaluate, reformulate, and give feedback. They provide what Mercer (1995) called the guided construction of knowledge. Narrative guidance and narrative construction are interdependent because the guidance provides the means for learners to construct their own narratives, and the additional support for narrative construction leads to greater engagement with the narrative guidance. Narrative is thereby coconstructed, and in this way, learners are able to get the story straight. As the quotation from Olson (1990) at the beginning of this chapter claimed, narrative serves to make events "comprehensible, memorable and communicable" (p. 104). Narrative is therefore central to the processes of understanding, remembering, and communicating that underpin teaching and learning. The design of interactive media is still a long way from being as sophisticated as teachers in this respect, and thinking about teaching and learning as processes of narrative guidance and narrative construction demonstrates just how formidable a task it would be to simulate this highly reciprocal relation. Nevertheless, these findings suggest that awareness of this interdependence would lead to improved design and benefits for learning.

ACKNOWLEDGMENTS

This research was conducted as part of MENO (Multimedia, Education and Narrative Organization) funded by the Economic and Social Research Council's Cognitive Engineering Programme, Grant no. L127251018. I am indebted to my colleagues on this project—Diana Laurillard, Rosemary Luckin, and Josie Taylor—and to the teachers and students involved in the studies. The "Galapagos" CD-ROM was developed by Matthew Stratfold.

REFERENCES

Arnheim, R. (1974). Art and visual perception: A psychology of the creative eye (rev. ed.). Berkeley: University of California Press. (Original work published 1954)
Bamberg, M. (Ed.). (1997). Narrative development. Mahwah, NJ: Lawrence Erlbaum Associates.
Barthes, R. (1977). Introduction to the structural analysis of narratives. In Image, music, text (pp. 79–124). London: Fontana.
Bordwell, D. (1985). Narration in the fiction film. London: Routledge.
Branigan, E. (1992). Narrative comprehension and film. London: Routledge.
Bruner, J. (1996). The culture of education. Cambridge, MA: Harvard University Press.
Bruner, J. (2002). Making stories: Law, literature, life. New York: Farrar, Strauss & Giroux.
Cazden, C. (1987). Classroom discourse: The language of teaching and learning. London: Heinemann.
Cobley, P. (2001). Narrative. London: Routledge.
Collins, W. A. (1979). Children's comprehension of television content. In E. Wartella (Ed.), Children communicating: Media and development of thought, speech, understanding. Beverly Hills: Sage.

Denzin, N. (2000). Narrative's moment. In M. Andrews, S. D. Sclater, C. Squire, & A. Treacher (Eds.), *Lines of narrative: Psychosocial perspectives* (pp. i–xii). London: Routledge.

Edwards, A., & Westgate, D. (1987). *Investigating classroom talk.* London: Falmer.

Goldman, S. R., Varma, K., & Sharp, D. (1999). Children's understanding of complex stories: Issues of representation and assessment. In S. R. Goldman, A. C. Graesser, & P. van den Broek (Eds.), *Narrative comprehension, causality and coherence* (pp. 135–159). Mahwah, NJ: Lawrence Erlbaum Associates.

Hardy, B. (1977). Towards a poetics of fiction: An approach through narrative. In M. Meek, A. Warlow, & G. Barton (Eds.), *The cool web* (pp. 12–23). London: Bodley Head.

Hastie, R. (1981). Schematic principles in human memory. In E. T. Higgins, C. P. Herman, & M. P. Zanna (Eds.), *Social cognition: The Ontario symposium* (Vol. 1, pp. 39–82). Hillsdale, NJ: Lawrence Erlbaum Associates.

Hoadley, C., & Enyedy, N. (1999). Between information and communication: Middle spaces in computer media for learning. In C. Hoadley & J. Roschelle (Eds.), *Proceedings of the Computer Support for Collaborative Learning (CSCL) 1999 Conference* (pp. 242–251). Mahwah, NJ: Lawrence Erlbaum Associates.

Kintsch, W., & Greene, E. (1978). The role of culture-specific schemata in the comprehension and recall of stories. *Discourse Processes, 1,* 1–13.

Laurillard, D. M. (1993). *Rethinking university teaching: A framework for the use of educational technology.* London: Routledge.

Laurillard, D. M. (2002, January/February). Rethinking teaching for the knowledge society. *Educause Review, 37*(1), 16–25.

Laurillard, D., Stratfold, M., Luckin, R., Plowman, L., & Taylor, J. (2000). Affordances for learning in a non-linear narrative medium. *Journal of Interactive Media in Education, 2.* Retrieved September 1, 2004 from www-jime.open.ac.uk/00/2

Learning Technology Standards Committee. (2001). Scope and purpose of IEEE P1484.12 Learning Object Metadata Working Group. Retrieved Learning Technology Standards Committee Web site: http://ltsc.ieee.org/wg12/

Luckin, R., Plowman, L., Gjedde, L., Laurillard, D., Stratfold, M., & Taylor, J. (1998a). An evaluator's toolkit for tracking interactivity and learning. In M. Oliver (Ed.), *Innovation in the evaluation of learning technology* (pp. 42–64). London: University of North London.

Luckin, R., Plowman, L., Laurillard, D., Stratfold, M., & Taylor, J. (1998b). Scaffolding learners' constructions of narrative. In A. Bruckman, M. Guzdial, J. L. Kolodner, & A. Ran (Eds.), *Proceedings of Third International Conference on the Learning Sciences (ICLS–98)* (pp. 181–187). Atlanta: Georgia Tech.

Luckin, R., Plowman, L., Laurillard, D., Stratfold, M., Taylor, J., & Corben, S. (2001). Narrative evolution: Learning from students' talk about species variation. *International Journal of Artificial Intelligence in Education, 12,* 100–123.

Lyle, S. (2000). Narrative understanding: Developing a theoretical context for understanding how children make meaning in classroom settings. *Journal of Curriculum Studies, 32,* 45–63.

Mallon, B., & Webb, B. (2000). Structure, causality, visibility and interaction: Propositions for evaluating engagement in narrative multimedia. *International Journal of Human–Computer Studies, 53,* 269–287.

McEwan, H., & Egan, K. (Eds.). (1992). *Narrative in teaching, learning and research.* New York: Teachers College Press.

McNeil, L. (1996). Homo inventans: The evolution of narrativity. *Language and Communication, 16*, 331–360.

McQuillan, M. (Ed.). (2000). *The narrative reader.* London: Routledge.

Meek, M. (1988). *How texts teach what readers learn.* Stroud, England: Thimble Press.

MENO. (2001). *Guidelines: Narrative in software.* Retrieved September 1, 2004 from http://www.becta.org.uk/page_documents/support_staff/narrative.pdf. British Educational Communications and Technology Agency Web site.

Mercer, N. (1995). *The guided construction of knowledge.* Clevedon, England: Multilingual Matters.

Nash, C. (1990). *Narrative in culture: The uses of storytelling in the sciences, philosophy and literature.* London: Routledge.

Nelson, K. (1996). *Language in cognitive development: The emergence of the mediated mind.* Cambridge, England: Cambridge University Press.

Olson, D. R. (1990). Thinking about narrative. In B. Britton & A. Pellegrini (Eds.), *Narrative thought and narrative language* (pp. 99–111). Hillsdale, NJ: Lawrence Erlbaum Associates.

Pedersen, E. M. (1995). Storytelling and the art of teaching. *Forum, 33*(1), 2–5. Retrieved September 1, 2004 from http://exchanges.state.gov/forum/vols/vol33/no1/

Plowman, L. (1992). An ethnographic approach to analysing navigation and task structure in interactive multimedia: Some design issues for group use. In A. Monk, D. Diaper, & M. D. Harrison (Eds.), *Proceedings of HCI '92: People and Computers VII* (pp. 271–287). Cambridge, England: Cambridge University Press.

Plowman, L. (1996a). Designing interactive media for schools: A review based on contextual observation. *Information Design Journal, 8*, 258–266.

Plowman, L. (1996b). Narrative, linearity and interactivity: Making sense of interactive multimedia. *British Journal of Educational Technology, 27*, 92–105.

Plowman, L. (1996c). What's the story? Narrative and the comprehension of educational interactive media. In T. Green, J. Cañas, & C. Warren (Eds.), *Proceedings of the 8th European Conference on Cognitive Ergonomics (ECCE8)* (pp. 167–172). Granada, Spain, September 1996. London: European Association of Cognitive Ergonomics Press.

Plowman, L., Luckin, R., Laurillard, D., Stratfold, M., & Taylor, J. (1999). Designing multimedia for learning: Narrative guidance and narrative construction. In *Proceedings of CHI '99, ACM conference on Human Factors in Computing Systems* (pp. 310–317). New York: ACM Press.

Rumelhart, D. (1975). Notes on a schema for stories. In D. G. Bobrow & A. Collins (Eds.), *Representation and understanding—Studies in cognitive science* (pp. 211–236). Orlando, FL: Academic.

Salomon, G. (1994). *Interaction of media, cognition, and learning.* Hillsdale, NJ: Lawrence Erlbaum Associates. (Original work published 1979)

Silverstone, R. (1999). *Why study the media?* London: Sage.

Steiner, G. (1996). The uncommon reader. In *No passion spent, essays 1978-1996.* London: Faber & Faber.

Thorndyke, P. (1977). Cognitive structures in comprehension and memory of narrative discourse. *Cognitive Psychology, 9*, 77–110.

White, H. (1981). The value of narrativity in the representation of reality. In. W. J. T. Mitchell (Ed.), *On narrative* (pp. 1–23). Chicago: University of Chicago Press.

Wiley, D. (2001). Connecting learning objects to instructional design theory: A definition, a metaphor, and a taxonomy. In D. Wiley (Ed.), *The instructional use of learning objects*, Online version. Retrieved September 15, 2004 from http://www.reusability.org/read/

4

Technology and the New Culture of Learning: Tools for Education Professionals

Lauren B. Resnick
Alan Lesgold
Megan W. Hall
University of Pittsburgh

If education is to equip young people to live the uncertain life, a concern with the changing nature of society and its corollary demands—with the eventual real-life capabilities and dispositions which will be needed—has to reach down into the microstructure of the teacher's momentary intentions and interactions.
—Claxton (2002, p. 27)

In this chapter, we present a view of the emerging needs for systemic changes in schooling and discuss ways in which technology can facilitate the needed professional development of the teachers and school leaders who must make these systemic changes. The changing needs come from a complex of societal factors. Many of the skills needed to adapt to adult life outside of school are different from those needed inside the school world. In an era of information overload and continuous multitasking, people have to learn how to manage attention, choose among multiple sources of information, and query the environment productively. Too much of schooling, however, assumes that children are being motivated at home to pay attention and to persist in complex cognitive activity. It is assumed that teachers, if motivated by various accountability provisions, will become able and willing to present learning opportunities of which children, because they are motivated by standards and by their parents, will afford themselves effectively.

All parties involved in this set of assumptions still carry the historic baggage of seeing much of being a good student as following directions, obeying orders, and producing work as required. Overall, the goals of education now include the ability to engage in extensive cognitive work independently, whereas the world outside of school is substantially less supportive of school-based learning—the task is harder both because of the desired outcomes and because of the changed inputs.

Fortunately, there is a science of learning that can provide a foundation for the new forms of teaching and learning called for by today's societal conditions. Cognitive science has provided rigorous new ways of defining knowledge and competence. There is also new evidence about how people develop and learn and hence new conceptions of effective pedagogy and teaching (cf. Bransford, Brown, & Cocking, 2000; Pellegrino, Chudowsky, & Glaser, 2001). The learning sciences today also propose a radically altered view of the nature of human intelligence and aptitude and of motivation for learning. Accompanying these changes in concepts of learning and cognition is a shifting view of the organizations in which people function as learners, citizens, and workers (cf. Nahapiet & Ghoshal, 1998; Resnick & Wirt, 1996; Wells & Claxton, 2002).

Effective improvement of schools toward the goal of producing active learners will require that teachers and school leaders have opportunities to reflect on the deep educational needs of children and to learn not only how to teach important concepts well but also how to use the day-to-day progression of active learning opportunities to foster learning skills, intellectual resilience, and the ability to persist in tough mental challenges. Active learning must be justified not just as a tactic for achieving small curricular goals but also as a fundamental goal of schooling—the production of students who can deal with the opportunities and uncertainties of modern life. If systematic changes in schooling can achieve this for all students regardless of how much their out-of-school environment contributes to the process they will represent a truly important contribution to education.

Technology can and almost certainly will play a role in this educational renewal process. However, ways of using technology will need to be adapted both to the new forms of learning that schools will want to foster and to the social and organizational school structures into which new technological tools are introduced. In this chapter, we begin by pointing to the new conceptions of knowledge, learning, and teaching that frame the challenge and the opportunity of educational renewal. We then consider the demands that these concepts establish for new forms of continuous professional learning and the particular roles that technology might play in redesigned systems.

Next, we offer analytic descriptions of several technology-based tools that we have designed specifically for use in new forms of professional education. In a final section of the chapter, we assess the current status of our efforts and look ahead to next steps in the project of bringing technological tools into the heart of professional functioning in education.

NEW CONCEPTIONS OF KNOWLEDGE, INTELLIGENCE, LEARNING, AND TEACHING

Knowledge and Competence

Consider first what counts as knowledge (see Fig. 4.1). Throughout most of the last century, psychologists considered knowledge to consist of bits of information linked in associative pairs: *bonds* in the terminology of associationist psychology and *stimulus-response pairs* in later behaviorist terms. Today, attention is focused on schemas and structures, that is, ordered domains of knowledge in which individual bits of information take their place within structures of meaning and relation. In cognitive neuroscience, for example, the search is for dynamic patterns of activation in which meaning emerges and not for isolated pairs and bits of information.

Other changes in conceptions of knowledge have more to do with the emergence of powerful information technologies than with theories of epistemology or brain functioning. One hundred years ago, there were few sources of knowledge and information and a relatively small number of individuals and institutions that determined what information was released to the public. Today, there are multiple sources and a near impossibility of controlling the release of information. Knowledge, then, which once seemed bounded and fixed so that it was possible to imagine compiling it all into an encyclopedia, is now understood to be emergent and exploding. No one "controls" it, and no one can master it once and for all. Both because of the volume of knowledge and because of its continually changing character,

Old conceptions of knowledge	New conceptions of knowledge
• Bonds and lists	• Schemas and structures
• Few sources	• Multiple sources
• Controlled	• Public
• Bounded/fixed	• Exploding/emergent

FIG. 4.1. Our understanding of what counts as knowledge has changed.

successful human living involves lifelong and just-in-time acquiring and analyzing of information.

With changes in the conception of knowledge have come powerful, often confusing shifts in what counts as competence (see Fig. 4.2). In the old days, being competent meant being able to perform some skill (e.g., solving algebra equations) with few or no errors or being able to give the expected (usually brief) answer to questions posed by an examiner. Competence was entirely an individual matter: Skill and knowledge resided in the head and hand of each person. Relationships between individuals were more like those in a catechism class—an expert posing questions to a series of individuals with no necessary relation among the series of questions asked and answered—than those in a conversation or debate. Now, one views cognitive competence as consisting at least equally of the capacity to engage in explanation, inquiry, or argumentation. Ability to participate in such conversations in which knowledge is distributed rather than centered in individuals is part of what one now means by cognitive competence.

Intelligence

For most of this century, American and European education has operated on the premise that inherited ability is paramount, that there are innate limits to what people can learn, and that the job of the schools is to provide each student with an education that befits his or her naturally occurring position on the statistical bell curve (see Fig. 4.3). Recent evidence has suggested that human capability is multidimensional (Gardner, 1983; Sternberg, 1985) and open ended (Neisser, 1988; Perkins, 1995): People can grow their functional intelligence through sustained and targeted effort (Resnick & Nelson-LeGall, 1996). There is mounting evidence coming from research in neuroscience, cognitive science, and social psychology to support this view, but no one really knows where the upper limits are. Especially important is the emerging realization that just about all people can learn if they engage in the right cognitive activities on a sustained basis, just as all people can become physically healthier if they engage in appropriate programs of physical activity.

Old understanding of competence	New understanding of competence
• Automated skill	• Explanation/inquiry/argumentation
• Q & A	• Conversation and argument
• Individual	• Distributed

FIG. 4.2.   Changing ideas about what constitutes competent performance.

Old ideas about aptitude and intelligence	New ideas about aptitude and intelligence
• Entity	• Incremental
• Intelligence limits learning	• Intelligence is learnable
• Bell curve: Few are highly capable	• Open capacity: Many can become capable

FIG. 4.3.   Old and new conceptions of aptitude and intelligence.

Cognitive scientists and psychologists have been working for several decades to understand the specific elements of intelligence and to learn how
these elements are acquired. There is broad agreement today that although
individual differences in biological endowment for learning exist, so much of
functional intelligence is learnable (and therefore teachable) that educators
have an obligation to treat the cultivation of functional intelligence as a central charge in their work. What is now understood to be learnable ranges from
specific knowledge and skills (e.g., figuring out analogies and word meanings
in context—e.g., Pellegrino & Glaser, 1982; Sternberg, 1977) to much
broader capacities of self-monitoring, elaboration, and self-management of
learning (e.g., Bereiter & Scardamalia, 1989; Brown, Bransford, Ferrara, &
Campione, 1983; Campione, Brown, & Connell, 1988; Glaser, 1996).

An extensive literature (e.g., Mueller & Dweck, 1996; Resnick &
Nelson-LeGall, 1996; Thorkildsen & Nicholls, 1998) has also revealed the
ways in which different children come to believe that their educational accomplishments or failures are due to aptitude rather than effort. In a world
where many believe that only the "able" students can learn, it is easy to decide that you failed to learn because you were not able, whereas successful
peers did well in school because they were more able. After all, if learning
failures come from lack of aptitude, then the student who fails is not at fault
but rather unlucky. A major step toward improved learning success for such
children must be convincing them that their investments of effort will pay
off in increased learning.

Social psychologists' research on achievement goal orientation shows
that people's beliefs about the nature of intelligence and their dispositions
toward learning are associated. It also shows that these associated beliefs
and dispositions and the practices they produce differ from person to person.
People who see intelligence as a thing that individuals possess in fixed
amounts and display in performance tend to avoid challenging situations
because they view working hard as a sign of low intelligence whereas people
who believe intelligence develops over time through hard work on challeng-

ing problems generally display continued high levels of task-related effort in response to difficulty (Mueller & Dweck, 1996). However, individuals are not purely learning oriented or performance oriented. People tend to be mostly one or the other, but their orientation—the way they describe themselves and the way they behave—can switch depending on the kind of environment they are in. This means that educators and those who set policies for education have the opportunity to create environments that foster learning-oriented achievement goals and the belief that intelligence is incrementally learnable. Just as people with minimal athletic inclination can be motivated to engage in more physical training and even to become able to run a marathon race, students with minimal learning orientation can be motivated to develop and more persistently apply powerful cognitive learning skills.

These diverse bodies of research now converge in support of the claim that human capability is open ended and begin to point the way to an educational approach based on deliberate activation of self-managed thinking. Increasingly, educators are seeking to build learning environments that create learning-oriented habits of mind and in so doing grow intelligence.

Learning and Teaching

As the nature of knowledge and competent performance and of intelligence and ability to learn have been redefined and expanded, so too has understanding of how learning takes place (see Fig. 4.4). When knowledge was believed to consist mainly of a smoothly performed skill or a list of specific facts, then practice and repetition were privileged means of learning, and pedagogical methods to enhance this practice were sought. Pedagogy was viewed as a matter of effectively and efficiently transmitting established knowledge to a receiver. The right answers to questions, the skilled bits of performance, were to be "stamped in" through praise or other rewards, whereas wrong answers and ineffective performances were to be "stamped

Old thinking about teaching and learning	New thinking about teaching and learning
• Practice and repetition	• Interpretation and explanation
• Transmission	• Construction
• "Stamping in" and "stamping out"	• Self-monitoring and self-management
• Individual	• Social

FIG. 4.4.   Changing notions about how teaching and learning take place.

out." For decades, following the lead of E. L. Thorndike (e.g., 1906, 1922, 1932) and other associationist and behaviorist psychologists, educators and scholars searched for the most effective ways of organizing practice, of stamping in and stamping out (should wrong answers be "punished" or merely allowed to languish in favor of well-rewarded correct answers?), and of maintaining "motivation" among students for attending to uninteresting or even downright boring learning activities.

Over decades, a well-crafted pedagogy of practice and recitation (sometimes even including "scripts" for teachers to follow) has grown up. This kind of teaching has over time become highly "engineered." Applied researchers have expanded on the basic science of associationist learning science to create effective programs for teaching basic skills and knowledge. However, these programs are unlikely to teach the kinds of knowledge and competence that are now recognized as the ultimate goal of school instruction. Indeed, few such programs even claim to be trying to do so, their advocates stressing instead the capacity of such programs to bring low-achieving and at-risk students up to a basic level of academic performance. Indeed, such programs do produce increased levels of minimal performance—even higher test scores on basic skills tests—but they are insufficient for achieving the newly needed goals of education for the information age because they focus only on the minimal information handling routines increasingly assigned to machines rather than people.

Today, with new conceptions of knowledge and competence, pedagogical methods are sought that are more likely to engage students in active interpretation of what they read or explanation of what they observe. Learning research has shown that learners need to manipulate and use the information they are offered and that in so doing, they will construct schematic representations that make sense of domains of knowledge. This sense-making activity by learners may lead to misunderstandings and misconceptions to which teachers must be alert, but few theorists of learning and instruction today would suggest that practice alone is the route to perfection. Changing ideas about motivation for learning accompany this activist, meaning-seeking view of learning. In today's theories of teaching, there is a substantial emphasis on self-monitoring and self-management of one's own learning. Students must go beyond simply absorbing predigested knowledge to learning how to make knowledge from the information around them.

Today's new pedagogies derive directly from the new conceptions of learning and competence described here. Instead of providing a diet consisting entirely of private drill and practice and perhaps guided by workbooks with many fill-in-the-blank exercises, researchers and practitioners of the new pedagogies now try to establish communities of learners who are engaged together in guided activities of interpretation and analysis leading to robust and correct theories of science, mathematics, history, and the like.

Instead of workbooks, we seek to develop case studies and annotation tools that will allow individuals to track their own developing knowledge and to share interpretations with others. From short-answer tests and exclusively external evaluation systems, we are evolving toward increasing amounts of guided self-evaluation based on open-response assessments or collections of students' best work for evaluation by committees of evaluators. Instruction is now understood as inherently social: engaging groups of learners in interpretation and explanation rather than drilling individuals who happen to be gathered in a group within a classroom.

> Consider a simple description of the complicated task the teacher faces in leading a group discussion. Imagine the purpose of this discussion is to foster students' participation in thinking through a particular problem. Let's assume that the teacher is committed to giving each child equal access to the intellectual enterprise, and that the students present a wide range of linguistic backgrounds, attitudes, and academic resources. The teacher must give each child an opportunity to work through the problem under discussion (whether publicly or privately) while simultaneously encouraging each of them to listen to and attend to the solution paths of the others, building on each other's thinking. Yet she must also actively take a role in making certain that the class gets to the necessary goal: perhaps a particular solution or a certain formulation that will lead to the next step in the academic task. She may need to make judgments about what to avoid, or to lead them away from topics or methods for which too many of them are not prepared, while not squelching those who made the problematic contribution. Finally she must find a way to tie together the different approaches to a solution, taking everyone with her. At another level—just as important—she must get them to see themselves and each other as legitimate contributors to the problem at hand. (Michaels, O'Connor, Hall, Resnick, & Fellows of the Institute for Learning, 2002, pp. 22–23)

PROFESSIONAL LEARNING
FOR NEW FORMS OF TEACHING

We turn now to the question of how to successfully inculcate in teachers and school leaders the beliefs, knowledge, and skill implied by the principles just discussed. It is important to remember that the goal is more than just conveying a body of factual knowledge. Given the evidence that the beliefs and capabilities of teachers with respect to high levels of learning need alteration, one can be sure that didactic approaches will be insufficient. Neither skill nor beliefs can simply be told.

Traditional forms of professional development are unlikely to produce the necessary change. They are too removed from the professional practice they are meant to develop. Moreover, they are based on the very forms of pedagogy that the new pedagogies we have described are trying to displace:

transmitting isolated units of knowledge and skill to passive groups of individual learners. What is needed instead are forms of ongoing, embedded professional development that themselves exemplify the kind of teaching and learning we hope students will participate in: deep engagement with texts and other forms of information, critical discussion in which ideas and opinions are tested in a social forum, application of knowledge to practice, and reflection on the practice as a platform for further polishing of skills.

One key to change is to build groups that can absorb the needed beliefs and coach each other's skill development. A second key is to anchor the groups' activities in examples of effective teaching and learning and also to tie their activities to examples from their own schools and classrooms. A third key is to provide opportunities for school people to engage in reflective conversation around specific cases using the vocabulary of the new approaches and making the new knowledge their own. The primary vehicle used for this purpose has been termed "nested learning communities" (Resnick & Hall, 1998). The idea is to organize a school system—or even consortia of school systems—into a hierarchy of learning communities where each learning community has a facilitator who is part of the next level's learning community. For example, a study group of teachers in a school might be facilitated by a principal or team leader who in turn belongs to a study group of school-level leaders. That group in turn might be facilitated by a district leader who in turn is a member of a central office study group. In our view, the teachers in a study group are also to see themselves as facilitators of their classrooms, which constitute a study group as well.

This approach has multiple advantages. First, all participants are both teachers and learners. This is both a strong statement about the professional roles of educators and a known effective technique for learning. Being a teacher provides opportunities to test the knowledge that one has acquired as a learner. Second, it provides a means for scaling up the kind of systemic change approach that is needed. The top level of the hierarchy of nested communities will be small enough to manage, and each layer underneath adds an exponential expansion of the number of participants. Finally, it provides a mechanism for cases to be accumulated that are relevant for the discussion of any given study group, namely, the reported experiences of each group member combined with what that member learns from the group he or she is facilitating.

One can gain theoretical perspective on this new form of professional learning by thinking of professional development as a kind of continuous apprenticeship in the craft of teaching built around adult communities of learners all trying to improve their practice just as we hope that schooling is for children a continuous apprenticeship in the craft of learning. In traditional craft apprenticeship (Lave & Wenger, 1991), young people learn by making things that matter (e.g., in West African tailoring apprenticeships—bags, hats, pants, and shirts that have an immediate market value) and reworking them until a criterion of usability (and marketability) has been reached. The workplace, which doubles as a learning place, is filled with visible models of acceptable products. These are used and talked about as the apprentice is coached through the revision process by a master craftsman or by more senior apprentices.

Since the mid-1980s, learning researchers (cf. Brown, Collins, & Duguid, 1989; Collins, Brown, & Newman, 1989; Lave, 1988; Lesgold & Nahemow, 2001; Resnick, 1990; Rogoff, 1990; Wenger, 1998) have been exploring the concept of "cognitive apprenticeship" and experimenting with school learning environments that include its key features: modeling and observation, active practice, scaffolding, coaching, and guided reflection. Applying these ideas to professional development of educators implies planning and "mental modeling" of teaching, reworking of teaching practice to identified criteria, observation and emulation of visible models, coaching by master teachers or advanced peers, and opportunities for analysis and reflection.

In such apprenticeship learning, the cognitive and the social are combined. Learning is embedded in a social community and in work that matters in the world. Teaching takes the form of assisting the performance of authentic tasks by novices. As a model for professional development, this notion of apprenticeship implies the need for educational organizations committed to continuous learning by—and social accountability among—all members of the community.

The term *assisted performance* was introduced by Tharp and Gallimore (1988) in their book, *Rousing Minds to Life: Teaching, Learning, and Schooling in Social Context*. Rooted in the same theories of situated learning as those of cognitive apprenticeship (Lave & Wenger, 1991; Resnick, Säljö, Pontecorvo, & Burge, 1997), an assisted performance approach to instruction treats teaching as assisting learners in the doing of something important and new (as opposed to just telling them how to do it) and then expecting them to perform with increasing degrees of independence. Learning takes place in activity settings that are conducive to productive instructional conversation, and instruction is targeted within the learner's "zone of proximal development" (i.e., the new knowledge and skills are beyond what the learner already knows well and can do alone, but within a range that the learner can perform with help and support—Vygotsky, 1978; Wertsch, 1985). Tharpe and Gallimore's (1988) "triadic model of assisted performance" (p. 89) described chains of reciprocal assistance in which A assists and is assisted by B, who assists and is assisted by C, and so on. This model is particularly pertinent to professional learning in communities of educational practice where teachers, principals, coaches, and other instructional leaders assist each other's performance. Stein and D'Amico (2002) observed such forms of assistance in a learning community of educators in New

York City Community School District Number 2 where professional development is anchored in the content of a district-mandated Balanced Literacy Program. The authors noted the importance of tailoring the amount and kinds of assistance to the needs of individual professional learners who are invariably at different stages in their development of expertise with respect to the new ways of teaching that they are trying to master.

This way of thinking necessitates a redefinition of the term *professional.* Traditionally, a professional has been someone who has acquired a body of expertise that she or he then delivers or makes available to others. The size and substance of that body of expertise fixes the person's value as a professional. Although professionals in many fields are required to participate in a certain amount of continuing education to keep their licenses or certificates current, educators often perceive that to admit that one is still learning is to announce a professional weakness. This understanding of professionalism suggests a view of ability as immutable. However, when ability is seen as an expandable repertoire of skills and habits, professionals are defined as individuals who are continually learning instead of people who must already know. When a professional is defined as someone who is continually learning, and learning is seen as a function of effort more than of aptitude, it is a person's willingness to participate in cognitive apprenticeship or assisted performance opportunities that defines his or her professional value.

We and our colleagues have been working on tools and methods to support the continual learning of school professionals—teachers, school leaders, and school system leaders. We believe that nested communities of learning should be a central and continuing part of the school world. Our goal is to learn and demonstrate how these communities can be created and supported and to produce tools to help these communities work effectively—to create the teaching side of the new educational workplace.

TECHNOLOGY-BASED TOOLS
FOR PROFESSIONAL APPRENTICESHIP

It seems natural to imagine using technology to help create the new educational workplace. It is, after all, the growth of information technology in society at large that at first permitted, then largely required, the development of participatory organizations and social processes among large groups of people. So as educators and those who work with them have begun to seriously take on the redesign of the educational workplace—as one requiring continuous learning embedded in the work itself rather than front loaded—it is natural that they have imagined and attempted to construct ways of using technology in the process. Many of the proposals for using technology to reconstruct education have focused on bringing high-end, state-of-the art information technology into classrooms. One goal had been to enable students and their teachers to engage in interactive forms of learning that access broad networks of information and people (e.g., shared computer-based notebooks, messaging tools, and information browsers). Another has been to utilize the data management, representational, and editing tools that are common today to build knowledge-building communities (e.g., word processors, groupware tools, spreadsheets, and presentation authoring tools). Most efforts have focused directly on student users. Teacher learning in such projects is viewed as ancillary—a matter of preparing teachers to support students in the use of the new technology-supported ways of learning. Very recently, however, several efforts to develop Internet supported distance learning programs for teacher training have begun to emerge.

Like these distance learning programs, the work we describe here is aimed at continuous education of educators. Different from most other efforts, our work is embedded in a larger institutional redesign effort aimed at building nested professional learning communities of the kind described earlier in schools and school districts. Our work has joined—sometimes imperfectly—direct "on the ground" work with efforts to build technology-based tools. The aim of our direct work is to transform large school districts' theories of learning and practices of teaching and to create organizational structures that will evoke and sustain these new practices. The purpose of our technology-based tools is to support these organizational and learning changes.[1]

Before turning to descriptions of our technological "solution," therefore, we begin with a brief analysis of what practicing professionals need to learn. If teachers are to function well within the kind of learning environments we have described, they need to engage in continuous activities around a core set of knowledge and skills. These constitute the core curriculum for a continuous, practice-based professional development system. We identify six such components, each calling for particular forms of enabling learning tools:

1. Building a coherent theoretical understanding and common vocabulary of teaching and learning. Educators need a shared understanding of—and a shared language for talking about—the new conceptions of knowledge, intelligence, learning, and teaching outlined at the beginning of this chapter.
2. Learning to observe and critique teaching. Educators need to be able to recognize instantiations of these new conceptions in their schools

[1]The on-the-ground work is carried out by the Institute for Learning (www.instituteforlearning.org) at the University of Pittsburgh's Learning Research and Development Center. Research, development, and production of the technology-based tools described in these pages were supported by NetLearn: Networked Learning Communities for Educational Reform under contract No. R303A980192 with the Technology Innovation Challenge Grant Program of the U.S. Department of Education, Learning Technologies Division.

and classrooms and to make connections between the theory and the practices that enact them.

3. Analyzing student performance as the criterion of successful teaching. If the quality of teaching practice is to be judged by the students' learning, educators need to develop a shared vision of what student products and performances look like when they meet the expected standards for a given grade level and content area.

4. Planning lessons using standards for student learning and research-based criteria of professional practice. Educators need to know how to pull together everything they know about their students, their subject matter, and good professional practice when they plan lessons. They need to be able to run a mental model of each lesson, anticipating how their students will respond and building a contingency plan for different sets of responses.

5. Analyzing and revising one's own teaching. Teachers need to reflect on what they and their students have done during lessons and to use what they learn from such reflection to inform how they will proceed in subsequent lessons and assignments.

6. Assisting others' professional learning. There is a particular function—beyond knowing how to enact excellent teaching oneself—that entails helping others learn to do the same. This is the role we envision for coaches, master or lead teachers, and in some cases, principals.

In the next section, we describe examples of tools we have built to support the first three of these components.

Building a Coherent Theoretical Understanding and Common Vocabulary of Teaching and Learning

To engage in professional learning communities, educators need a common base of understanding of the science of learning as it bears on teaching practice in the school subject matters. The new theories of knowledge, learning, and instruction that we discussed in the opening sections of this chapter have begun to penetrate the education system, having become part of virtually all teacher-preparation programs. However, educators came through these programs at different times and different institutions. As a result, individuals know incomplete and different versions of these theories and are often not able to discuss issues of teaching and learning with one another in a sustained way using a common vocabulary that is clearly related to teaching practice. A first step in building professional practice communities is to build a common base of understanding and to begin a regular practice of professional talk.

To support this kind of learning practice, we have built a series of CD-ROMs around nine Principles of Learning distilled from 25 years of research on teaching and learning. These might best be construed as a practitioner-friendly version of the theoretical ideas presented in the National Research Council's recent reports on the science of learning and cognitive assessment (e.g., Bransford, Brown, & Cocking, 2000) joined with a small set of organizational practices aimed at creating equitable opportunities to learn for the full spectrum of students populating today's schools. Figure 4.5 provides a brief summary of the Principles of Learning.

The CDs are intended for use by study groups of about six people, possibly including an expert facilitator. Containing a browser-accessible "web site" of text, images, and media clips, the CDs set forth the rationale and substance of the principles and illustrate how they play out in classrooms. They use the affordances of the medium to (a) enliven and illustrate expositions of the principles; (b) teach the meaning of key concepts of learning and teaching through multiple examples of instructional practice that can be compared, contrasted, and intensively analyzed using support tools built into the CDs; (c) engage groups of educators in intensive case studies of particular examples of practice; and (d) simulate some aspects of live communities of practice in more socially protected settings.

Organizing for Effort

Everything within the school is organized to support the belief that sustained and directed effort can yield high achievement for all students. High standards are set, and all students are given as much time and expert instruction as they need to meet or exceed the expectations.

Clear Expectations

Clear standards of achievement and gauges of students' progress toward those standards offer real incentives for students to work hard and succeed. Descriptive criteria and models that meet the standards are displayed in the schools, and the students refer to these displays to help them analyze and discuss their work.

Fair and Credible Evaluations

Tests, exams, and classroom assessments must be aligned to the standards of achievement for these assessments to be fair. Further, grading must be done against absolute standards rather than on a curve so that students can clearly see the results of their learning efforts.

Recognition of Accomplishment

Clear recognition of authentic student accomplishments is a hallmark of an effort-based school. Progress points are articulated so that, regardless of entering performance level, every student can meet the criteria for accomplishments often enough to be recognized frequently.

Academic Rigor in a Thinking Curriculum

In every subject, at every grade level, instruction and learning must include commitment to a knowledge core, high thinking demand, and active use of knowledge.

Accountable Talk

Accountable Talk means using evidence that is appropriate to the discipline and that follows established norms of good reasoning. Teachers should create the norms and skills of Accountable Talk in their classrooms.

Socializing Intelligence

Intelligence comprises problem solving and reasoning capabilities along with habits of mind that lead one to use those capabilities regularly. Equally, it is a set of beliefs about one's right and obligation to make sense of the world, and one's capacity to figure things out over time. By calling on students to use the skills of intelligent thinking—and by holding them responsible for doing so—educators can "teach" intelligence

Self-management of Learning

Students manage their own learning by evaluating feedback they get from others; by bringing their own knowledge to bear on new learning; by anticipating learning difficulties and apportioning their time accordingly; and by judging their progress toward a learning goal. Learning environments should be designed to model and encourage the regular use of self-management strategies.

Learning as Apprenticeship

Learning environments can be organized so that complex thinking is modeled and analyzed in apprenticeship arrangements. Mentoring and coaching will enable students to undertake extended projects and develop presentations of finished work, both in and beyond the classroom.

FIG. 4.5. The Principles of Learning are distilled from 25 years of research on teaching and learning.

An introductory CD, *Principles of Learning: Study Tools for Educators* (Resnick, Hall, & Fellows of the Institute for Learning, 2001), is mainly designed to set forth the core theories and build common ways of using the language of teaching and learning. The "e-book" section of the CD introduces and illustrates the principles of learning. Audio segments expand on some of the background for the principles, and video segments provide classroom examples that illustrate points made in the text. Users are advised to read this document from beginning to end, probably on their own, playing the audio and video clips where indicated. Several full-text articles and references to further reading are included to support deeper study. Figure 4.6 shows a typical page from the Principles of Learning e-book.

Another section of the *Principles of Learning* (Resnick et al., 2001) CD presents the "Instruction and Learning Profile." This section allows users to study a particular principle in greater depth. The Profile sets forth an encapsulated definition of each principle. The features of classroom activity that reflect use of each principle are presented along with indicators that can be watched for when observing classroom practice. The Profile provides multiple video examples from a mix of grade levels and subject areas to help users build their understanding of how the principle might look when enacted in

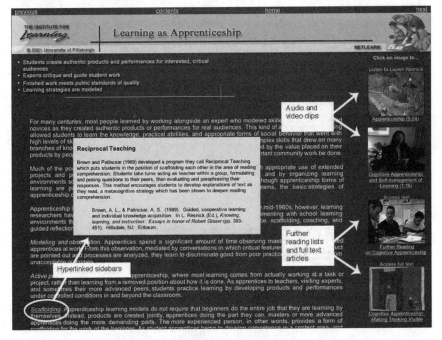

FIG. 4.6.   This page from the e-book section of the *Principles of Learning* CD features audio and video clips, references to further reading, full text of a foundational article and a hyperlinked sidebar.

schools and classrooms. Figure 4.7 shows the introductory page of the Profile from which users can select the principle they want to study. Figure 4.8 shows one of the principles ("Academic Rigor in a Thinking Curriculum") with its features and indicators, a bank of video illustrations, and the pop-up window for one of the videos. When a video is selected, it is accompanied by a written transcript to assist people in following the language and a set of suggested discussion questions to guide users' consideration of how the segment exemplifies the principle.

Additional CDS focusing on individual principles of learning—*Clear Expectations: Putting Standards to Work in the Classroom* (Resnick, Bill, & Fellows of the Institute of Learning, 2000) and *Accountable Talk*^{SM}: *Classroom Conversation That Works* (Michaels et al., 2002)—provide study groups with the means of further developing a shared theory of instruction and learning. Each CD set presents an overview of the principle either in text format or as an extended video presentation as well as materials for in-depth study of specific aspects of the principle. Each also contains extended case studies.

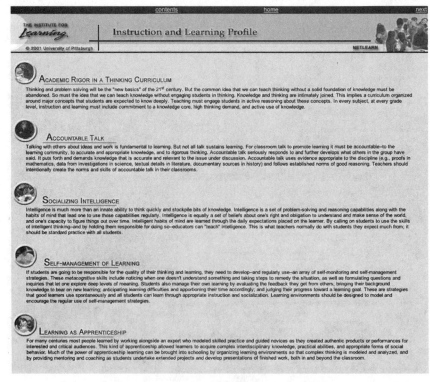

FIG. 4.7. The top page of the *Instruction and Learning Profile* presents encapsulated definitions of the nine Principles of Learning. From this page users can select a principle to explore in greater detail.

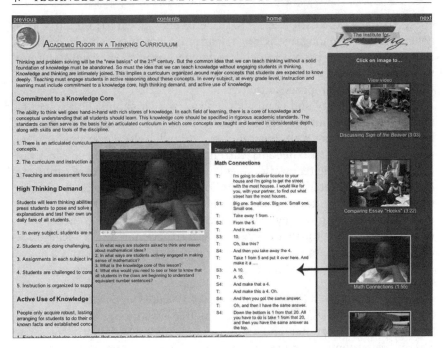

FIG. 4.8.   The profile for each individual principle details its features and indicators and provides multiple video illustrations accompanied by transcripts and discussion questions.

All are supported by suggested activities for individuals and study groups along with observation sheets (to be printed out) to help ground the conversation and provide a record of issues discussed.

Learning to Observe and Critique Teaching: Structured Professional Talk About the Principles of Learning in Practice

In the preceding, we have illustrated how the resources of the interactive CD medium can be used to teach core principles of instruction and learning and to help educators connect a theory of instruction and learning to specific, selected features of instructional practice. However, in the real world, no example of teaching ever neatly illustrates a particular principle or practice. If one observes a classroom for longer than a few minutes, one sees multiple things happening. Teachers may pose problems and start discussions, but—with rare exceptions—matters do not unfold according to a script. Students' responses may lead in a direction not fully planned by a teacher, efforts to make expectations clear to students may appear to interfere with a goal of students' managing their own learning, a complex and academically rigorous lesson may become much less demanding in the teacher's attempt to help weak or shy students, and different students may react differently to the same teacher-proposed activities.

All of this variety and complexity means that it cannot be enough to teach educators about specific features of effective learning and teaching— even when these are well illustrated by carefully selected examples from practice. Educators also need to learn how to analyze the "messy" instructional practice of the real world—deciding which principles of learning are illustrated (or violated) and learning how to discuss examples of practice that may be en route toward but still somewhat distant from the "best practices" one is aiming for. They also need to learn how to function "in community"—that is, how to treat discussion of instructional cases as legitimate opportunities for comparing ideas and sharpening concepts. Our CDS are structured to supply such opportunities and to scaffold discussions.

LearningWalks[SM]: *Building Communities of Practice.*[2]   One approach to building communities of instructional practice is for groups of educators to visit classrooms together and then confer about what they have seen. Shared classroom observations provide an anchor for discussion that grounds the conversation. A skilled facilitator can further guide the discussion, and shared protocols for observation can help to direct the initial observations—including examination of students' work and sometimes conversations with students—in productive directions. At the Institute for Learning, we have developed protocols for the LearningWalk and have trained educators in a number of U.S. school districts in the processes of facilitating these professional visits (Goldman et al., 2001).

Despite this available training, LearningWalks can sometimes prove socially disruptive, especially when school communities are new to the process. In particular, educators whose main experience in observing teaching (or being observed) is supervisory or evaluative often turn the event into a "checklist" process that does not build the group's analytic capabilities and can alienate teachers who believe that they are being evaluated outside the formal system that has been negotiated for such evaluations. For the most part, this kind of distortion of the intended function of the LearningWalk occurs because people have had inadequate advance experience in how to conduct a LearningWalk that is indeed focused on learning rather than evaluation. It can help substantially to be able to "practice" LearningWalk activities in a "virtual" environment prior to entering real classrooms in a real school.

---

[2]Funding for development of the LearningWalk and related leadership tools, protocols, and activities has been provided by DeWitt Wallace-Reader's Digest Fund.

The *Clear Expectations* (Resnick et al., 2000) CD provides an example of how such virtual practice can occur. Users see on the screen a map of a simulated school (see Fig. 4.9). By passing the cursor over a particular classroom, one can get a visual preview of what is inside (classroom activities and artifacts such as students work, standards, criteria charts, and rubrics). By clicking on the classroom, users can "enter" the room and look more closely at each of the artifacts. Figure 4.10 shows the pop-up window that appears when one clicks on the criteria chart in the image map. The window also contains guiding questions to support analysis of the artifact itself and how it might function to establish Clear Expectations in the classroom. Clicking on a different image might bring up a video of one of the interactive classroom activities—along with transcript and discussion questions such as we have seen earlier (see Fig. 4.8).

Case Studies: In-Depth Discussion of Examples of Instruction.   Learning-Walks take people into the reality of a school. Yet—especially in the case of virtual LearningWalks—observations are still limited to a very small slice of instructional activity. Because the time in any single classroom is extremely brief, the full complexity of even a single lesson is missing. Furthermore, because much of the power of a LearningWalk derives from the group's common focus on one or two preselected aspects of instruction, participants do not have the experience of analyzing a complete, complex instruction and

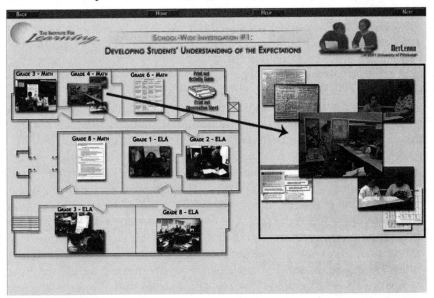

FIG. 4.9.   The *Clear Expectations* CD allows users to go on a "virtual" Learning WalkᴿM where they can practice observing classroom interactions and artifacts such as student work, standards, rubrics, and criteria charts.

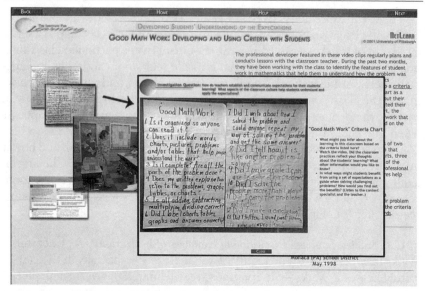

FIG. 4.10.   Clicking on an image in the cluster of classroom "snapshots" causes a pop-up window to appear. The enlarged image is accompanied by guiding questions to support analysis of the artifact itself and of Clear Expectations in the simulated school.

learning event. Some of this complexity can be introduced through carefully designed case studies (cf. Stein, Smith, Henningsen, & Silver, 2000). Such case studies are built into all of these CDS.

A relatively simple version appears in the *Principles of Learning* (Resnick et al., 2001) CD. Here, the case studies are designed to help study groups detect several principles in an ongoing flow of instruction. The case study activities are also organized to help study groups conduct discussions in which they combine information from several points of view. As shown in Fig. 4.11, the group begins by watching a video (typically 15 min in length) together. Individuals or subgroups next select a Principle of Learning as their lens for further, detailed observation. The group then splits up, each printing out an observation sheet that provides a transcript of the entire video and coding information specific to the principle they have chosen (see Fig. 4.12). Individually or in small groups, users watch the video again with as many starts and stops as they wish and use the observation sheet to record instances of "their" principle. Next, the participants reconvene and develop a group composite observation sheet that constitutes their shared interpretation of the episode as a whole.

There is more to a lesson than can be seen just by watching it—even in its entirety. What happens in a given class period grows out of teacher re-

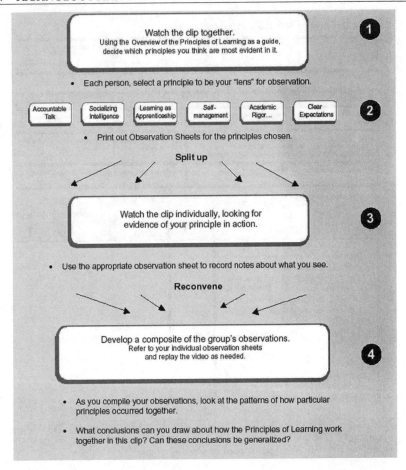

FIG. 4.11. The *Principles of Learning* CD employs relatively simple case-study activities to help study groups detect several principles in an ongoing flow of instruction, and to collectively draw conclusions about how the Principles of Learning work together.

flection on what has gone on in prior sessions, out of consideration of past student work, and out of a plan for what is meant to follow in the way of student activity. A fuller case study would include opportunities to consider all of these in addition to the videotaped lesson itself. The case studies in the *Accountable Talk* (Michaels et al., 2002) CD set provide these opportunities. In addition to lesson videos, they include extensive related resources such as teacher commentary, student work, classroom artifacts, and excerpts of the texts that students are reading or the problems that have been set for them. Each case offers three separate "inquiries" focusing

Video Observation Sheet: Socializing Intelligence

Name	Date Watched

Key to features of Socializing Intelligence	
SI1=Students acquire and use strategies for learning and problem solving	SI2=Students acquire and use strategies for appropriately get and giving help in learning
SI3=Staff communicate to all students that they are already competent learners and are able to become even better through their persistent use of strategies and by reflecting on their efforts	SI4=Classroom practice holds students accountable for using learning, problem solving, and helping strategies
SI5=Students are persistent when working on challenging problems	SI6=Students regularly expect to do "better than before"

Polygon Investigation	Features (from the key above)	Explanation (How you think the video shows the feature)
1. T1: Okay, the next part of the activity is I'm gonna give you a sheet. It's called "Student Sheet 1 – Is it a Polygon?" And with your partner, I want you to, to look at the shapes, and I want you to sort these shapes into two different categories. The first category is, "yes, it's a polygon." And the second category is, "no, it is not a polygon." And I want you to go ahead and write the word "yes" next to the shape, or the word "no." The second thing I want you to do, is I want you to write *why* you say, "yes," and *why* you say,		

FIG. 4.12.   Observation sheets accompanying the Mini Case Studies on the *Principles of Learning* CD include transcripts of the video and coding information specific to the principle each study group participant chooses as a lens.

on different key concepts, which guide users through a particular sequence of case resources (see Fig. 4.13). The activity sheets are similar to those we have discussed previously—printouts of the transcript on which users can take detailed notes focused on a particular question. "Supporting Documents" (Fig. 4.14) provide users with excerpts from the actual materials teachers and students on the video are working with, giving users the background they need to interpret what is going on in the segment. Also available are examples of student work (Fig. 4.15) including marked up copies of the text they are reading, journal entries, notes from lectures and discussions, and drafts of papers. Most case studies also include video of the teacher commenting on specific aspects of her instructional plan, her understanding of students, and strategies for using student talk to further their learning.

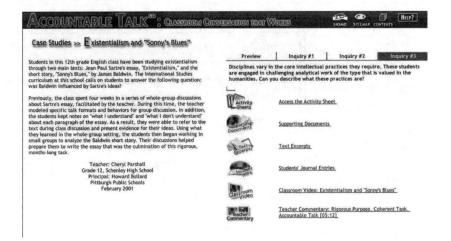

FIG. 4.13. Each *Accountable Talk* case study offers a preview activity and three different guided "inquiries." Each inquiry includes a particular sequence of contextual resources to help users interpret the centerpiece video.

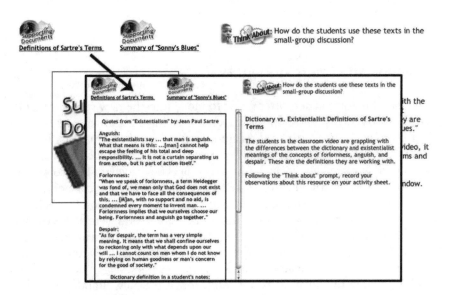

FIG. 4.14. Among the resources accompanying each *Accountable Talk* case study are supporting documents that give users the background they need to interpret what is going on in the video.

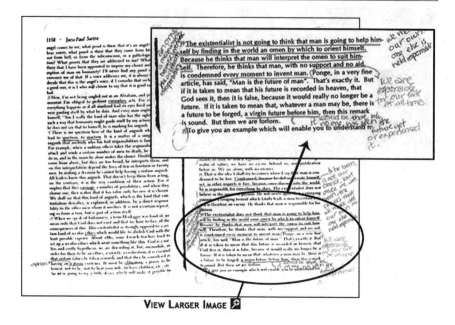

VIEW LARGER IMAGE

FIG. 4.15.   Examples of student work, such as these notes in the margins of a text that students are analyzing in the Accountable Talk "Existentialism" case study, help study group participants develop a more nuanced interpretation of the classroom videos.

Tools for Analyzing Student Work

A crucial skill for teachers attempting to move into the new world of high-level cognitive instruction for all students is to have clear expectations in their own heads about where they are trying to lead their students. In the United States, educators traditionally have not been accustomed to examining student work in light of established criteria. They have not had common standards for what student work should look like. In recent years, officially mandated performance standards have become the norm in most U.S. school districts. However, to make sense of the standards and be able to assess where their learners are in relation to a given standard, educators need models of actual student work that exemplify what the standards mean. Few state or local standards documents are accompanied by such examples.

One attempt to fill this gap has been through the New Standards books outlining expectations for reading, writing, speaking, and listening in kindergarten through third grade (New Standards Primary Literacy Committee, 1999; New Standards Speaking and Listening Committee, 2001). Although the primary purpose of the New Standards committees of re-

searchers and practitioners was to set forth explicit and rigorous performance benchmarks that would be widely accepted and congruent with
many state and local standards, committee members understood that for
those standards to mean anything, they would have to be tied to student
work and to ways of analyzing the work with respect to the standards. Because many of the student performances that needed to be demonstrated
were oral, they had to be captured on videotape. The video examples were
packaged on CDs and distributed along with the standards books. Figure
4.16 shows a screen from the first-grade reading standard for fluency. The
video of the student's reading performance is accompanied by the text of the
standards, written analysis, teacher commentary, and links to similar work
at adjacent grade levels.

MAKING TECHNOLOGY WORK:
SOCIAL DESIGNS FOR PROFESSIONAL LEARNING

The tools we have described represent promising steps toward the forms of
professional support that will be needed to assist teachers as they attempt to
adopt new forms of teaching. These tools are capable of taking educators

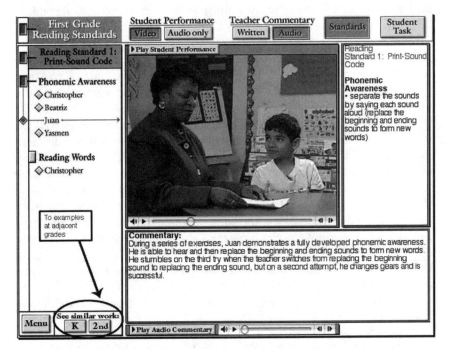

FIG. 4.16. On the CD of New Standards Primary Literacy Standards, video of a student's reading performance is accompanied by the text of the standard, written analysis, teacher commentary, and links to similar work at adjacent grade levels.

into authentically situated study of teaching, helping them become "reflective practitioners" (Schön, 1987) of their craft. Beyond supervised pilot experiments, do people use these tools as we intend? In fact, do they use them at all? Or will these tools suffer the fate of so many other technological innovations in education—taken up by a few dedicated and technologically sophisticated users but mostly unable to penetrate established routines and ways of thinking in the schools (Schofield & Davidson, 2002)?

The Institute for Learning is just beginning to implement these tools on a large scale. However, a pilot trial carried out in three school districts gives a good early indication of what the difficulties and possible successes are likely to be. During the 2001 to 2002 school year, the *Principles of Learning* (Resnick et al., 2001) CD was given a trial run in three medium-size school districts in the United States. All are districts that were already working with the Institute for Learning, although they had been engaged for different periods of time and in different ways. Senior leadership in each district knew about the Principles of Learning and were committed to making them the foundation of a district-wide reform effort. Senior administrators in these districts also were fluent in the language (although not necessarily the practice) of nested learning communities. That is, they knew that they needed to find ways of establishing study groups and other professional community-building activities in their schools. Each was already holding principals' meetings focused on the Principles of Learning and how to teach in accord with them. It seemed logical to use the *Principals of Learning* CD as part of their effort to take their intended reform into schools and classrooms across the district. A plan was made in each district to introduce the CD to principals and to provide multiple copies for school use.

When RAND evaluators visited each district to examine how well the trial was working, their interviews and observations led to radically different assessments in the three districts. In one of the districts, the evaluators were able to observe active study groups using the CDs in some schools and heard reports from principals and teachers in many schools about successful use of the CD. There was considerable—although not universal—enthusiasm for the CD as a powerful tool for initiating or supporting teacher study of the Principles of Learning. Fewer complaints about technical flaws were heard compared with the other districts. In those two other districts, by contrast, there was little use of the CDs in evidence in schools. Indeed, principals and others throughout these districts often reported that the CD was technically flawed—that it couldn't be opened, that navigation through the different parts of the CD was not smooth or didn't work at all, and that videos wouldn't play or sound was inadequate.

How could the same tool receive such different evaluations by potential users? A first possibility, of course, was that in fact two technically different products had been distributed—that something had gone wrong in production or shipping and a flawed batch of CDs had been sent out to two of the districts. With the Institute for Learning tool development team, we checked that possibility and were able to reject the technical flaw hypothesis. All districts had received technically sound CDs. This meant that we had to try to account for the observed differences by examining differences in the individual capabilities of people working in the three districts or in the social structures into which the CDs were introduced. The Institute's field trial was not a controlled experiment, so we were not able to draw firm conclusions. However, we can sketch some strong hypotheses worthy of future investigation.

First, there were no great differences in technological sophistication among the people in the three districts. Most of the target users in all three districts were a bit "shy" of technology at the outset—but, as we have seen, in one of the districts, this initial reluctance was mostly overcome. Nor were there enormous difficulties in the availability of appropriate equipment or technical help. In one of the two nonuser districts, there was little technical help offered, but in the other nonuser district, adequate help was available.

There were some differences in the initial presentation of the CDs to principals. In the first, high-use district, the CD was presented with confidence at a principal's meeting, and there was some practice in using the CD with small groups of peers. In the low-use districts, the CD was presented only in a group demonstration with some hesitancy on the part of the presenter. Most important, there was no modeling of small study group use.

The biggest difference among the districts was in how the CD was situated as part of an ongoing professional development sequence. In the high-use district, participants were given "homework assignments" in which they were asked to go back to their schools and lead study sessions using the CD and its printable activity sheets. They were expected to collect "artifacts" from these sessions—filled-out activity sheets, for example—that would be shared and discussed at the next principals' meeting. Several cycles of assignments and artifact discussion ensued, making it highly likely that even the initially reluctant principals would find a way to launch the CD project in their schools.

None of this social facilitation and demand was present in the two low-use districts. There, at the end of the introductory sessions, principals were told that the CDs could help in their efforts to establish ongoing professional development in their schools; but no particular expectations for use were established, and there was no follow-up, hence no reason for the initially skeptical or those who were not fluent in the technology to expend the effort to even get started. In addition, it is likely that "war stories" from those who tried but did not experience immediate success or satisfaction spread a view through the community of principals that discouraged others from beginning.

This is not a new story in the annals of efforts to introduce new technologies. Each new information technology has seen a similar situation in the business world. Remember, for example, that it was first felt that word processing was only for trained people (indeed, word processor was a human role in industry for a while). Both in the school world and in the business world, there was a period in which one prepared materials for subsequent entry into word processors. During that period, few executives used the tools themselves.

Over time, executives came to understand the value of the tools and eventually to realize that it was more efficient in some cases to just type directly rather than to require the extra human scaffolding of a word processor person. Similarly, many people acquired skill in using various office information processing tools long before they were able to help the workers they led to start using the same tools.

Today, novel software systems for critical functions generally are introduced through the use of special training courses that groups of potential users attend together. Over time, the business world has learned that this level of social scaffolding is needed to get systems into widespread use. Further, technology for the business world tends to start out with interfaces that emulate existing business artifacts (the new Tablet PC devices even emulate standard business writing pads and can be tuned to match the exact ruling of those pads). This match to the social structure being penetrated can be faded away, but it is important to initial acceptance and continued use.

The same approach is needed for educational technology, both for student technology and for the professional development technology we are introducing. As much as possible, our technology needs to match with what people already do together. In the high-use school district, a culture of school-based study groups had already been introduced and it was not very hard—even in the face of some technical difficulties with the CDs and local equipment for running them—to incorporate the new tools. Most users then became enthusiastic proponents of the new technology. In the other districts, it was hoped that the technology might promote the development of school-based study groups. That did not happen. Instead, normal ways of acting in the school coupled with pressures of time and competing activities drove out the technology.

This is a sobering message for advocates of technology in education. Many advocates tend to promote technology not just as a way of making current practices somewhat more efficient but as a way of fundamentally reforming professional practice. Our experience at the Institute for Learning and the experiences of others working in similar ways, suggests that relying on technology to change social practices is unlikely to work. If the basic practice of education is going to change, including the ways in which educators engage in continuing professional development, fundamental social redesign will be required. Technological tools can support new professional learning practices—but availability of the tools cannot be expected to create those new practices.

REFERENCES

Bereiter, C., & Scardamalia, M. (1989). Intentional learning as a goal of instruction. In L. B. Resnick (Ed.), *Knowing, learning, and instruction: Essays in honor of Robert Glaser* (pp. 361–392). Hillsdale, NJ: Lawrence Erlbaum Associates.

Bransford, J. D., Brown, A. L., & Cocking, R. R. (2000). *How people learn: Brain, mind, experience, and school.* Washington, DC: National Academy Press.

Brown, A. L., Bransford, J. D., Ferrara, R. A., & Campione, J. C. (1983). Learning, remembering, and understanding. In P. H. Mussen (Series Ed.), & J. Flavell & E. M. Markman (Vol. Eds.), *Handbook of child psychology: Vol. 3. Cognitive development* (4th ed., pp. 515–629). New York: Wiley.

Brown, J. S., Collins, A., & Duguid, P. (1989). Situated cognition and the culture of learning. *Educational Researcher, 18*(1), 32–42.

Campione, J. C., Brown, A. L., & Connell, M. L. (1988). Metacognition: On the importance of understanding what you are doing. In R. I. Charles & E. A. Silver (Eds.), *The teaching and assessing of mathematical problem solving* (pp. 93–114). Hillsdale, NJ: Lawrence Erlbaum Associates.

Claxton, G. (2002). Education for the learning age: A sociocultural approach to learning to learn. In G. Wells & G. Claxton (Eds.), *Learning for life in the 21st century: Sociocultural perspectives on the future of education* (pp. 21–33). London: Blackwell.

Collins, A., Brown, J. S., & Newman, S. E. (1989). Cognitive apprenticeship: Teaching the crafts of reading, writing, and mathematics. In L. B. Resnick (Ed.), *Knowing, learning, and instruction: Essays in honor of Robert Glaser* (pp. 453–494). Hillsdale, NJ: Lawrence Erlbaum Associates.

Gardner, H. (1983). *Frames of mind: The theory of multiple intelligences.* New York: Basic Books.

Glaser, R. (1996). Changing the agency for learning: Acquiring expert performance. In K. A. Ericsson (Ed.), *The road to excellence: The acquisition of expert performance in the arts and sciences, sports and games* (pp. 303–311). Mahwah, NJ: Lawrence Erlbaum Associates.

Goldman, P., & Resnick, L., with Bill, V., Johnston, J., Micheaux, D., & Seitz, A. (2004). *LearningWalk*^{SM} *sourcebook.* Pittsburgh, PA: Institute for Learning, Learning Research and Development Center, University of Pittsburgh.

Lave, J. (1988). *Cognition in practice: Mind, mathematics and culture in everyday life.* Cambridge, England: Cambridge University Press.

Lave, J., & Wenger, E. (1991). *Situated learning: Legitimate peripheral participation.* Cambridge, England: Cambridge University Press.

Lesgold, A., & Nahemow, M. (2001). Tools to assist learning by doing: Achieving and assessing efficient technology for learning. In D. Klahr & S. Carver (Eds.), *Cognition and instruction: Twenty-five years of progress* (pp. 307–346). Mahwah, NJ: Lawrence Erlbaum Associates.

Michaels, S., O'Connor, M. C., Hall, M. W., Resnick, L. B., & Fellows of the Institute for Learning. (2002). *Accountable Talk*^{SM}: *Classroom conversation that works* [CD-ROM]. Pittsburgh, PA: Institute for Learning, Learning Research and Development Center, University of Pittsburgh.

Mueller, C. M., & Dweck, C. S. (1996). Theories of intelligence: Evaluations of ability and effort in achievement. *International Journal of Psychology, 31*, 454–476.

Nahapiet, J., & Ghoshal, S. (1998). Social capital, intellectual capital, and the organizational advantage. *Academy of Management Review, 23*, 242–266.

Neisser, U. (Ed.). (1998). *The rising curve: Long-term gains in IQ and related measures.* Washington, DC: American Psychological Association.

New Standards Primary Literacy Committee. (1999). *Reading and writing grade by grade: Primary literacy standards for kindergarten through third grade.* Washington, DC & Pittsburgh, PA: National Center on Education and the Economy and the University of Pittsburgh.

New Standards Speaking and Listening Committee. (2001). *Speaking and listening for pre-school through third grade.* Washington, DC and Pittsburgh, PA: National Center on Education and the Economy and the University of Pittsburgh.

Pellegrino, J. W., Chudowsky, N., & Glaser, R. (Eds.). (2001). *Knowing what students know: The science and design of educational assessment.* Washington, DC: National Academy Press.

Pellegrino, J. W., & Glaser, R. (1982). Analyzing aptitudes for learning: Inductive reasoning. In R. Glaser (Ed.), *Advances in instructional psychology* (Vol. 2, pp. 269–345). Hillsdale, NJ: Lawrence Erlbaum Associates.

Perkins, D. N. (1995). *Outsmarting IQ: The emerging science of learnable intelligence.* New York: Free Press.

Resnick, L. (1990, Spring). Literacy in school and out. *Daedalus, 119*(2), 169–185.

Resnick, L., Bill, V., & Fellows of the Institute for Learning. (2000). *Clear expectations: Putting standards to work in the classroom* [CD-ROM]. Pittsburgh, PA: Institute for Learning, Learning Research and Development Center, University of Pittsburgh.

Resnick, L., & Hall, M. W. (1998). Learning organizations for sustainable education reform. *Daedalus, 127*(4), 89–118.

Resnick, L., Hall, M. W., & Fellows of the Institute for Learning. (2001). *Principles of learning: Study tools for educators* [CD-ROM]. Pittsburgh, PA: Institute for Learning, Learning Research and Development Center, University of Pittsburgh.

Resnick, L., & Nelson-LeGall, S. (1996). Socializing intelligence. In L. Smith, J. Dockrell, & P. Tomlinson (Eds.), *Piaget, Vygotsky and beyond* (pp. 145–158). London: Routledge.

Resnick, L. B., Säljö, R., Pontecorvo, C., & Burge, B. (Eds.). (1997). *Discourse, tools, and reasoning: Essays on situated cognition* (Vol. 160). New York: Springer (in cooperation with NATO Scientific Affairs Division).

Resnick, L., & Wirt, J. G. (Eds.). (1996). *Linking school and work: Roles for standards and assessment.* San Francisco: Jossey-Bass.

Rogoff, B. (1990). *Apprenticeship in thinking: Children's guided participation in culture.* New York: Oxford University Press.

Schofield, J. W., & Davidson, A. L. (2002). *Bringing the Internet to school: Lessons from an urban district.* San Francisco: Jossey-Bass.

Schön, D. A. (1987). *Educating the reflective practitioner: Toward a new design for teaching and learning in the professions.* San Francisco: Jossey-Bass.

Stein, M. K., & D'Amico, L. (2002). Inquiry at the crossroads of policy and learning: A study of a district-wide literacy initiative. *Teachers College Journal, 104*, 1313–1344.

Stein, M. K., Smith, M. S., Henningsen, M., & Silver, E. A. (2000). *Implementing standards-based mathematics instruction: A casebook for professional development.* New York: Teachers College Press.

Sternberg, R. J. (1977). *Intelligence, information processing, and analogical reasoning: The componential analysis of human abilities.* Hillsdale, NJ: Lawrence Erlbaum Associates.

Sternberg, R. J. (1985). *Beyond IQ: A triarchic theory of human intelligence.* Cambridge, England: Cambridge University Press.

Tharp, R. G., & Gallimore, R. (1988). *Rousing minds to life: Teaching, learning, and schooling in social context.* Cambridge, England: Cambridge University Press.

Thorkildsen, T. A., & Nicholls, J. G. (1998). Fifth graders' achievement orientations and beliefs: Individual and classroom differences. *Journal of Educational Psychology, 90,* 179–201.

Thorndike, E. L. (1906). *The principles of teaching: Based on psychology.* New York: A. G. Seiler.

Thorndike, E. L. (1922). *The psychology of arithmetic.* New York: The Macmillan Company.

Thorndike, E. L., and the staff of the Division of Psychology of the Institute of Educational Research of Teachers College, Columbia University. (1932). *The fundamentals of learning.* New York: Teachers College, Columbia University.

Vygotsky, L. S. (1978). *Mind in society: The development of higher psychological processes.* Cambridge, MA: Harvard University Press.

Wells, G., & Claxton, G. (2002). *Learning for life in the 21st century: Sociocultural perspectives on the future of education.* London: Blackwell.

Wenger, E. (1998). *Communities of practice: Learning, meaning, and identity.* Cambridge, England: Cambridge University Press.

Wertsch, J. V. (1985). *Vygotsky and the social formation of mind.* Cambridge, MA: Harvard University Press.

5

Modeling the Perceptual Component of Conceptual Learning—A Coordination Perspective

William J. Clancey
*Institute for Human and Machine Cognition
and NASA-Ames Research Center*

Visual forms are not discursive. They do not present their constituents succes-sively, but simultaneously, so the relations determining a visual structure are grasped in one act of vision. Their complexity, consequently, is not limited, as the complexity of discourse is limited, by what the mind can retain from the beginning of an apperceptive act to the end of it. Of course such a restriction on discourse sets bounds to the complexity of speakable ideas. An idea that contains too many minute yet closely related parts, too many relations within relations, cannot be "projected" into discursive form; it is too subtle for speech. A language-bound theory of mind, therefore, rules it out of the domain of understanding and the sphere of knowledge.

—Susanne Langer (1942/1958, p. 86)

Although a picture may be worth a thousand words, modeling diagrams as propositions and modeling visual processing as search through a database of verbal descriptions obscures what is problematic for the learner. Cognitive modeling of language learning and geometry has obscured the learner's problem of knowing where to look—what spaces, markings, and orienta-tions constitute the objects of interest? Today, educational researchers are launching into widespread use of multimedia instructional technology without an adequate theory to relate perceptual processes to conceptual learning. Does this matter? In this article, I review the symbolic approach to modeling perceptual processing and show its limitations for explaining difficulties children encounter in interpreting a graphic display. I present an alternative analysis by which perceptual categorization is coupled to behavior sequences where gesturing and emotional changes are essential for resolving impasses and breaking out of loops. I conclude by asking what kind of cognitive theory researchers need to exploit communication technology. Is it correct to assume that pedagogy must be grounded in an accurate psychological model of knowledge, memory, and learning?

THE ZBIE MODEL OF LANGUAGE LEARNING

In a pioneering computer model, Siklóssy (1972) developed a model of language learning that Vera and Simon (1993) believed refuted the claim that knowledge is not stored as descriptions in the human brain.

> Clancey [1993] says, "Regularities develop [in behavior] but without requiring us to represent them as rules or graphic networks or pictures. The obvious example is of a child learning to speak before being taught an abstract grammar." (p. 103)

> Now the best example we know of a theory of how a child learns to speak is the program, ZBIE, written by Siklóssy (1972) which does just that. It learns language by seeing sentences in juxtaposition with the scenes they denote, and gradually acquires both vocabulary and grammar, together with the ability to produce sentences never before experienced, when presented with new scenes. The grammar (stored in the simulated child's memory) is not in the form of rules that the child is aware of and can state; it is in the form of active procedures that are gradually built up through experience as an integral part of a changing program—all done with a purely symbolic representation. An empirical demonstration of a phenomenon provides a convincing refutation to a "proof" of impossibility. Can any existing SA [Situated Action] theory perform this learning task? (p. 128)

I look at ZBIE and see whether it fits Vera and Simon's (1993) claims. To begin, Siklóssy tells us that the inspiration of ZBIE's design is I. A. Richards et al. (1961) language-through-pictures series:

> Pictures are associated with sentences in an NL [natural language] to be learned. The pictures are to act as a general representation that has uniform meaning for all human beings (*English through pictures*, Book I is prefaced in 41 languages). The student is supposed to use the pictures as clues to the meanings of the sentences and, by successive comparisons of the sentences, to infer the vocabulary and grammar of the NL studied.

> The student's own mother tongue is bypassed, thereby avoiding problems of translation from one language into another; instead the student learns to translate situations directly from "reality" into a new NL. (p. 289)

Siklóssy (1972) wrote that the idea of language-through-pictures is to associate meanings with pictures, rather than descriptions in another language. In this way, "the student's own mother tongue is bypassed" (Siklóssy, 1972, p. 289). Instead of translating between languages, "the student learns to translate situations directly from 'reality' into a new NL" (Siklóssy, 1972, p. 289).

This theory has some merit, although the learning process is not "translation." If there were sufficient context, such as in a cartoon strip relying on a common cultural background, a student could to some extent understand the meaning of the pictures and relate this to the words of the NL. Indeed, language learning must involve some aspect of coordinating nonlinguistic conceptualizations (images, gestures, interpersonal relationships, etc.) with linguistic statements.

Amazingly, Siklóssy (1972) noted parenthetically that language-through-pictures learning does not work in his experience or that of other people he knows:

> As an aside, the author tried to learn Hebrew, absolutely unknown to him beforehand, from *Hebrew Through Pictures*. He had the advantage of having previously read several other known languages; nevertheless he had great difficulty in determining the meanings of the pictures or the clues to be derived from them, and finally abandoned the endeavor. Several other persons reported identical difficulties. (p. 289–290)

If the pictures are insufficient, how could a computer implementation of this approach work? ZBIE's input consists of descriptions of the pictures, so the process is indeed translation and no visual perception is required. Siklóssy (1972) glossed the difference from the original problem:

> The philosophies between ZBIE and I.A. Richards' booklets are similar. ZBIE uses a functional language (abbreviated FL) to represent situations; FL has the same function in ZBIE as the pictures have in Richards. By successive comparisons of situations, as represented in FL and as expressed in an NL, respectively, ZBIE tries to express other situations represented in FL and, failing that, to use its previous knowledge to learn how to express the other situations. The learning sequence presented to ZBIE is taken from Russian Through Pictures with slight modifications. (p. 290)

Table 5.1 illustrates how ZBIE represents a situation in FL, corresponding to the NL expression the person is supposed to be comprehending.

TABLE 5.1

Foreign Language (FL) Representation for Corresponding Natural Language (NL) Statement Describing a Picture

Language	Expression
FL	(be (on hat table))
NL	The hat is on the table

Siklóssy (1972) wrote that "FL has the same function in ZBIE as the pictures have in Richards" (p. 290). That is, the linguistic statement "(be [on hat table])" serves the same function of providing a reality to be related to words as a picture in Richards' booklets.

Here Siklóssy (1972), like Vera and Simon, made no distinction between a description of a picture and the picture itself: "It [ZBIE] learns language by seeing sentences in juxtaposition with the scenes they denote, and gradually acquires both vocabulary and grammar, together with the ability to produce sentences never before experienced, when presented with new scenes" (Vera & Simon, 1993, p. 128).

However, ZBIE does not see scenes at all! ZBIE relates linguistic statements in FL to linguistic statements in NL. I have thus related an assumption in Siklóssy's (1972) chapter that FL statements serve the same function as pictures to a retelling in Vera and Simon's (1993) article that ZBIE sees pictures themselves.

The distinction is crucial. The ZBIE model of language learning, which Vera and Simon (1993) called "the best example we know of a theory of how a child learns to speak," operates by mapping statements to one another. For this to be a model of language learning, as Vera and Simon claimed, it is first necessary to learn (or have inborn) the FL and to have a way of mapping perceptual categorizations to the words of FL.

Vera and Simon (1993) emphasized that ZBIE's manipulation of translation patterns corresponds to subconscious processes in a human being. "The grammar (stored in the simulated child's memory) is not in the form of rules that the child is aware of and can state; it is in the form of active procedures that are gradually built up through experience as an integral part of a changing program—all done with a purely symbolic representation" (p. 128).

Although there is no distinction in the model between FL and NL statements and translation rules—all are statements—the interpretation of the model, according to Vera and Simon (1993), is that the translation rules are not accessible to the person.

Although the idea of designing programs so they can "introspect" to read internal models and grammars has been the dominant approach for machine learning and expert systems design, Vera and Simon (1993) were correct that a scientist need not design a program in this way:

> This example also helps clarify a source of Clancey's confusion about conflation. He appears to be under the impression that any "rule" that appears in the computer memory of a simulation program (i.e., a production in the Category 4a symbol structures) must be accessible to the simulated person, and verbalizable as a Category 3 structure. Of course, this is false. (p. 128)

Granting Vera and Simon's (1993) point, the fact remains that there is nothing in Siklóssy's (1972) theory of memory, perception, learning, or reasoning that distinguishes ZBIE's translation patterns from the FL and NL input: All three are statements in a language and all are manipulable by the program to produce new statements. That is, just as ZBIE can generate new NL statements and store them in memory, it can generate new translation patterns and store them in memory. Hence, the theory of comprehension (understanding FL or NL statements) is purely a process of mapping between and assembling statements. Nothing in the nature of the statements, their storage in memory, or how they are used prevents their accessibility.

Setting aside the issue that plagues all exclusively descriptive (symbolic) theories of cognition—how are the initial translation patterns learned— one must make sense of Siklóssy's (1972) experience in attempting to learn Hebrew from Richards' (1961) booklet. How can relating pictures to NL (which Siklóssy abandoned as too difficult for a person to do) be equivalent to relating FL to NL (which Vera and Simon [1993] claimed is the best example of how a child learns to speak)? Siklóssy's experience suggests that the process of language learning in humans is surely not what ZBIE is doing. Rather, ZBIE succeeds at its task because it is mapping between descriptions. Siklóssy failed at learning Hebrew from pictures precisely because he was operating on pictures, not descriptions of what the pictures represent.

Indeed, to understand the relation of ZBIE to learning language through pictures, one must analyze the difference between Siklóssy's (1972) and ZBIE's tasks in language learning more carefully.[1] Siklóssy's task in using Richards' (1961) booklet involves attempting to determine what the pictures mean:

[PICTURE] ↔ interpretation of picture ↔ NL string

---

[1]Ironically, having inaccurately described ZBIE, Vera and Simon (1993) failed to see how my conclusions depend on careful analysis of existing computer programs. Instead, Vera and Simon (1993) said "These are examples of another mode of fallacious argument in which Clancey indulges. In this case, his arguments are simply based on misconception about the actual construction and operation of symbolic systems" (pp. 128–129).

ZBIE's task involves mapping three linguistic expressions to each other in a syntactic parsing process:

FL string ↔ formal translation rule ↔ NL string

Siklóssy's (1972) difficulty arises because the meaning of the picture is open to many descriptions. ZBIE's ease derives from being given a description to work with, "(be [on hat table])." Siklóssy needed to create a suitable description by finding a way of viewing and conceiving of the picture—which are not exclusively linguistic processes. ZBIE is given the suitable description, indeed, already in the vocabulary to be learned!

Siklóssy (1972) acknowledged these limitations in his model. Furthermore, Siklóssy (1972) pointed out that the FL representations (as well as the pictures in Richards' books) capture "an Indo-European's 'vision of the world' " (p. 322) and as such are not a neutral, universal input by which a student who speaks any language at all could understand the target language.

However, according to the symbolic view, the cultural variation of interpretation is merely a matter of different background knowledge, which is to say the initial patterns in ZBIE affect what the program can do. One is back to the same dispute: The symbolic view says that background knowledge consists of more descriptions. An alternate view is that the background knowledge consists of ways of seeing, speaking, and conceptually coordinating activity—not just descriptions of these (Clancey, 1997a, 1999).

Is it possible to step outside of this argument? How can it be shown that human comprehension of text or pictures depends on a conceptualization that itself cannot be reduced to descriptions? Rather than starting with descriptions of arrangements—forms that a teacher claims are significant—I examine how students create their own significant forms. I study the process by which people perceptually and physically segment space to create forms that they claim are meaningful. Fundamentally, I examine how this process of "viewing as" and interpreting is inseparable in human experience, so seeing something meaningful and conceiving what it means occurs together and is only subsequently followed by a coherent linguistic statement by which the meaning is represented.

In the following example, I turn around Vera and Simon's (1993) challenge: Can any existing computer program do what these children accomplish?

HUMAN LEARNING: A GREEN GLOBS EXPERIMENT

In this example, two students are working on an exercise intended to teach them about the properties of linear equations. The students (Pam [P] and Susanna [S]) are following and completing a worksheet that directs their use of a graphing program (called *Green Globs*[2]). Along the way, the students get confused about what a straight line is and miss the intended point of the lesson.

{Asked to predict how the line for Y = 5X + 1 will appear, P and S first write "that the equation is going to get thicker." However, after seeing the screen (Fig. 5.1), they modify the answer—"not" is inserted above and before "going," and "thicker" is smudged out above "straight"}

What do you think will happen if you type in Y = 5X + 1?
That the equation is not going to get ~~thicker~~ straight.

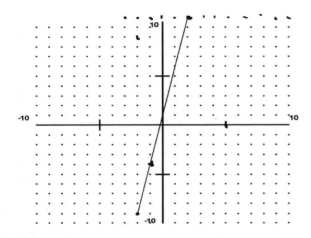

FIG. 5.1. Green Globs graph of Y = 5X + 1.

Sketch your prediction on this empty graph and then try it on the computer. What happened? The line is not really straight.

211	P	Did it get thicker? Yes. Didn't it? No, wait! Then it didn't get ... **It's getting bigger.**	Both are gesturing on the screen. P might be saying that it didn't get straight or that it got "bigger" and not "thicker" as she predicted.

[2]The Green Globs program and the experiment described here are the work of Susan Magidson, Judit Moskovich, and Alan Schonfeld. The term *green globs* refers to the dots connected when a line is drawn (Dugdale & Kibbey, 1982). This educational game was designed to relate algebraic equations to their graphs. In the original configuration, students were given a graph with 13 randomly placed points (green globs) and asked to enter an equation that would pass through as many points as possible. A previous analysis (Clancey, 1993b) examined the first part of the Pam and Susanna interaction.

212	S	I know. **It's getting bigger.** But how do we get that?	Agreement. Apparently now believes that prediction is wrong, correct answer is "bigger," but doesn't know how to justify this observation post hoc.
213	P	I don't know. Wait. Wait, wait, wait. (laugh) "Sketch … " What's sketch? "Sketch your prediction (S: Put it here …) on this empty graph and then try it on the computer." But what? "What happens?"	
214			S laughs
215	S	Reads "Sketch your prediction on this empty graph and then try it on the computer."	
216		(A brief exchange, inaudible. Laughter.)	
217	P	Not that, we can't do that. I don't know.	P rifles through sheets; S takes them.
218	S	Let's do it this way.	S possibly suggests filling in response after seeing the results.
219	P	We can't!	Possible reference to crossing out earlier answer. At lines 469 and 471 she says that they cheated.
309	S	It's just (inaudible) **It's not (P: it is …) a straight.** **(P: It is) See, it's not.**	S aligns worksheet plot shown above with ruler. Now is possibly saying "a straight"; before was clearly saying "as straight."
310	P	It *is!*	Oddly, perhaps because reference is to the drawn diagram and not the computer screen, P says line is straight for the first time.
311	S	Look. It's not a straight!	
312	P	It *is!*	(P takes the paper from S.)
313	S	See, it's over here. It's between this point and the other one.	S points to screen with pen. Apparently emphasizing that it is not on the Y axis?
314	P	It is. Wait. It *is.*	

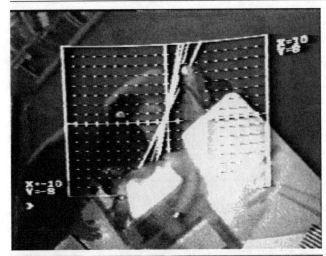

FIG. 5.2.
S moves finger up the line $Y = 5X + 1$ and says "That's why this ...."

FIG. 5.3.
S continues gesture by indicating at top of screen how $Y = 5X + 1$ is inside two others with her thumb moving across "... not inside ... that—."

315	S	It's not as straight. **That's why this ... not inside ... that—**	S gestures as shown in Figs. 5.2 and 5.3.
316	P	Susanna, it's *straight*!	Very loud and certain.
317	S	Oh, but it ... it'd have to be ... it'd have ... oh ... well, it's not	Broken speech, difficulty articulating what she is seeing. Does not fit idea of vagueness as an uncertain choice between defined alternatives.
318	P	It is.	
319	S	It's not.	
320	P	It *is*. How can it—	

321	S	Okay, okay, all right.	Clearly resigns. P later refers back to this agreement?
322	T	Okay, it's straight.	Pleasant, somewhat humorous lilt. She's overhearing from the side.
323	S	(laughs) Okay, what happened?	Goes back and changes p. 5 prediction to add "not" and "straight" (difficult to reconcile with teacher's remark)
324	P	What happened? We got a (3, 9).	
325	S	It is … wrong. **The equation is going to get** thicker.	S says their prediction was wrong.
326	P	I don't know. **The equation is going to get straighter.**	Unsure tone. Insists on straighter.
327	S	No, the equation is going to get … **it's not going to get** straight.	Revised prediction. Insists not straight.
328	P	It's not?	
329	S	No.	
330	P	**The equation is** … (S: inaudible) **The equation is not** …	
331	S	**The equation is** going—	Chooses positive wording, disagreeing with P again.
332	P	**Is not going to get—**	P follows along with negative phrasing.
333	S	**Is not going to get** straight.	
334	P	That one. How could it … ? (inaudible)	
335	S	It's not a straight.	Possibly says "as straight."
336	P	It's straight!	
337	S	Okay, okay. Put it's straight. (Inaudible.)	S gives in.
338	P	(Inaudible.)	
339	S	**Is this line straight?**	(spoken to teacher)

340	P	It *is!*	Note her willingness to answer so certainly, before hearing the teacher's response.
341	S	It's not.	
342	T	**What do you mean by straight? Do you mean, like, as in this is straight,** [gestures vertically on paper] **and that's not?** [gestures at 45 degree angle on paper]	Contrast T's presentation of alternatives with P and S's argument.
343	S	Yeah.	
344	T	So then, **it's getting close**, but it's not quite, is that what you're saying?	T gestures to the near the Y axis; uses the term "close"; she overheard S say this?
345	S	Mm hm. (turns to P) See? **So can we put here** [T & S laugh] **the line is not, is not really straight?**	
346	T	Mm hm. (long pause) I came in to tell you that you've been working for just about an hour. So if you've had enough and you'd like to stop, you can stop. If you'd like to work a little longer, you can work a little longer.	Acknowledges, meaning "you can write that." T exits after a discussion about continuing.
353	P	Yeah. **I think you said straight.**	P gestures with pen upwards, vertically on the page. Suggesting that S has contradicted her agreement (#337).
354	S	It's not straight, you know why? **Because it has to be like this with the points.**	S shows willingness to explain, more confident, apparently reflecting sense that T has confirmed her point of view.
355	P	I thought you said *que* straight; it wasn't a straight line.	P gestures to vertical.
356	S	**It is a straight line when you use a ruler**, but it's not when you do like this	S gestures with pen making points on paper; suggesting that freehand lines are crooked? Referring back to discussion with Teacher? Possibly "straight" means vertical (#55); "straight line" means not crooked (#38).
357	P	Real funny.	Tone is that S is indeed strange & humorous in her point of view.

What do you think will happen if you type in **Y = 1X +1**? **The line is going to get straighter.**
Sketch your prediction on this empty graph and then try it on the computer.

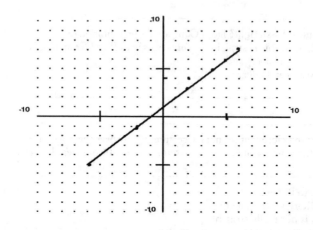

FIG. 5.4.   Green Globs graph of Y = 1X + 1.

364	P	What do you think? You have to answer it first.	Again P insists on "not cheating."
365	S	Um … **the line's gonna get straighter.**	
366	P	So write it.	Gestures to worksheet. Plays with pen in hair. Clearly not engaged.
367	S	Do another one with the same equation. Don't get mad!	Entering points on graph of Y = 1X + 1 on paper (above).
368	P	I'm not mad. Who said I was mad? There's not going to be (inaudible) right here.	
369	S	Try this one. **See, it's getting straighter.**	S notices that the line intersects grid cleanly?
370	P	No.	
371	S	You want to bet?	
372	P	**How weird, the lines get straighter … dots.**	P agrees now, apparently sees the line differently. Dots refers to grid.
408	S	It has to be 3 … 3 … here. They have to be here. No, wait. Here. My fault. 5. **The line's getting straighter; I told you.**	

409	P	Yeah ... What do you mean, "straighter"? Like straight like the straight line right here?	First serious attempt to negotiate a definition. Possibly echoing the teacher's question? P gestures along vertical axis, referring back to the teacher's interpretation.
411	P	It's straight, but if you put it like this ... [turns the paper to 45 degrees]	Again, apparently repeats teacher's contrast; trying to show that being straight is not relative to the Y-axis, but a property of the line as an object?
412	S	Ha! (laughs)	
413	P	Isn't this vertical?	Suggests that the word for being aligned with the Y-axis is "vertical," perhaps to contrast with P's use of the term "straight."
414	S	Forget it. Forget it.	Forced to decide, S opts out.
415	P	What's horizontal? Like this [draws horizontal line on paper] or like that? [draws a vertical line on paper]	P pursues the point. Offers a clearer contrast about meaning of "vertical."
416	S	Horizontal's like this ... [draws a horizontal line]	
417	P	Y like this? [draws a vertical line]	
418	S	Alright. Let's just forget about it. **But it is straight.**	S holds her forehead, expressing frustration. Apparently refuses to acknowledge that Y-axis is called vertical and not straight. Possibly referring back to Y = 1X + 1 is straight.
419	P	If you say so.	Tone of resignation.
420	P	Wait ... 1 ...	Clears the screen
421	P	No! Yes. Huh.	
422	S	–1 ...	
423	P	Yes. Don't do any more!	
424	S	See! **See, it's getting straighter.**	
425	P	**Okay. Now, enough, enough.**	P gestures "stop" with her hand and puts her hand on her forehead
426	S	Wait, let me put it here.	Graphing Y = 1 X + 1 on computer

427	P	All of them thing?	Referring to the dots of the grid.
428	S	(Inaudible.) What ... See? **It is a straight.**	Term "a straight" would suggest a property of the object, as in "a perpendicular"; S is noticing that there aren't any jagged segments?
429	P	**Oh, yeah, it is! I get it now. I understand what you're saying. I understand.**	Shifts point of view. Graph shows Y = X + 1, with the line clearly intersecting the grid (contrast with Y = 5X + 1 with grid points *near* the line).
430	S	Okay.	
431	P	**The dots, huh? The little dots, no?**	This is her second reference to the dots. Little dots refers to the grid?
432	S	Mm hm.	
433	P	Now I understand.	Apparently a true agreement.
434	S	Good.	

Were you right? Explain. **Yes, because the dots got on a straight line.**
{*"Line" was replaced by "dots," which is written over several times.*}

435	P	I'm sorry. "Were you right?" **Yes.** "Explain."	P touches S.
436	S	**Yes, because the line** got straight.	S focuses on a line, possible reference to pixels.
437	P	[writing] **Yes, because the line** ...	
438	S	**got**	
439	P	**got** what?	Subsequent remarks suggest she wants to describe the dots, not the line.
440	S	**Straight!**	Humorous. After all this ...
441	P	The dots ... were on ... the straight line.	Speaks very slowly and deliberately. Says "the straight line" suggesting that the line was always straight? Salient feature is that the dots are on the line. Refers to grid?

442	S	Yeah. Erase that.	S agrees to mention "dots."
443	P	The line ... The line ... The dots ...	
444	S	Yes, because **the dots ...**	S uses the word "dots" for the first time.
445	P	The line ... The dots, huh?	Acknowledges agreement that they are describing the dots.
446	S	No, **the line**! (laughs)	But S immediately rejects the focus on dots ...
447	P	The dots were ...	
448	S	Because I put here, "the line is going to get straight."	...because her prediction was about the line $Y = 1X + 1$, not the dots.
449	P	The dots were on a straight ... are on a straight line	
450	S	Okay, okay. **The dots are in a straight line.**	S emphasizes "are" and "in"
451	P	Were on a straight line. "Got?" Yes.	**P emphasizes "were" and "on" while writing.**
452	S	Yeah.	
453	P	The ... Hmmm! **The dots got on a straight line.** **The dots got on a straight line.** I understand it.	P reflects on the description and says that it makes sense.
454	S	(reading) **"Because the dots got on a straight line."** Isn't that ... is that a sentence?	But S isn't sure she can parse it.
455	P	Yes. I guess.	
456	S	*Mira, tue eso* (mumbles).	*(Look, you are ...*
457	P	*Callate.*	*(Shut up.)*
458	S	That's why Sofia ... saw you (mumbles then laughs).	

Try some numbers greater than 5.
What do you think will happen as your numbers get larger?

462	S	Okay, 6 … let's put 6.	S suggests Y = 6X + 1.
463	P	No, we don't have to write anything. (laugh) (reading) "What do you think will happen as your numbers get larger?" **The … um … The … [snaps fingers] …(S: the line) … the dots are not going to be on that straight line.**	Possible reference to the 45 degree line they just drew. Almost a humorous delay in her pauses, as if trying to be funny … S interjects with line focus again; P contradicts immediately.
464	S	Okay, put that.	

Write down your prediction.
The line is not going to be straight.

Now try it on the computer. Were you right? Explain.
Yes, because the line was not straight.

470	S	Let's try it on the computer. "Were you right?" Yes.	
471	P	Yes. We cheated.	They simply wrote "not straight," nothing about the dots here.

Now let's try some small positive numbers (numbers between 0 and 1).
What do you suppose these lines will look like?

The lines will look straight.

Let's try it. Clear the screen and type in these equations, one at a time:
    $Y = 1/2X + 1$
    $Y = 1/3X + 1$
    $Y = 1/4X + 1$
What do you notice? **That the lines are not straight.**
What stays the same?

515	P	[reading with S] "What stays the same?" (they laugh) I don't understand.	
516	S	**What stays the same? The dots? No.**	S means that the grid is unchanged?
517	P	That they … Nope.	

| 518 | S | "What stays the same?" The line .... (P: no.) "Let's skip that one" | |

What changes? **The lines**

519	P	"What changes?" (both laugh) Ah, look, **these little lines** are getting ... *asi mas* wide. (S: What?) Look, that thing are getting *mas*—	P gestures to the jagged segments with her pen. Trying to find another interpretation
520	S	**Wider? Thicker? Bigger?**	S brings back the earlier terms used to describe the jagged lines on the computer.
521	P	Uh huh.	
522	S	No, I don't think that's the correct answer.	S indicates that these descriptions aren't likely to be what the teacher intended.
523	P	(whispers) Okay now?	
524	S	I don't really know. I'm confused. Just— "what stays the same?"	Worksheet question is driving their interaction.

What do you think will happen if you type in **Y = 1/5X + 1**?
Sketch your prediction on this empty graph and then try it on the computer.
We think that the line is going to get closer to be straight.

Let's try some numbers smaller than 1/5. What do you think will happen as your numbers get smaller? Write down your prediction.
We think that the line is going to be straight.
Now try it on the computer. Where you right? Explain.
Yes, the lines didn't get any closer to be straight.

532	S	The lines—	S types Y = 1/5X + 1 again
533	P	**I told you that they're getting bigger. The lines will get closer to the straight line.**	P refers back to claim that they the "little lines" are getting bigger. But she describes lines as getting closer to the X-axis. The progression of equations suggests focusing on what's different rather than the common Y intercept.
534	S	To the what?	S says "the."
535	P	**To a straight line.**	P says "a."

536	S	Yeah.	They agree from here to the end because P drops her observation about the little lines getting wider.
537	P	Write it down.	
538	S	It doesn't (inaudible)	
539	P	"What do you think will happen"—	
540	S	Okay. I think—or we think. We think. We think that the line is going to, is going to get, we think the line is going to get close to being—	S changes "I" to "we" in worksheet. Manifests her sense that they agree. Says "close" again.
541	P	to be a ...	emphasizes "be"
542	S	—to be a straight line	possibly no "a"
543	P	We think that that is going ...?	
544	S	We think that we, that the, that that is ... we think that that that is going ... (laughter) **I have no idea what I'm thinking.** (Laughs.)	S struggles with wording. Indicates that she doesn't understand the lesson.
545	P	(Laughs.) Oh, God.	P looks up to the ceiling
546	S	Do you want to go now? It's four fifteen.	
563	P	Call her.	
564	S	Let's get out of here. Do you know where the garbage can is?	

ANALYSIS OF THE GREEN GLOBS INTERACTION

What is happening here? First, the students were never told what features to look for in the graphed lines but simply to compare them. The text opens by using the word *straight* twice: "these equations are straight lines ... will produce a straight line." So what is a nonstraight line? If told that straightness is a property of some equations, perhaps the students can discover equations producing lines that aren't straight?

P and S's interaction can be studied from many perspectives. Some of the questions to consider are the following:

- What do they experience that's difficult to describe?

- What is their practice of description? Why and how are new terms introduced, shared, and written?
- What are the differences between the students in adopting different views, seeking and giving explanations, promoting collaborative interaction, introducing new terms, adhering to the worksheet, gesturing, and so forth.
- How do the students assess their own understanding?
- How do different modalities (nomenclature, diagrams, instructions, computer graphics, gestures) relate in the activity to foster understanding?
- Are the dynamics of their interaction confirming each other's perceptions or leading to opposition? Why, if one student "gets it," do they end up with different interpretations?
- What are the interactions between the different aspects of activity (Leont'ev, 1979)?: social interactional ("what I'm part of"), representational cognitive ("what I'm inferring and planning"), or operational behavioral ("what I'm doing here and now").
- How are they generating equations to graph? Are they testing hypotheses?
- How does the worksheet's design direct, help, or inhibit their understanding?

A conventional analysis might focus on the logical argumentation, evident for example in lines 411 through 418 in which P confronts S with two defined alternatives. However, my interest here is in *conceptual transformations*, aspects of nondescriptive understanding in images, gestures, and emotion, which are dialectically developing with the spoken and written descriptions. (By dialectic, I mean that conceiving—a neurological process—and describing causally influence each other.) I am especially interested in development of sequences (e.g., as full sentences are written in the worksheet [lines 325–333]), repetition in behavior sequences ("it is"—"it is not straight"), and means by which the students resolve impasses (e.g., dismissing, laughing, shifting levels).

I begin with a summary of the interaction and then consider in turn aspects of perception, reference, description, collaboration, and breakdown. I conclude the analysis by considering how describing relates to conceptual coordination.

Summary of Interpretations

P and S give many explanations for why the lines are straight or not. Besides S's belief that a vertical line is straight, both P and S notice that lines between 45 and 90 degrees are jagged, an effect caused by coarseness of the screen display (number of pixels per inch). Early on, S also notices that their hand-drawn lines are not straight. At the very end, P notices that the equation $Y = 1X + 1$ intersects the dots of the grid (which evidently S agrees is straight because the jagged segments disappear).

The following aspects of the interaction are of special interest:

- P's understanding shifts between jagged segments and alignment to the grid. S appears to shift between three interpretations, holding most firmly to verticality.
- S appears to use the word *straight* in two ways at the same time, corresponding to "being in a line" (definition of straight line) and "being vertical" (a kind of straight line; line 418).
- S's insistence on "the dots" near the end apparently prompts P to look again; she sees "the little dots" as being relevant for first time (lines 427–431).
- P introduces the terms "thicker" (line 133[3]), "width" (line 171), "bigger" (line 195), "dots" (line 372), "vertical" (line 413), "horizontal" (line 415), "little lines" (line 519). S does not introduce new terms (indeed, she cannot remember the word *vertical*).
- S's descriptions are qualifications on "straight"—"always straight" (line 116), "stay straight" (line 142), "straighter" (line 147), "not very straight" (line 194), "not as straight" (line 195), "not a straight" (line 309), "going to get straighter" (line 326), "getting straighter" (line 369), and "got straight" (line 436). S's qualifications are relative to an ideal reference (being in a line or the vertical) and consistently mention change in appearance.
- P's explains by naming a particular configuration ("straight like the straight line right here?"; line 409) and mimics the teacher (line 342) by drawing vertical and horizontal lines to illustrate her meanings (lines 417–418). She attempts to disambiguate S's meaning.
- S explains by classifying an instance as a member of a category ("it's not a line"; line 38), pointing to a visual property ("it has to be like this with the points"; line 354), and describing an action ("when you do like this"; line 356). She shows P what she means but doesn't confront her with choices.
- S is tuned to the requirements of the teacher and the worksheet (line 212), what is a plausible response (lines 325, 522), and the timing of the session (line 546). P appears more oriented to understanding S.

Perceptual Reorganization.   What symbols are given in this problem? In some sense, only pixels are given. If the input were obviously straight lines,

---

[3]Some quotations appear earlier than the transcript reproduced in this chapter. Line numbers are shown for reference to indicate relatively where they appeared in the interaction.

as intended by the teacher, P and S would only be "symbolic information processors." Rather, what they see, understand, and how they talk arise together, codetermining each other. My objective in what follows is to provide evidence for this claim and show how visual categorizing, referring, and describing develop together.

In Bamberger's (1991) terms, the question for the children is what figure should be seen as straight. The process is not simply classifying lines but constructing configurations into objects by which the word *straight* can be given an interpretation. These configurations are perceived at different times during the process of making sense of each other and the worksheet. They include a thick bundle of lines, jagged "little lines" (line 519), and little dots (the grid).

In itself, referring to "the little dots" is a figure-ground shift. The grid is now no longer just a background but perceived as objects to be described (the little dots get lined up)—there is shift between "in-ness" and "on-ness" when viewing the display as a configuration. In effect, the students agree that straightness has something to do with "being lined up," but it's unclear what gets lined up with what. Figure 5.5 summarizes some interpretations.

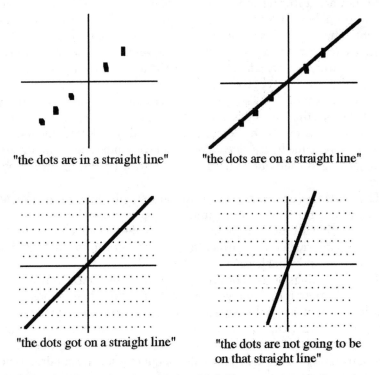

"the dots are in a straight line"   "the dots are on a straight line"

"the dots got on a straight line"   "the dots are not going to be
                                          on that straight line"

FIG. 5.5.   Graphic interpretations of what the children are seeing (the forms they are perceiving and relating) when they describe alignment (see transcript lines 441 and 453 and 448 and 450).

New interpretations are based on perceptual regrouping: In considering how the points of the equation are lined up, the dots of the grid are irrelevant. However, when one includes the dots of the grid, a previously straight line is no longer lined up. Thus, different ways of talking are grounded in different images. The meaning of straight depends on what objects are perceived and grouped in the scene and the relations of these objects to each other. Significantly, an "object" may be a space between two lines (Fig. 5.3).

In traditional schema theory, the meaning of new terms given by a teacher is defined in terms of old terms by generalization and specialization as well as by correspondence to a given, stable scene in the world. However, because the vast majority of symbolic models (such as ZBIE) do not engage in visual processing, researchers didn't acknowledge the perceptual reorganization that might be involved in learning new meanings.

The Construction of Reference

To carry this analysis further, I consider what the students are conceiving when they are gesturing and using indexicals like "it," "this," and "that." A classic example is shown in Figs. 5.3 and 5.4, when S says, "It's not as straight. That's why this … not inside … that—" (line 315).

In general, perception is occurring on several levels: where to look and what constitutes an object, and which is the topic of description (the reference of "this" or "it's"). Once directed to an area by a gesture, one still must know what level of detail is relevant. For example, P says "the little dots" (line 431) and "these little lines" (line 519) to refer to the grid and the jagged segments in contrast with the plotted dots and the plotted equations. Yet now, in seeing some figure, one is conceiving of a difference. This difference is not a thing in itself but a change or a contrast (Bateson, 1972; Roberts, 1986, 1993).

The students describe their conceptions by calling attention to a figure, some particular object or configuration of objects, which they describe by contrasting it with the surroundings in terms of temporal change, location, shape, and internal configuration. Indeed, these contrasts are multidimensional, as shown by Table 2.

Three meanings of straight line are described by contrasting a figure in terms of location, form, change over time, and internal relations (e.g., the little lines that make up the big line). Such descriptions, combined with gestures in a shared visual space, enable the children to coconstruct figures. These figures (ranging from a bundle of lines that is getting thicker to the dots of the grid) constitute a particular detail that for the children is new, a basis for reconceiving the meaning of straight. Put another way, conceptualization is visible in this interaction as the description of changes and contrasts the children perceive. Their describing and gesturing first acts to

TABLE 5.2
**Varieties of Difference or Contrast Described in Explaining
Conceptions of a Straight Line**

Variable	Meaning of "Straight"	Temporal Change	Internal Relation
Location	Vertical or aligned to the grid	"Straighter," "closer"	"On the straight line," "not inside that"
Form	Not bent	"Thicker," "wider"	"Little dots," "little lines"

separate figure from ground and secondarily to define straight in terms of the contrast they perceive.

Indeed, the difficulty of the interaction between P and S appears to lie in S's proclivity to describe contrasts and P's proclivity to describe figures. P must then work to understand what S perceives is changing (because S says "this," "that" is changing, getting closer, getting on, etc.). In general, S adopts P's contrast words ("thicker," "wider") but never introduces her own names for focus details.[4] The following exchange is typical:

170	S	The line gets …
171	P	**The length.** No. **The width.**
172	S	Gets …
173	P	… width
174	S	**Width gets thicker**
175	P	Yeah
176	P	The lines get thicker?

Indeed, every single reference to "it" or "this" in S's discourse refers to "the line," "the lines," or "the equation" (which refers to the graphical form on the screen). S resists or rejects every single attempt to enter a statement in the worksheet in which the subject is something else including the dots, little lines, or bundle. When P nevertheless enters such statements, S accepts them passively.

---

[4]By *focus detail,* I mean perceptual figures that are being incorporated in a description such as dots and lines and their perceived attributes; the term is used by Bartlett, (1932/1977) in characterizing storytelling when remembering.

Given that the worksheet is calling for the children to say that the slope or angle of the lines and the Y-intercept is changing, this resistance to adopt another focus detail is a fundamental problem for S. P is wandering around looking for another figure by shifting grain size and making a figure-ground shift; S is fixated on describing the lines as wholes. One might say that S's preferred contrast, that the lines are getting closer to the vertical, is "conceptually close" to the idea that the angles are changing. However, S's contrast is with respect to a fixed reference, and she is focusing on the ends of the lines. P and S are simply not looking at what is occurring in the spaces between the lines down near the origin. They need to see the space as a figure (which we call an *angle*); this perceptual reorganization never occurs.

To reiterate, understanding that all the lines on the screen are straight does not mean merely relating some concept description to "instances" that are on the screen. A descriptive model of perception views seeing and recognizing as this kind of feature matching and mapping (e.g., see Larkin & Simon, 1987). Roberts (1993, pp. 16–25) referred to this as "reference *qua member*" in which some figure is claimed to be an instance of a general thing (this is a straight line) or to have a property of a type (this line, like all lines, is straight). One can find examples of such descriptions in P and S's interaction such as when S says, "It's always straight" (line 117).

However, Roberts (1993, pp. 16–25) pointed out that the construction of reference occurs as "reference *qua particular*" in which a figure is described via a contrast as a thing. By this view, seeing and recognizing is a process of creating features and inherently involves visual reorganization (Clancey, 1997b). The concept of the general thing is then developed dialectically by the inclusion of this example. Describing within the process of learning is not just pointing, naming, and defining but separating something out from the background and describing the figure as a contrast. That is, the figure is not something that stands alone, but is only known as a difference over time, of form, or within a larger configuration.

As Bateson (1972) emphasized, the contrast and hence the visual concepts are not located in particular things. The reference is not to an object per se but to a difference: The lines are getting closer, wider, thicker. "The dots got on a straight line"; "the little lines are getting wider." A contrast is an experience occurring over time or within a process of looking. A visual contrast is within a particular area but is not a property of a particular thing in isolation. In saying that the lines are getting "closer," for example, S focuses on the difference in distance of the line (segments) from the vertical; in gesturing (Fig. 5.3), S shows us that she perceives this space as a figure for which the lines are now a ground.

A ground is also a visual conception. In line 316, S is attempting to describe how the figure she is currently seeing (referred to by "it") is different from another visual conception—how she sees the meaning of straight.

When the ability to put her experience in words fails—she plainly knows that a contrast exists—she falls back on denying the applicability of P's description. The conversation then becomes a shouting match.

Finally, referring back to Table 5.2, the dimensional analysis of the multiple interpretations of "straight line" suggests that S is able to hold to both "vertical" and "not bent" because they arise from different visual organizers—one conceiving difference in location and the other difference in form. S appears to smoothly move from seeing the hand-drawn lines as not straight (line 101) to seeing the thickness (jaggedness?) of the lines as not straight. However, she is shifting her point of view when she agrees with the teacher that the Y-axis is straight (line 342)—a matter of location and not form.

At the end, when they graph $Y = 1X + 1$, S is perhaps still seeing the line in terms of form—she had previously indicated that smaller numbers (with slope approaching $45°$) the line is getting straighter (line 147). Ironically, the salience of intersection with the grid leads P to see this line as straight but for a different reason, one based on location not form. Hence, P and S can agree on the description, a $45°$ line is straight, but are unable to agree on the definition because they are contrasting their experience on different dimensions.

Therefore, the inability to communicate stems from not articulating these different ways of organizing the visual field. S never acknowledges that she is viewing straight as a matter of form at one time and location at another time. This same difference is replicated in P and S's conception at a given time and exacerbated by S's tendency to merely agree when P says something she apparently doesn't understand (line 432).

The analysis of the relation of description and visual conception of contrast is fundamental for understanding the interaction of P and S. However, there are many subtle aspects of how these descriptions are created through the interaction of different modalities. In particular, the children are coordinating different actions (speaking, drawing) and coordinating their own interaction (filling in the worksheet, taking turns). In subsequent sections, I consider how the conceptualization I have just described occurs within larger, coordinating frameworks that serve to constrain and supply resources for what the children see and say.

Aspects of Representing

Broadly speaking, representing includes much more than describing or drawing. Besides names and phrases, P and S are creating other forms that are intended to represent their understanding of the worksheet's questions and what is happening on the display screen. Representing, as an activity, involves a number of different activities using different modalities:

- Spoken phrases ("the little dots").
- Drawing ("Y like this?"; line 417).
- Gesturing (Fig. 5.3)
- Calling attention to details ("Look! Which one is that?"; line 167) and looking again to verify a hypothesis (line 211).
- Following worksheet directives (line 203).
- Focusing a written response on some figure (lines 443–447).
- Commenting on a partner's representation ("No! The lines are getting bigger"; line 195).
- Abstracting perceptual patterns ("Ah, look, these little lines are getting ... *asi mas* wide"; line 519).

These activities are not all descriptive in origin and nature. As Bamberger and Schön (1991) emphasized, the students are engaged in a "conversation with materials." They are taking turns writing and interacting with the computer, they are choosing equations to display, and they are coordinating ways of understanding each other as they are following the worksheet's directives. As Dewey (1902/1981) emphasized, P is reinterpreting and looking for other features. She is attempting to reconcile her view that the lines are not straight (line 116) with the worksheet, the teacher (line 344), and S's disagreements. Probably she would not have come up with ideas about the little dots and little lines if S had agreed with her at the end.

The symbolic approach claims that all these actions are driven by subconscious descriptions. However, S's stumbling and repeated references to "this" and "that" as she points suggest that she has no words for what she is seeing, the figures and contrasts that are of interest to her. At a basic level, one sees that the work of representing is adapting and learning words that describe personal experience.

Collaboration

At the beginning, the teacher said "I'd like you both to work together, so I'd like you to take turns typing and take turns writing." Indeed, their sharing is remarkable. On the other hand, the obligation to fill in the worksheet prompts heated discussion and sometimes forced resignation. Of special interest is how they suggest words for the worksheet, which for the observer conveniently reveals their different focus of attention ("the dots," "the line"; Garrod & Anderson, 1987).

Although the worksheet is the product of two people collaborating, the students have a marked sense of independence. Beside the obvious banter—"it is" "it is not"—P and S have clearly indicated their identities on the worksheet by how they dot the letter "i." Furthermore, their activities are oriented in different ways. S assumes responsibility for satisfying the worksheet: She is the only one who asks questions of the teacher, she points out inconsistencies between what they observe and what they predicted, and she turns to the worksheet more often for direction ("Okay, what happened?"; line 323; "what stays the same?"; line 524). P worries a bit more about reaching a shared understanding: She deliberately seeks explanations for S's claims both by reinterpreting the display and presenting choices to S to interpret.

The high degree of interactively is most pronounced in their typing and exchanges when filling in words (lines 142–153, 169–186, and 437–449). An example of how P and S type an equation $(Y = -5/3\, X + 7)$ appears in the following transcript:

Line		Statement	Gestures
79	P		P types Y =
80	S		S types 5 / 3
81	P	Wait! It's negative.	brushes S away from keyboard; erases 5 / 3; types – 5
82	S		S types /; P reaches forward; S types 3; P reaches forward; S erases 3
83	S	X there.	gestures to X
84	P		P types 3 X; S gestures to +; P has both hands on keyboard; P types =; erases =; types + 6 . .; erases .; types 7; S gestures to return; P presses return.
85	S	Yeah.	

However, there are as many examples of discord. On several occasions, the children give up in their attempt to work together but allow the partner to proceed with her preferred action. S gives in by saying "Okay, okay" (lines 321, 337, 450). P gives in by telling S to write the statement she prefers: "Write it!" (lines 197, 366). Both children express exasperation at different times, looking up at the ceiling and holding their heads in their hands (lines 418–425).

Learning may be collective and based on communication and interaction. Yet nobody can learn for somebody else.[5] At a certain point, each child

---

[5]Thanks to Janni Nielsen for this observation.

expresses her individuality and present understanding by calling a halt to an exchange and moving on. Thus, the task of filling in the worksheet is satisfied, and the individual's sense of personal understanding is preserved—at the expense of not understanding the partner and not representing for the experimenter-teacher what each person understands.

Breakdown, Action, and Talk

Disagreements occur when different conceptualizations lead to different ways of describing. Impasses result not only because P and S can't agree what to call something (or the correct syntax) but because as I have discussed previously, they see different figures or conceive of the figures in different ways.

At different times, each child finds that she cannot continue the activity because she is unable to resolve this conflict. When these discussions are not focused around how to fill in the worksheet but are instead squarely about their concepts, a breakdown may be resolved by simply calling a halt to the activity. Perhaps the best example is when P is leading S through the definition of vertical and horizontal, which S halts by saying "Alright. Let's just forget about it" (line 418). At other times, a breakdown may be resolved by asking the partner to give her more time (P says, "Wait"; lines 142–143) or by marking an inability to understand (P says, "How weird"; line 372).

An impasse is a *discoordination*, a breakdown between how ways of seeing, conceiving, and talking are dynamically related. Experience of an impasse is often accompanied by an emotion or attitude that Bartlett (1932/1977) emphasized accompanies a new orientation. Because a person must be experiencing something, the emotion appears to substitute for the previous (ineffective) conceptualization. For example, in lines 309 through 320 the girls contradict each other six times, interposed with requests to look and explanations. S finally breaks out by simply saying "Okay, Okay, all right." The teacher breaks in at this moment with a humorous lilt, "Okay, it's straight," and then S laughs.

Here is a summary of how impasses are resolved in P and S's interaction:

- Try to control or end the offending event. In the face of S's insistence that the 45° line is getting straighter, P says, "Don't do any more!" (line 423) to get S to stop plotting points.
- Laugh or dismiss the behavior; "Real funny" (line 357).
- Ask for a justification; "I know … but how do we get that?" (line 212).
- Appeal to logic and authority by referring to the worksheet's directives, their previous responses, or the teacher; "I don't think that's the correct answer" (line 522).

- Request a clarification of the reference: P, "It's straight"; S, "Where?" (line 126).
- Suggest a rephrasing for clarification of the figure and contrast: S, "Width gets thicker"; P, "The lines get thicker?" (line 176).
- Force the partner to look again accompanied by gestures and descriptions of focus details; "Look. It's not straight!" (line 311). (See also the gestured explanations in lines 211, 313, 315, 342, 356, 409, 411–417, and 519.).
- Wait for later resolution and move on with a simple acknowledgment: S, "The little dots, no?"; P, "Mm hm" (line 431).
- Classify the activity as irrelevant: S says, "Forget it …. Let's just forget about it" (lines 414, 418).
- Move to a larger coordinating conceptualization of the relationship: S tells P not to get mad (line 367) and reminds P of an incident with a friend (line 458).

Impasses may lead to new conceptualizations for coordinating the activity. For example, after a point, it becomes apparent to P and S that their predictions of how lines will appear on the screen do not fit their perceptions of what is happening. Consequently, they must adjust their conceptualization of their activity: accept that some of their work is wrong or "cheat" by looking at the result on the computer first (or erase previous responses). Thus, the procedure for how to fill in the worksheet develops in the course of the activity. This is what I mean by a new coordination. The disagreements are not rooted in just the definition of straight but in differing conceptions about how the experimental session is to be carried out.

Coordinating Multiple Interpretations in Two Languages

To understand how concepts and words are related, one must consider the possibility that S is using a single English word (*straight*) for several concepts she associates with different Spanish words, her first language. The effort to coordinate a single word with multiple concepts and hence multiple ways of seeing may be the cause of her difficulties.[6]

In particular, S may be conceiving of straight in the everyday sense of *derecha* (*una linea derecha*), which is the opposite of crooked or oblique. This meaning incorporates the sense of standing up straight (i.e., vertically), straightening a picture that is askew (i.e., making it perpendicular to the floor), driving straight through the city (i.e., in the same direction), and so on. In this sense, the Y-axis, the nonjagged computer lines, and the lines drawn on paper with a ruler are straight because they are *derecha*.

---

[6] I am indebted to Sue Magidson and Judit Moskovitch for the initial analysis that appears in this section.

Spanish, unlike English, uses a different word for the mathematical sense of straight, *"recta"* (*una linea recta*). Repeatedly, S refers to "a straight" (lines 309, 311, 335, 410, 428), suggesting that she knows this meaning, too.[7] In this sense, all lines are straight (line 117), so the word *line* in "a straight line" is redundant.

Furthermore, *"recto"* in Spanish means both "straight" and "right" (as in *rectángulo*). In English, we use the Latin *rect-* prefix without realizing the double meaning (*rectilinear* means "straight-lined," but *rectangular* means "right-angled"). In this sense, one may say that the Y-axis is a paradigmatic *recto*, for it indicates the right angle in the graph (90°) and is a straight line.

So when S says at the very beginning, referring to the drawing on paper, "It's not a line" (line 38), she probably means it's not *una linea recta* because it's not *derecha*. When she says, "It's always straight" (line 117), referring to the lines graphed by the computer, she means that they (*linea recta*) are always *derecha*. In both cases, *derecha* is conceived as an inherent property of *una linea recta*. However, when P shows that the lines are getting thicker, S shifts to viewing *derecha* as a description of appearance, which may or may not apply to a given *linea recta*. Indeed, when first describing this appearance, she shifts from saying "the line" to "the *lista*," meaning "strip" (line 179), a figure on the screen. Significantly, she immediately afterwards refers to this figure as "the equation" (lines 207, 325–331), showing lack of distinction between the mathematical entity and what she sees on the screen. At this point, her understanding appears to be that some equations actually do have the property of being thicker than others.

It is difficult to tie S's interpretations into a neat bundle. The evidence suggests that S shifts between interpretations of straight as she conceives of different meanings corresponding to different Spanish words. She appears to know the meaning of *una linea recta* in Spanish, given her repeated use of the phrase "a straight." Her sense of redundancy in the English phrase "a straight line" may have brought the contrast between *derecha* and *recta* into the foreground: Some lines do not appear straight. Given the messiness of their initial drawing (Fig. 5.6) and P's subsequent claims about thickness, S conceives the lesson as characterizing which *recta* (equations) are not *derecha* and why.

Coordinating Acts of Redescription

I have listed multimodal aspects in the activity of representing, but I haven't considered how these are brought together. First, following Dewey (1896/1981), one would want to explore the hypothesis that conceptualiz-

---

[7]Listening to the videotape, one is faced with a perceptual problem. One can almost shift between hearing S say "not as straight" and "not a straight" at will. However, I found five occasions in which the phrase sounded more like "a straight" and no occasions in which "as straight" appeared more likely.

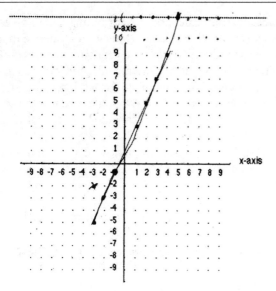

FIG. 5.6. Actual plot produced by P and S with teacher's help. Notice that freehand drawing of the line is not straight.

ing, experiencing, talking, and manipulating are occurring as one coordination. That is, these aren't independently occurring processes or variables but arise as an interactive product. Describing is not just saying or expressing something in words but one observable aspect of the process of coordinating activity. One can observe these recoordinations when the children recast previous descriptions, both in looking back at a response and in adopting and modifying each other's terms and phrases.

The traditional approach of modeling concepts as networks of words would suggest that S has a subconscious description of what she is seeing. According to the symbolic view, S is not very good at explaining her reasoning—the meanings are organized inside but perhaps are inaccessible or inconsistent. A more parsimonious explanation is that nonverbal experience is organizing S's action, and she simply does not have any words to describe what she is seeing.

S's stumbling is not evidence of "reading out" or deductive inference. This is what representing for the first time looks like (line 544): "We think that we, that the, that that is ... we think that that that is going ... (laughter). I have no idea what I'm thinking. (Laughs.)."

The work of recoordinating visual conception in comprehending and recasting descriptions is evident in the alternatives offered by the children: in/on, the/a, the dots/the line, being/be, thicker/width. Choosing a term is choosing a point of view—not describing what is already seen and certainly not merely translating what is already described.

In contrast with the kind of chronological sequencing in music learning discovered by Bamberger (1991), language affords more reordering. Words can be rearranged more easily than the body. Reorderings themselves change the meaning of the parts (a dialectic effect). Just as a sequence in a melody defines the hearing of the individual tones, rearranging words is creating a configuration within which the parts relate meaningfully. Just as individual tones cannot be "recovered" unchanged, the children are not manipulating words (atomic meanings) that have some fixed (atomic) meaning independent of their use. A rephrasing is an act of constructing a meaning.

The students' striking turn taking in typing frequently occurs when they are composing sentences. Several aspects of conceptual coordination of sequences are manifest:

- Use of anchors such that phrases are repeated from an accepted head (i.e., repeating what has been agreed).
- Incorporation of perceptual details, that is, agreeing what needs to be described and what are the defining perceptual characteristics of an abstract mathematical definition.

This phenomena is strikingly evident in the transcript. In the sequence lines 325 through 329, only an adjective is at issue. Notice how they keep repeating the sentence from the beginning and then "not" becomes a focus detail. In the next sequence (lines 330–333), the anchor shifts from the subject to the verb. Notice how both students incrementally add to the sequence and how P twice introduces "not," but S persists, producing a result identical to line 327. Sequence lines 435 through 454 shows the problem of agreeing on a focus detail, a figure, which needs to be described. In terms of conceptually coordinating sentence construction, the problem is to agree on a subject anchor—is the topic the dots or the line?

The incremental constructions reveal negotiating about the subject (dots vs. the line). Interaction line 448 brings the two girls back exactly to 441, with P's statement, but now "the dots" has been fixed and the focus shifts to the verb *were* versus *got*. S had introduced "got" (line 438); P acknowledges this (line 451) and then accepts it. However, the result is ultimately P's view (contrast line 454 with line 436); for S it isn't clear that this is even a sentence, let alone correct.

Again, my interest here is to go beyond simply observing that turn taking occurs to examine the sequence as revealing conceptualizations that organize the interaction and conceptual transformations occurring within it. In particular, the preceding sequence shows repeated questioning about the subject and verb, as both girls are directly involved in constructing a written sentence. Although P's viewpoint dominates (she is writing), she incorporates S's verb. So the apparent individual choices (P, the dots were; S, the line got) become composed as "the dots got."

An attempt to construct a meaningful statement may also fail (see lines 515–518). Here, as in lines 441 through 444, P and S both make bids for a figure—"that they" and "the line." P interrupts S ("No"), and S acknowledges the evaluation. So they decide to skip this question. In effect, the children are unable to coordinate some meaning of *same* because neither can conceive of an appropriate figure.

To summarize, to understand conceptual change, one cannot assume that problems are merely texts and diagrams. The children's problems consist of much more than comprehending text; impasses are not merely matters of understanding a referent of an already conventional representation. To understand perception, one must not assume that the world is given as objects with inherent properties. To understand the nature of description, one must not assume that concepts are named and described properties stored in memory.

CONCLUSIONS: LESSONS LEARNED FOR "INTELLIGENT TUTORING SYSTEMS"

The sometimes confusing interaction between P and S is sobering for designers of computer interfaces and instructional text. Clearly, more guidance about what to look for on the screen would have been possible and might have helped. Yet in practice, it is impossible to anticipate all the alternative ways of seeing the screen. Understanding what straight means is not a matter of memorizing a definition but of coordinating (and creating) possible meanings of the words with what you are seeing. For example, suppose we told Paula and Susanna that "straight means that the dots you plotted are lined up." What does "lined up" mean? Do "the dots you plotted" include the intermediate dots the computer filled in for you, that is, the pixels you caused to appear on the screen? I would hope that P and S's interaction would dismiss any designer's assumptions about simply engineering the system to avoid student misconceptions.

To understand better the student's point of view, one must focus on how people create representations, perceive symbols, and attribute meaning in physical manipulation of materials. I begin with a new contrast: teaching a pre-formalized curriculum versus studying how a new language develops. Attempting to relate levels of analysis—perceptual, deliberative, and social —leads one to reconceive the nature of misconceptions as well as the resources enabling successful learning. Successful design does not depend on only—and ultimately cannot rely on—careful choice of words and diagrams. The realization that contrasts, perceived in experiences over time, are the source of new conceptualizations provides a fundamental shift in how educational researchers view lesson planning. Although it has been known for sometime that ordering lessons is important, the focus has generally been on logical prerequisites based on the idea of composition and re-finement of descriptions. To step out of this "representational flatland," we must understand learning as a process of multimodal recoordination during interaction with physical materials. That is, we must develop lessons around the shift in figure contrast that occurs as meaning is constructed. Such a reframing of the learning problem may indeed help us to consolidate arguments about the many methods of instruction—coaching, discovery, tutor-ing—that are otherwise viewed as competing alternatives.

Equating human knowledge with descriptions (e.g., expert system rules) eliminated the grounds and origin of belief and greatly oversimpli-fied the complex processes of coordinating perception and action. Put simply, a learner participates in the creation of what is to be represented and what constitutes a representation. This dialectic process can be modeled by schema transformations of assimilation, refinement, and so forth (Norman, 1982) in which descriptions are logically combined in an individual mind. However, such a mechanism posits a set of descriptive primitives out of which all expressions are formed. The analysis here sug-gests that although these primitives may exist, they are so general and open to reconfiguration (as in figure-ground shifts) that an additional theory is required to explain how such primitives are configured to form a visual conceptualization.

Specifically, a theory based on mere recombination of primitives map-ping to a "perceptually obvious" world (Larkin & Simon, 1987, p. 88) doesn't explain how new representational languages are created or con-ventional notations are learned. The analysis shown here suggests that it is insufficient to posit that descriptions are controlling how visual primitives are assembled; rather, the learner's common experience is that she sees fig-ures on the basis of contrasts she cannot yet describe. A mechanism grounded in descriptions and visual primitives also fails to account for in-dividual differences because it assumes that there is one objective world of features that everyone can perceive. In short, the exclusively symbolic ap-proach fails to acknowledge or explain what is problematic to the learner, namely, determining what needs to be understood.

However, what kind of cognitive theory do educational researchers need to exploit communication technology? Have we been correct to as-sume that pedagogy must be grounded in an accurate psychological model of knowledge, memory, and learning?

Ironically, the same constraints that made ZBIE appear successful may be employed to some degree in a computer instructional system: One may offer a predefined list of descriptions in menus and operations, which channel the student into the terminology and distinctions of value in the coordinate sys-tem being taught. For example, rather than a free-form workbook in which students write responses, what if P and S had been given multiple choices such as "the line is closer to the Y-axis (vertical)," and "the line is closer to the X-axis (horizontal)"? Suppose that this were hypertext so the students could select terms such as X-axis for further information. By having examined a variety of student responses, such as those by P and S, the designers could anticipate a broad range of difficulties (not only misconceptions) and thus craft a flexible system.

I believe better engineering has merit and could generate a more productive interaction than the handwritten worksheet. Of course some caveats are mandatory: First, there is no guarantee that such a system would work for all students. Second, the problem of modeling the student's understanding and offering assistance on that basis is finessed, and this second point is what bears some discussion.

Here are the points I take to be most salient:

- A human teacher cannot expect to follow, understand, and correct all aspects of a student's behavior.
- Even after dozens of hours of analysis over the course of a decade, I have not fully understood what P and S are experiencing and doing.
- P and S find their own individual experience problematic, uncertain, and frequently at loose ends. That is, they are lost.
- At key junctures, P and S's behavior appears to be ill determined (without coherent organization, not conceptually coordinated in a single way).
- Even when behavior is apparently well directed, as when the students quickly respond to each other in constructing worksheet responses, one cannot assign unique justifications—their behavior is a blend of conceptual and physical constraints, not a reasoned plan or articulatable units (breakable into parts).

More could be said along this vein, but consider the implication so far: The theoretical basis of intelligent tutoring systems, namely, driving all program behavior by a correct explanatory model of student behavior, is false. No existing model fits the bill, and strong theoretical reasons can be given for the practicality of constructing such a model (on the basis of information available during an interaction) as well as for the theoretical possibility of constructing such a model (on the basis of the nondescriptive aspects of perception and conceptual coordination).

This leads to several possible revisions in the strategy of designing computer-aided instruction systems:

- Incorporate a perceptual categorization model based on neural networks (e.g., Edelman, 1992), that is, retain the strategy of instruction through explanatory models.

- Tell a different story about the nature and role of cognitive models in instructional systems; for example, say that it's like a teacher with a strong point of view who keeps guiding the student back onto the preferred path (without attempting to exhaustively understand the student's difficulty).
- Reject the use of cognitive modeling for instruction; instead, focus on providing a multimedia, hypertext system, perhaps linking student projects through a network.

I can imagine reasonable arguments for each of these alternatives in terms of research goals and practicality. However, here I am more interested in the fundamental turning point: The education, psychology, and computer science community cannot proceed with the assumption that cognitive (student) modeling is useful because it causally explains student behavior. At the level of argumentation in which perceptual details, terminology, objectives, and values are captured in a descriptive language, there should indeed be a mapping between the program's model and a person's representational manipulation—indeed, this is what cognitive modeling has shown. However, and it's a large but, the computer model is replicating the person's expressive behavior (formation and manipulation of descriptive models), not the internal conceptual coordination process. Thus, the person's behavior is always more open to blending of perspectives, recognizing of exceptions, and handling of contradictions. Second, such a set of assumptions does not hold in instructional settings in which perceptual details (where to look), terminology, objectives, and social values are all uncertain and requiring new conceptualization to coordinate.

To restate the conclusion, use of student models in instructional systems should be viewed as being like the use of models in any expert endeavor—a means of classifying a situation so as to conveniently and efficiently determine action plans without requiring a full understanding of the particulars of a case and their causal relations. Thus, a librarian can help you find a book without needing to know the particulars of your motivation. A physician can diagnose and treat a rash without investigating your home environment in detail, and a teacher can provide guidance without understanding how you have gone astray. The point is that expert assistance is always heuristic and need not be scientifically thorough. This relation between observation, modeling, and action is called *heuristic classification* (Clancey, 1985) and constitutes a description not only of expert systems but a characterization of human expertise in broad terms (Clancey, 1997a).

Where artificial intelligence (AI) and educational psychologists went astray was to identify the heuristic classification model with human knowledge, suggesting that inference over such models is all that knowledge and reasoning consists of (ignoring the perceptual, cross-model, conceptual coordination aspects). Thus, both the knowledge to be taught and the method for teaching were wrongly identified with descriptive models. A nicely closed system results: The nature of expertise was misconstrued, and consistently, the nature of instructional expertise was misconstrued in the same way. Knowledge consists of more than descriptive models, and successful teaching consists of more than manipulating descriptive models (of the student and the domain).

Thus, any of the three alternatives just listed are justifiable: Continue to build an AI if you wish (but you need to understand the nature of conceptualization); tell a different story, viewing the models as "active systems" that guide a student down the well-trodden path (chiefly by being blind and ignorant of alternatives); or find other uses for multimedia technology and models. I like all three alternatives and hope they will each stimulate a broad community of researchers.

ACKNOWLEDGMENTS

The Green Globs example presented here was originally presented by Sue Magidson and Judit Moskovitch at a video interaction analysis laboratory at the Institute for Research on Learning (IRL) during the early 1990s. I produced the transcript and screen shots from the original video. Some of the ideas about dots and lines, including especially the bilingual analysis of *straight*, were collaboratively developed in the group discussions at IRL. This work was supported in part by the NASA's Computing, Communications, and Information Technology Program, Intelligent Systems subprogram, Human-Centered Computing element, managed by Mike Shafto. I received useful comments from Terry Grant.

REFERENCES

Bamberger, J. (1991). *The mind behind the musical ear*. Cambridge, MA: Harvard University Press.
Bamberger, J., & Schön, D. A. (1991). *Learning as reflective conversation with materials*. London: Sage.
Bartlett, F. C. (1977). *Remembering: A study in experimental and social psychology*. Cambridge, England: Cambridge University Press. (Original work published 1932)
Bateson, G. (1972). *Steps to an ecology of mind*. New York: Ballantine Books.
Clancey, W. J. (1985). Heuristic classification. *Artificial Intelligence, 27*, 289–350.
Clancey, W. J. (1993). Situated action: A neuropsychological interpretation (Response to Vera and Simon). *Cognitive Science, 17*, 87–107.
Clancey, W. J. (1994). Situated Cognition: How representations are created and given meaning. In R. Lewis & P. Mendelsohn (Eds.), *Lessons from learning* (pp. 231–242). Amsterdam: North-Holland.

Clancey, W. J. (1997a). The conceptual nature of knowledge, situations, and activity. In P. Feltovich, R. Hoffman, & K. Ford (Eds.), *Expertise in context* (pp. 247–291). Menlo Park, CA: AAAI Press.

Clancey, W. J. (1997b). *Situated cognition: On human knowledge and computer representations.* Cambridge, England: Cambridge University Press.

Clancey, W. J. (1999). *Conceptual coordination: How the mind orders experience in time.* Mahwah, NJ: Lawrence Erlbaum Associates.

Dewey, J. (1981). In J. J. McDermott (Ed.), *The philosophy of John Dewey* (pp. 136–148). Chicago: University of Chicago Press. (Reprinted from *The reflex arc concept in psychology. Psychological Review, 3,* 357–370, 1896)

Dewey, J. (1981). In J. J. McDermott (Ed.), *The philosophy of John Dewey* (pp. 511–523). Chicago: University of Chicago Press. (Reprinted from *The child and the curriculum,* by John Dewey, 1902, Chicago: University of Chicago Press.)

Dugdale, S., & Kibbey, D. (1982). *Green globs and graphing equations.* Pleasantville, NY: Sunbirst Communications.

Edelman, G. (1992). *Bright air, brilliant fire: On the matter of the mind.* New York: Basic Books.

Garrod, S., & Anderson, J. R. (1987). Saying what you mean in dialogue: A study in the conceptual and semantic co-ordination. *Cognition, 27,* 181–218.

Langer, S. (1958). *Philosophy in a new key: A study in the symbolism of reason, rite, and art.* New York: Mentor Books. (Original work published 1942)

Larkin, J. H., & Simon, H. A. (1987). Why a diagram is (sometimes) worth ten thousand words. *Cognitive Science, 11,* 65–100.

Leont'ev, A. N. (1979). The problem of activity in psychology. In J. V. Wertsch (Ed.), *The concept of activity in Soviet psychology* (pp. 37–71). Armonk, NY: M. E. Sharpe.

Norman, D. A. (1982). *Learning and memory.* New York: Freeman.

Richards, I. A. (1961). *Russian through pictures, Book 1.* New York: Washington Square Press.

Roberts, L. D. (1986). The figure-ground model for explanation of the determination of indexical reference. *Synthese, 68,* 441–486.

Roberts, L. D. (1993). *How reference works.* Albany: State University of New York Press.

Siklóssy, L. (1972). Natural language learning by computer. In H. A. Simon & L. Siklóssy (Eds.), *Representation and meaning: Experiments with information processing systems* (pp. 288–328). Englewood Cliffs, NJ: Prentice Hall.

Vera, A., & Simon, H. (1993). Response to comments by Clancey on "Situated action: A symbolic interpretation." *Cognitive Science, 17,* 117–133.

6

Metacognition, Distributed Cognition, and Visual Design

David Kirsh
University of California, San Diego

An e-learning environment like other environments of human activity is a complex constellation of resources that must be managed by agents as they work toward their goals and objectives. Designers help students manage these resources by providing them with tools, supports, advice, and high-quality content. Ultimately, much of the success of a learning environment turns on the dynamic relation that emerges between learner and environment: how well students interact with their environment; how well they read documents; how well they explore concepts, facts, illustrations; how well they monitor progress; and how well they solicit and accept help. As educators and designers, how can we fashion the conditions that will lead to improved learning? How can we improve the quality of this dynamic relation between student and e-learning environment?

Experience in web usability has shown that the success of an e-learning environment depends as much on the details of how tools, contents, and supports are implemented and visually presented as on the simple fact of their presence. Discussion forums and frequently asked questions, a classical method for providing advice, will go unused if not noticed when a student is in a receptive mood. Key areas of content will regularly go unvisited if the links that identify them are not well marked, distributed widely, or collected at the bottom of web pages. It is one thing to be primed to recognize information as useful, it is another to actually notice it or to know where to quickly find it. The same applies to chat rooms and other interactive possibilities. These learning opportunities risk becoming irrelevant if they are not visually apparent. Navigational cues and page layout can significantly affect student behavior.

I expect broad agreement that visual design is more than an aesthetic choice in the design of learning environments and that it can have an impact on learning outcomes. It affects the usability, simplicity, and clarity of content. It also effects the way users conceive of interactive possibilities. Because usability is known to be an important factor in how deeply, how easily, and how successfully a user moves through the content of an environment, the more usable an e-learning environment is the more successful it will likely be.

There is a further reason, rarely if ever mentioned, why good visual design can facilitate learning. It can improve metacognition. That is my main objective here. It is not standard to associate visual design with metacognition. *Metacognition*, in its most basic form, is the activity of thinking about thinking. Because thinking is often taken to be a mental activity, largely a matter of manipulating internal representations, there has been little reason to look to the structure of the environment as a factor in thinking. If people are told that libraries are good places to think, it is because they are quiet, offering few distractions, and have wonderful reference material. The relevant attributes are social or content oriented rather than structural or interactive. Seldom do we hear that libraries facilitate thinking because they have large tables, or because they have good lighting, or because books are laid out according to the Library of Congress classification. Helpful features such as large surfaces are recognized as being useful for working as are thoughtful classification systems. But all too often thinking and working are treated as separate activities.

This, of course, is an outdated idea. Thinking is as much concerned with the dynamic relation between a person and the external environment he or she is interacting with during the thinking process as it is with the internal representations being created and processed inside that person's head. We do not live in a Cartesian bubble when we think; we live in a world of voices, books, paper, computers, and work surfaces. But then if thinking and cognition are better understood as interactive processes should we not also reconceptualize metacognition in a more interactive fashion?

For the educational community, I expect that, again, there is little news here. Metacognition in education, for instance, is associated with the activities and skills related to planning, monitoring, evaluating, and repairing performance. Sometimes these do take place entirely in the head, as when, as readers, we realize we have just skimmed a paragraph and not really understood it, or when thinking of homework we decide that if we don't spend two hours working now, we'll never finish. But, as often as not there are external resources around that can be recruited to help. We look at the clock to see how quickly we are making progress. We look ahead to see how many pages are left in our text or whether there is an example of how to do the assignment we are stuck on. These supports, distributed in our work environment, are there to help us manage our work, our thought. So are the scraps of paper we store intermediate results on. They enrich the environment of activity. The same is true for the annotations we make on documents, such as problem sheets, or the timetables that we are encouraged to prepare, the to do lists we make, the study plans and checklists we tick off to mark progress. All these are structures in the environment that are involved in metacognition. They help us track where we are, understand what remains to be done, offer indicators that we do not understand something, and so on.

Because most of these "external" supports must be designed, it is likely that better designed supports will be more effective than less well-designed ones. Hence, if some of these supports are metacognitive aids, the better they are designed the better the metacognition. This becomes even more evident when one considers "interaction design."

The expression interaction design refers to the controlled display of affordances (Kirsh, 1997). Designers try to reduce the complexity of choice perceived by a user by shaping visible properties. They attempt to simplify the perception of options a user sees when choosing what to do next. They shape the affordance landscape.

The idea of an affordance was first introduced by J. J. Gibson (1966, 1979) to designate perceivable attributes that humans and creatures view in a functional or dispositional light. For Gibson (ibid), we can actually perceive a door handle as graspable, as turnable, that is, as an opportunity for action. If it seems odd to call the process of identifying functional attributes a type of perception, it is because, from a purely ocular standpoint, our retinas can only be sensitive to the structural and visual properties of objects. Visual perception, viewed from an optical perspective, must be a matter of extracting three-dimensional shape from time sequenced two-dimensional projections on our retinal cortex. But, according to Gibson (ibid), visual perception is active, interactive and so actually involves an integration of motor and visual systems. On this view, our ocular muscles, our neck, head, body, and legs are part of the retinal control system that governs the sampling of the optical world. What we see, therefore, is not independent from how we move. Vision, consequently, is really visual activity; and visual categorization—the "projection" of properties onto our activity space—emerges from the way we as acting creatures interact with our world. Because one of the things we regularly do in our world is to open doors, we come to see door handles as turnable and doors as openable. When we approach entrances, we actively look for visual cues telling us where the handle is and whether it must be pushed, pulled, or rotated.

Affordances, and the way affordances are displayed, are an important part of user experience, whether in e-learning environments or others. Good design becomes a matter of displaying cues and constraints to bias what users will see as their possibilities for action—the action affordances of a space. The challenge of design is to figure out how to guide and direct users by structuring the affordance landscape. This is not all there is to design; designers also build in aesthetic attributes and, where possible, indicators of where or how close to a goal a user is. But to a first order, both visual and interactive design are about structuring the affordance landscape.

An example may clarify the idea of structuring the affordance landscape. If a user needs to configure a complicated piece of software, such as installing Adobe® PhotoShop™, it is customary to walk the user through the installation process with a "wizard," which is essentially a set of windows or screens, each of which represents a step in the installation or configuration process. The art of design is to constrain the visual cues on each screen to a small set that "signals" to the user what to do next: Just follow the affordances. This has the effect of breaking down the configuration process into modular stages that each have a semantic cohesiveness—an easy to understand integrity. The consequence for users is that they have the feeling that they understand what they are doing and where they are in the process; they are not just blindly following rules or being asked to make complicated choices about what to do next. They can see what they are supposed to do and notice when they are off course. Wizards do not reduce complex processes to the same level of simplicity and intuitiveness as turning a door handle, but they share that objective. When done well, wizards regulate interactivity in ways that reduce error, enhance user experience, and simplify complex processes.

It does not take much to appreciate that visual design plays a major role in the effectiveness of wizards. Intuitiveness comes from controlling the cue structure of each screen. However, visual design is not all there is to interactivity design. Designers still must understand how to decompose a functionally complex system into a collection of functionally simple systems. This takes skill and careful planning. But the two design fields, visual and interactivity design, are related because in both cases, the end goal is to control how the user registers what to do next. Good visual design should expose the cues that shape interactivity.

The hypothesis I argue for here is that just as visual design can reduce the cognitive effort involved in managing interfaces (and the complex systems those interfaces regulate), so too can visual design reduce the cognitive effort involved in managing the learning process, especially those aspects of the process that depend on metacognition. Well-designed affordance landscapes make metacognition easier.

The basic form of my argument is as follows:

1. Metacognition, like first-order cognition, is a type of situated cognition. Metacognition works, in part, by controlling the interaction of person and world. It is not just a mental control mechanism regulating Cartesian mental performance. It is a component in the dynamic coupling of agent and environment. Sometimes the way interaction is controlled is by biasing what one looks at such as when a student actively looks for important words or phrases in a paragraph. Sometimes the interaction controlled has to do with what one does in a more motor sense such as when a student underlines a phrase or lays out materials on a table. Sometimes the interaction controlled is more sophisticated, concerned with managing schedules, checklists, notes, and annotations. In every case, metacognition is highly interactive, a matter of regulating the way learners are dynamically coupled with their environments. Once metacognition is reconceptualized in this more situated, distributed manner, it follows that the principles that apply to improving first-order cognition should also apply to metacognition. Good design is one of these principles.

2. The rhetoric of metacognition is about internal regulation, but the practice of designers focuses on external resources. When one looks at the actual mechanisms and recommendations that educators give to students to improve their performance, they focus on re-representation or on manipulating external aids. Metacognition recruits internal processes but relies as well on skills that are oriented to controlling outside resources and mechanisms.

3. Good visual designs are cognitively efficient. The cognitive effort involved in metacognitive activity is no different in principle than the cognitive effort involved in first-order cognition. A poorly written paragraph requires more cognitive effort to comprehend than a well written paragraph. A well marked paragraph, with key words or phrases italicized, with topic clearly visible and standing out from the rest of the text, will make it easier for metacognitive activity to improve performance. In both cases, the way visual cues are distributed affects the cognitive effort required to notice what is important. Good design helps to manage student attention and train students to expect semantically important cues such as topic sentences or useful summaries to be visually prominent. Good designs are good because they are cognitively efficient.

4. Good visual design supports helpful workflow. Because learners typically have multiple tasks to perform, they need to plan, monitor, and evaluate their progress. Just as wizards reduce the complexity of multiphase processes by decomposing them into modular steps, each with appropriate visual affordances, so assignments can be made more step-by-step (at first), and helpful reference materials can be spatially distributed to the places on a page where they will be most useful. Once again, students can be trained to expect and to find the resources they have

learned are useful. Consequently, when they enter less well-designed environments in which the affordance landscape is less useful for learning tasks and metacognition they will come to these environments with well-established expectations of what they want and need. Because one major element in metacognition is realizing what one doesn't know and what one needs to know, it is helpful to have trained the knowledge expectations of students by exposing them to environments that are well set up. They then will develop expectations of the kind of information that is useful to have when engaged in a specific task such as solving a geometric or engineering problem.

5. Good visual design is about designing cue structure. Because the cognitive impact of good visual design depends on regulating visual interactivity, it is largely about cue structure. Cues, however, are more complex than simple visual attractors. In addition to cues that reveal affordances, there are cues that serve as indicators, letting students or users know when they are getting closer to one of their goals. By looking at complex documents, especially e-newspapers in which the lessons of addressing the needs of consumers has led to a rapid evolution in design, one can see how experience has taught designers to control user behavior.

I turn now to an account of metacognition that incorporates the insights of the theories of situated and distributed cognition.

A MORE SITUATED, DISTRIBUTED VIEW OF METACOGNITION

Metacognition, from a distributed and situated approach, is concerned with managing resources. These resources may be processes involved in internal cognitive functioning, but as likely as not they are objects and processes in one's immediate environment. This is consistent with current thinking in psychology in which the activities and skills typically associated with metacognition are also associated with a faculty called the *central executive*, which is thought to be localized in the prefrontal cortex. Executive function is assumed to be involved in planning, monitoring, and controlling certain aspects of reasoning as well as the action and behavior that that reasoning is linked with. So although metacognition, in psychology, is usually associated with internal regulation of internal cognitive processes, there is no prohibition on viewing metacognition to be also involved in the regulation of external processes associated with processes like planning, monitoring, evaluating, sequencing, and repairing.

The idea that metacognition is associated at least sometimes with external processes, is a necessary step in reinterpreting it in terms of a more situated and distributed approach to cognition. To explain what is involved in the reinterpretation, I review some of the key tenets of the situated distributed approach. The five tenets I elaborate are those most relevant to my purposes here. I make no claim that these are a sufficient set or, for that matter, that they are the set most commentators would choose as the core set, although I do think they capture the major themes.

The first tenet may be stated like this: The complexity of deciding what to do next, which is essentially the central problem of intelligent action, is made considerably less complex than the general problem of rational choice because we may assume that the environments people successfully operate in are richly imbued with cues, constraints, and indicators that reduce the complexity of those problems and serve as hints about what to do. Most of our everyday problems arise in environments rich in cues and resources that help us solve them. This explains the familiar war cry of supporters of situated cognition that people are not good at tasks that require abstract reasoning or intensive recall but are by contrast rather good at tasks that can be solved by recruiting perceptually salient attributes to jog memory or allow recasting a seemingly abstract problem into a concrete one. Humans excel at using resources especially representational resources, in systematic but creative fashion to work their way to solutions. They are good at using and manipulating structures. For instance, a short-order cook may convert a dozen orders, each with resource and scheduling implications, into an arrangement of ingredients laid out in a systematic manner on plates and burners to reduce memory load and calculation of what to do next (Kirsh, 1995). The scheduling problem, which in the abstract is computationally complex, can be reduced to the concrete problem of encoding ingredients in spatial arrangements. Once so encoded, the cook can read off from the moment-by-moment arrangement where in the process he or she is and what remains to be done. This method of pushing the abstract into the concrete serves to recruit the practical skills that people are good at.

Metacognition, from this standpoint, should be concerned with concrete factors, not with abstract ones to do with general notions of processing effort, mental resource consumption, and so on. For instance, the cook should be aware that given the pressures of the orders on call and the current layout of ingredients, pots, pans, and burner activity, the overall process must be sped up or else some clients will wait beyond what is acceptable. The metacognitive activities of monitoring and evaluating are tied to the specific cues of the situation. The metacognitive activities of replanning and repairing are also situated in the way the current setup constrains what can be done to rush things. Knowledgeable cooks know tricks and shortcuts for speeding things up, but these tricks are themselves typically dependent on how resources are laid out and processed in the kitchen. It won't help to use a cuisinart to chop vegetables that otherwise would be cut by hand if the cuisinart first has to be washed. Cognition and metacognition are tied to the concrete particulars of the workplace.

The second tenet draws a further implication from the idea that humans lean on environmental structure for cognitive support. The environments we work and operate in are primarily cultural environments. The work surfaces we use; the paths, roads, and buildings we move in and over; the tools and implements we rely on; our food; and even most of our soundscape is the product of technology and culture. All these elements have been adapted to us just as we ourselves have adapted and continue to adapt to them. Consider the activity of dining. We sit down to a table using chairs that are the appropriate height, and we rely on well-crafted implements that have been modified over centuries to meet the functional requirements of eating off of plates, of spearing food on distant platters, and of spreading viscous liquids such as butter. Even the food we lay out in bowls and containers has been adapted to suit our cultural requirements. Salads have been prepared so that they are bite sized or nearly so, meat has been precarved so that we can be confident it will fit on our plate. There is a great deal of social subtlety and cultural knowledge assumed at dinner. However, because the environment is so exquisitely structured, so well populated with tools and well-designed resources, the daunting task of feeding ourselves in a culturally appropriate manner is simplified enough to be readily learned.

Metacognition is affected by this assumption too. Because the presence of metacognitively exploitable properties ought to improve performance, we expect that well-designed environments will make these available also. Some of the culturally supported cues, constraints, affordances, and functionalities that simplify work, will be targeted at improving metacognition. In kitchens this is clearly true. Good cooks do not overcook. They monitor and evaluate, or they rely on a cooking process that itself guarantees proper cooking. To support monitoring and evaluative needs, pressure cookers have whistles, microwaves have buzzers and automatically turn off, ovens are designed with glass fronts and internal lights; burners are open and easily viewable; and there are meat probes, temperature indicators, clocks, and timers. The virtue of such tools is that they make explicit key indicators that simplify tracking how close to being cooked the target dishes are. Monitoring can be simplified even further if setting alarms is incorporated into one's cooking style. In that case, it can be hard to decide when a cook is simply following his or her normal first-order cognitive procedures and when he or she is adding metacognitive elements. The better designed an environment is the more blurred the distinction between metacognition and cognition.

The third tenet that marks a distinctly situated or distributed approach is that we assume that humans (and other animals) are causally coupled so closely with their environments that cognition is effectively distributed over mind and environment (Clark, 1998; Hutchins, 1995; Kirsh, 1999).

This tenet is primarily a claim about the meaning of terms such as *thinking* and *planning*. In my earlier discussion of the conceptual closeness of working and thinking, the point was made that thought is not just *expressed* in work, it is *executed* in work. C. S. Peirce, in his prescient way, was fond of saying that a chemist as much thinks with test tube and beaker as with his brain (as cited in Hartshorne & Weiss, 1960). Peirce's insight was that the activity of manipulating tools—in the chemist's case, manipulating representation rich tools and structures such as measuring devices, controllable flames, the lines in diagrams, and written words—is part of the overall process of thought. There is not the inner component, the true locus of thought, and its outer expression. The outer activity is a constituent of the thought process, although for Peirce it had to be continually reinterpreted to be meaningful. Wittgenstein (1953) too was eager to make this point: When people express their thoughts out loud, there is not the internal process called *thought* and an outer manifestation that is logically distinct. The speech itself is a constituent of the thought. It is part of the thinking process, and how we express ourselves out loud fits into the causal chain of reasoning from premise to premise.

Metacognition, on this account, will often be a process that is partly in the world and partly in the head. If agents plan by making to do lists or by using a day planner or working with a computer-based planning program, the nature of their planning process will be misunderstood unless attention is paid to the way their planning is constrained by those external resources. The process of planning is as much driven by the requirements and affordances of the tools as it is by the stated goals and intentions of the human planner. This means that it is as important to design metacognitive tools that cue and prompt effectively as it is to get students to use them. Design a homework tracker sensitively and it will fit right into the activity of students, helping them to allocate time and locate references more effectively. It becomes another element in the many-sided activity of doing homework. Design it badly and it is just an extra thing for students to do. It is not an essential part of their first order activity.

The fourth tenet I consider here is that this close causal coupling holds true at different temporal levels (Kirsh, 1999). People interact in a dynamic manner with their environments at frequencies that range from 50 or 100 ms in fast paced games to seconds and minutes such as when we cook, surf the web, or drive a car. This coupling is close despite the difference in temporal range.

In fast paced activity, such as computer games, expert players become so sensitized to regularities in display and action that they respond to small visual cues in strategic ways. They are attuned to the goal relevant cues in their gaming environments, so they are able to rely on optimized perception action routines (Agre & Chapman, 1987; Kirsh & Maglio, 1995). These routines go well beyond rapid eye-hand coordination. They are goal sensitive, semiautomatic processes that are permeable to the interests and concerns of the agent. They are typically well below 500 ms.

Gaming lends itself to discussions of active vision in which goal-directed agents actively probe the environment looking for cues that are related to their goals (Blake & Yuille, 1993). Because active vision is assumed to be partly the product of statistical or implicit learning of the visual features and patterns that are goal relevant, it is thought to be going on all the time in games (and elsewhere), most often unconsciously. It reflects a dynamic coupling between the eyes and hands of an agent and the environment of action. Agent and environment are locked in a high-frequency dance.

The same type of dynamic casual coupling also occurs at slower temporal frequencies, such as seconds, tens of seconds, or even minutes. In cooking, the cues that must be attended to and then acted on need not manifest quickly and then disappear. They may take time to become noticeable and then linger. Food gives off slowly changing aromas, it changes color with heat and oxidation. Good cooks are attuned to these cues. Gradual changes may be hard to notice but are still changes that must be monitored. This coupling between cook and kitchen, this trained sensitivity to cues, indicators, and prompts, is at a temporal frequency slower than gamers. This makes it possible to take a more explicit approach to active vision and ask cooks about the cues that matter.

Until now, I have not asked whether monitoring, evaluating, and selecting action is a conscious process or an unconscious one. Experience teaches that it can be both. At high frequencies, it seems to be mostly automatic or semiautomatic; at lower frequencies, it may be more self-aware. Obviously, slower cues give agents more time to talk about what they are looking for and to watch them emerge. Slower cues are easier to learn explicitly and easier to teach. They tend to be more conscious. This does not preclude active vision at an unconscious level being a part of the learned skill, however. Cue and indicators must be still be tracked. Because the pattern recognition involved may be quite complex, the unconscious tricks of active vision—saccade strategies and microfeature recognition—are especially useful. Accordingly, it is incorrect to assume that active vision at an unconscious level is irrelevant in monitoring just because the important cues are slower to manifest.

A reverse line of thought applies to high-speed contexts: It is incorrect to assume monitoring to be unconscious just because it is very fast. Even in the quickest of games in which most of the strategies of active vision are unconscious, players can still exercise conscious scanning. They can discuss games after the fact and make a conscious effort to note new cues. They can remind themselves to be on the look out for certain indicators and chastise themselves later for missing the telltale signs. This suggests that training can have both an explicit and implicit component even in games. It is primarily a matter of degree. In cooking, the conscious approach is typical. People are explicitly trained by others to look for certain things. The way I learned to cook pancakes was by being told explicitly to look for the little bubbles on the upper surface of the batter and to use those bubbles as timers indicating when the pancakes should be flipped. These slowly developing changes in the appearance of pancakes are cues I was explicitly taught to observe. However, no one taught me how to look for the appearance of the bubbles. I was never instructed in the art of scanning a dozen pancakes to track when each was done. My saccade strategies are not open to explicit review, suggesting that even in conscious searching, there is an unconscious or implicitly learned component.

The import for metacognition is that monitoring and evaluation are likely the product of both explicit and implicit learning. In tasks in which practical skills are most important—and I have been arguing that these are more common in intellectual and educational contexts than often appreciated—experienced agents may become implicitly tuned to some of the key indicators and cues they need to track. Others of these indicators and cues may be explicitly taught. Students and teachers know they are attending to these items and they discuss them. The challenge for teachers is knowing how to balance explicit with implicit teaching, instruction with practice.

For instance, a well-designed reader (i.e., a book) might use visual devices to call attention to topic sentences, key words, and ideas; it might summarize at helpful intervals, pace the student, and incorporate questions in its prose in a manner that encourages reflection. Teachers might explain these devices to students explicitly, using them as aids in explaining what comprehension is or as aids in explaining how to read. Yet students still must practice reading, and even without explicit instruction, students may become more sensitized to the semantic elements given special visual prominence. Good visual design, when combined with good writing, should make it easier for readers to process more deeply. Some of this deeper processing may be the result of conscious direction, or metacognition in the classical sense. Some of it may be the result of implicit reaction to cues, a blend of unconscious metacognition and conscious monitoring.

The final tenet that signals a situated or distributed approach has to do with coordination. Coordination is about dynamic fit; it is about parts moving in harmony, in synchrony, matched. Because people are coupled to their environments at many temporal frequencies, sometimes aware sometimes unaware of the nature of their active perceptual engagement, they should be seen more as managers of their interaction, as coordinators locked in a system of action reaction, than as purely rational agents evaluating possible actions on the basis of predicted consequences. This move toward seeing the key interactive relation as one of coordination rather than of planful control is meant to revise the scientific concept of agency.

It is on this point that the theories of distributed and situated action are in need of clarification. Coordination comes in many flavors, each with its own variety of mechanism. Metacognition ought to figure in some of these mechanisms as one class of ways we as humans coordinate our activities with the environments we are in tune with. Sometimes it does. But once again seeing metacognition involved in this revised notion of agency requires a revision of assumptions about metacognition.

For instance, in soccer play, the changing location and trajectory of the ball is a great focusing element for each player and each side as a whole. It helps coordinate players by fixing the vectors around which they should move into formation relative to the other team. Given the rules of the game and the objective of play, projected ball location helps to coordinate teams and also the activities of individuals. However, details seem to be missing about how players adjust to a change in ball position. Obviously, the ball helps to manage attention; players continuously monitor its location. Is this type of location monitoring metacognitive? As the ball moves the team reconfigures, leading to moment-by-moment repairs to strategy. Again, is this reaction to the dynamic state of the game metacognitive? Certainly coaches teach their team plays, positions, and ways of moving with the ball. So a player's repositioning in response to a change in ball dynamics may well be conscious and unambiguously metacognitive. Yet as skill increases or when one discusses the matter with "natural" players, it seems that sense of position is harder to separate from just playing. Responsive players have good ball sense, knowing where to move to be well positioned. They are beautifully coordinated with their team. Do they perform less metacognition or more?

Representations are another and even more powerful coordinator. When a student picks up her book of math homework with its exercise pages, the next 20 min of student activity is highly constrained. It is hard to predict what the student will do at each moment. We can be confident, however, that she will come back to the spaces that have to be filled in and slowly put in marks of a certain sort. Representations are potent behavior coordinators. Empty cells in a table cry out to be filled. Yet again, although the structure of behavior is nicely characterized and indeed explained in a macro sense, little is said about the specific mechanisms by which the representation interacts with the student to drive her in the direction of fulfilling the representation's requirements. Does she monitor the incompleteness of the representation? Presumably. But is that type of monitoring metacognitive or is it first-order cognition?

The same question of order on a level arises with other tools and resources for students. To do lists, checklists, forms, and other representations containing blanks that need to be filled serve to constrain, prompt, and coordinate activity. They set in motion activities as soon as the student takes notice of them. Is this noticing, which is in part the outcome of surveying or monitoring what is present in the environment, a metacognitive or simply cognitive process? If we call it metacognitive, doesn't that show that most of intelligent behavior has a significant metacognitive component to it? Another example will help to elaborate this question.

Musicians, much like students in a learning environment, work to keep their performance at a high level. Musicians take pain to be in synchrony, in step, with their orchestra. In step here means in tune, in tempo, in volume, and in tonality. Each of these attributes is marked in part by words or symbols in the score. However, the real meaning of in tune, in tempo, in tonality and volume are given by the emergent properties that arise from the joint activity of conductor and orchestra. Individual players regulate their own tempo to fit the orchestra's. They dynamically regulate their volume, their pitch, and tonality. There is no sense to the idea that the orchestra is not in tempo, but some of the players are. Tempo is a holistic, an emergent property of the group, just like marching in step is. This means that for good musicians, the process of registering tempo and adapting to the dynamic state of the orchestra is something they must do almost automatically. This is not to imply they are unaware of their effort. Musicians have a developed vocabulary for talking about tempo, and the conductor must set the right tempo and keep the group in time. Yet although musicians are always able to be aware of their adaptation to group tonality and tempo, it is clear from discussion with expert players that they are not always aware of all their adaptations. Sometimes they simply conform to tempo because of the feeling of beat. This is not always a conscious thing. The same holds for volume. As the community changes volume so do the individuals. Mass behavior is not always conscious behavior (Canetti, 1962). When adaptation is unconscious can it be metacognitive? Is it intelligent? However, if not intelligent, why do our most expert performers embody it best?

The implication for metacognition of all these tenets is that for agents operating in well-designed environments, the activity of maintaining coordination, of monitoring, repairing, and deciding what to do next may not be a fully conscious process and certainly not require attention to one's current internal thinking process. Because the thrust of the situated and distributed approach is that cognition is distributed between agent and environment, it follows that even when there is conscious awareness of mental activity, the aspect of cognition being attended to need not be some internal mentalistic entity, such as the auditory imagery accompanying thought, but may instead be the externalization of that thought as expressed in speaking, diagraming, and so forth. But then since cognition is often interactive, metacognition must be too. This ought to shift the focus of research on metacognition in education away from ideas based on classical theories of planning, monitoring, and repairing to ideas concerned with the way learning environments distribute cues, indicators, constraints, and prompts. It opens the door to studying how environments can improve metacognition by design.

CLASSICAL TOOLS FOR IMPROVING METACOGNITION

To see just how much of metacognition is concerned with external structures, I turn now to some of the ways metacognition is taught and engendered in school. As is evident, the rhetoric about metacognition portrays it as an internal process. In practice, though, metacognition is taught using external resources as an interactive process. Of the many forms of metacognition that teachers want their students to practice, I briefly discuss just two: metacognition that improves comprehension and metacognition that improves time management.

To begin, assume that the primary objective of teaching metacognitive skills to students is to provide them with a bundle of strategies that will make them more active information processors, students who monitor and control their learning activities, making local adaptations as required to ensure attaining key learning objectives. In comprehension, this may mean teaching students that during reading or immediately after reading a passage, they should

- Try to summarize the passage.
- Paraphrase key ideas.
- Try to imagine the situation.
- Analyze what the ideas mean.

Sometimes it means recommending that during reading, students should

- Take notes.
- Highlight.
- Underline key points.
- Make diagrams.
- Annotate the material in some other way.

All these activities seem well designed to force deeper processing. Because they are constructive, they require the student to generate a more personal understanding of material most often by externalizing that understanding in a product such as a note, mark, oral comment, or new representation. This drives semantic processing deeper and forces better comprehension—clearly a good idea. Constructive efforts are almost always conscious and deliberate.

Do these activities take place in the head, or in interaction with external resources? In virtually every case, students are being asked to rerepresent or elaborate the material studied. They create new representations of the material either by writing paraphrases, writing summaries or analyses, or by flights of fancy. Excepting the last method, in which activating internal imagination is the mechanism for metacognition, each metacognitive process requires that students act on the world. This means that many of the skills that are being called on are not simply internal skills, they are interactive skills such as: knowing how to look back and forth between reference passage and the summary, paraphrase, or analysis being written; knowing how to work with a text to annotate it; how to make a diagram using pen and paper; how to draw in the margin; and how to take notes, identify, and mark down key ideas. All these are interactive skills engaging external resources. In fact, part of the power of these exercises comes precisely because they force students to revisit the text with a specific externalization task in mind. Evidently, most metacognitive strategies for reading, at least at first, involve some form of externalization. Is it any surprise that beginning readers are required to read out loud and to talk about what they are reading?

The same focus on coordinating the use of external resources can be found in metacognition related to improving time management. Relying on the notion that those who are better managers of their thinking are better thinkers, learning environment designers have worked to add reminders, questions and exercises, checklists, and a host of other artifacts to improve students' tracking of their time and progress. Each involves students' using external aids to help structure time and activity.

Making a to do list, for example, may be as simple as writing a set of tasks on a scrap of paper. In one sense, it hardly alters a student's learning environment conceived as a classroom, a computer, or workbooks. Yet once this scrap has been dropped in the environment, then future tasks, which until now have existed as prospective memory elements alone, are reified as a list whose items can be checked off. The list becomes part of the persistent state maintained by the environment. This has the effect of making time easier to structure because a student can now see what remains to be done and what priority each task has. To do lists remind, cue, facilitate evaluation, and simplify planning by making it easier to keep track of what has to be done.

Lists are only one of many such external aids. They are effective when a student has the freedom, time, and inclination to consult them. In some environments, though, this is not the case. In exam settings, for example, there are restrictions on what can be brought into the environment and constraints on time that may make list making counterproductive. Yet metacognitive skills are crucial in exam-taking, and often taught explicitly. Students are told to scan all questions in advance, to select the easiest and most valuable ones to do first, to leave for later questions that are taking longer than recommended. They are expected to keep track of the time left, to compare it with the number of questions they have left, and if necessary, make strategic repairs to their exam plan. Are these metacognitive strategies external? Are they interactive?

From a distributed cognition perspective, all such strategies are interactive. The exam itself provides cues or prompts for metacognition. Questions are modular; they have a certain credit value. The duration of the exam is announced, and the proctor updates the notice of time left. These external aids are not arbitrary. They are present in the exam-taking environment specifically to help students manage their time better. It is as if the system made up of the student, the exam, and the resources in the exam-taking context are working together to encourage time management. Naturally, the better the exam and the context are designed, the better the coordination between student and his or her exam taking will be. That goal of coordination between environment, scaffolding, and student is precisely the moving target that designers of e-learning environments are trying to create for the many phases of learning. Sometimes it involves supplying resources, such as explicit exam planners, that students fill in themselves; but most often it involves enriching the environment with cues, metrics, and monitors that students can exploit moment by moment without writing anything down.

GOOD DESIGN IS COGNITIVELY EFFECTIVE

I have been arguing that metacognition is a more situated and distributed process than traditionally assumed. Most learning environments already incorporate many of the principles of good pedagogy by providing cues, prompts, hints, indicators, and reminders to students in the hope that these will trigger better, more adaptive, learning behavior. Metacognition is an integral part of many of these adaptive behaviors. In this section, I turn to questions of layout and affordance structure as factors that can effect metacognition. Because the manner of displaying cues, prompts, indicators, and so forth has an effect on what, when, and how students notice aspects of their environment, good designers need to present these stimuli in a cognitively effective fashion. They need to shape the affordance landscape.

Consider the two layouts displayed in the figures below. Why is Fig. 6.1b—a layout of text properties from the early 1990s—obviously better than Fig. 6.1a, a layout from the 1980s and the days of Microsoft® DOS?

One answer focuses on aesthetics. In the language of graphic artists, one is cleaner; it uses "white space" better, it has more "air." Another focuses on efficiency and effectiveness. In the language of cognitive scientists, Fig. 6.1b is cognitively more efficient/effective than Fig. 6.1a. Why is this?

Although the term *cognitive efficiency* does not have a universally accepted meaning, intuitively, a given representation, layout or visual design is cognitively more efficient than another if it can be comprehended, parsed, perceived, or used "faster without more errors." The better the design the

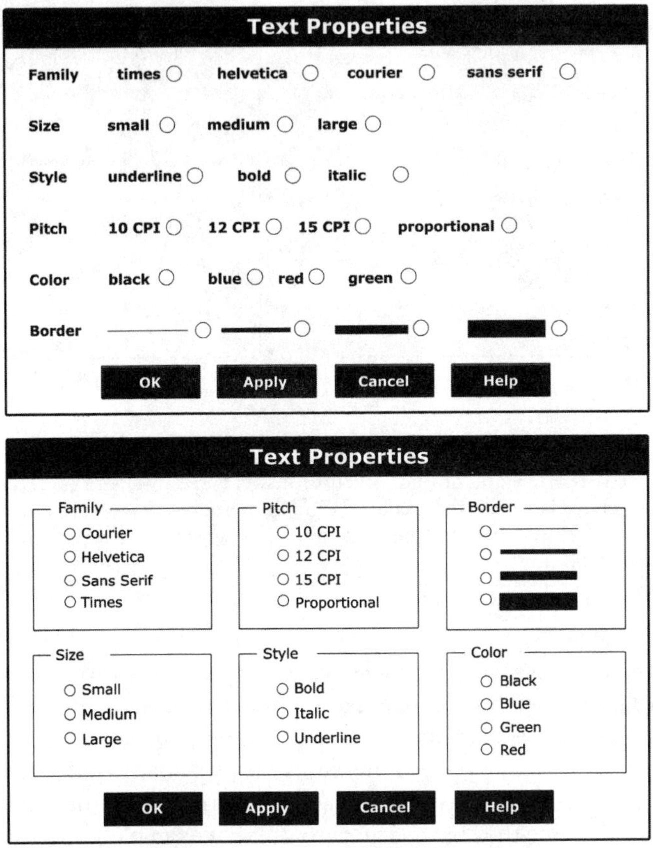

FIG. 6.1. Fig. 6.1a (top) is a form layout typical of the 1980s. Fig. 6.1b (bottom) is a form layout typical of the 1990s.

better the speed accuracy curve. That is, users can increase the speed at which they extract the same content without increasing their error rate; or conversely, they can reduce their error rate without reducing speed (see Fig. 6.2a).

The term *cognitive effectiveness* also does not have a universally accepted meaning. When technicians talk of effectiveness, they usually mean probability of correctness as in "effective algorithm," which refers to algorithms that guarantee a correct answer. Outside of algorithmics, effectiveness implicitly carries the idea of normal conditions. The addition of normal or boundary conditions is important because in simple speed accuracy diagrams, Fig. 6.2a, there are no assumptions about an acceptable or normal temporal window. That means that a given structure, such as the display in Fig. 6.1a, might have

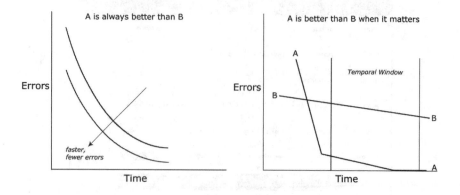

FIG. 6.2.   In Fig. 6.2a, (left side), the graphic structure represented by A is universally better than B if participants are more likely to answer correctly regardless of presentation duration. In Fig. 6.2b (right side), the graphic structure represented by A is not universally better than B, but it supports more correct answers in the region reflecting the normal conditions of use.

an acceptable speed accuracy profile over a portion of the timeline but be unacceptable for the temporal range that matters in a given context. This more pragmatic notion of effectiveness makes a better metric. For design, the effectiveness of a structure or process measures the probability that users will correctly comprehend, perceive, extract the meaning, or otherwise use the structure in the time they have (see Fig. 6.2b). For example, the display in Fig. 6.1b is cognitively more effective than that of Fig. 6.1a because users are more likely to understand their options quickly and correctly, and make effective decisions using Fig. 6.1b than using Fig. 6.1a. This means that the graphic in Fig. 6.1b is more usable and more effective.

Cognitive efficiency and effectiveness are empirical measures of the goodness of a visual design. At a deeper level, however, what makes one design better than another for a particular task is that the better design has a better structured affordance landscape.

Consider again what makes Fig. 6.1b so much better than Fig. 6.1a.

First, and most significant, Fig. 6.1b arranges visual elements so that it is easier to see what goes with what. Just as a well-written paragraph is easier to comprehend than a poorly written one, so a visually well-structured design is easier to comprehend and use than a poorly structured one. The reason Fig. 6.1b is better than Fig. 6.1a is that the way the semantic clusters are laid out in two dimensions with boxes and labels heightens their visual independence and subtly redirects users to chunk their configuration task into steps that match the boxes. The choice points are well marked and the options within each choice point are easy to compare. This makes planning, monitoring, and evaluating easier.

The principle at work is this: what goes together semantically goes together visually. Every (visible) representational structure has a referential or semantic domain it is about and a set of visual elements—syntatic features—that can be assembled and positioned. The visual elements in Fig. 6.1a and 6.1b include such things as circles, small squares, boxes, positioning, words, buttons, and lines. The referential domain contains elements such as fonts that are bolded, italicized, underlined, 10 points in size, Times New Roman, and so on. The reason Fig. 6.1b is more successful than Fig. 6.1a is that the inherent connection between the semantic elements is visually portrayed in an easy to understand style. For example, the terms *bold*, *italics*, and *underlined* are all visually bounded by a box. This box itself is labeled with the semantic category these options belong to, that is, font style. This perceptual grouping effect is enhanced further because each semantic sibling, each option, lines up cleanly, and as a group, is centered in the labeled box. Curiously, the box itself is not a semantic element; it is a visual aid that facilitates perceptual grouping. It is a visual scaffold.

A second reason Fig. 6.1b is superior to Fig. 6.1a is that it is less cluttered. It has less visual complexity.

Visual complexity is one of those terms like effectiveness that remains ill defined outside of a narrow domain of algorithmics. One explanation for this semantic imprecision is that visual complexity, like descriptive complexity, depends on the pattern recognition repertoire of the observer. One structure that looks random to one viewer may be familiar and hence patterned to another. Accordingly, it will take fewer bits to specify a structure to a practiced observer than for an unpracticed one. This measure—the number of bits needed to specify a structure—is the standard one used in descriptive complexity theory (Chaitin, 1975; Li & Vitanyi, 1997). In normal circumstances, bit size will vary depending on the assumptions made about the interpreter. In computer science, descriptive complexity refers to the fewest possible bits in principle needed to specify a structure.

For design work, an in principle measure of visual complexity will not work. Designers need to design to a user community acting in natural settings with their own specific goals and interests. In natural settings, vision is not independent from the semantic and pragmatic context framing how visual input will be interpreted.

The source of this contextual framing lies in the tasks the user is engaged in while looking and the recent linguistic and behavioral history of user. For instance, a desk littered with papers may seem complex to a visitor viewing the desk for the first time but be highly structured to its owner. Past history with those papers, especially by being the person who arranged them, provides an interpretive frame for the desk not shared by newcomers. Sometimes language can help. A few helpful comments about an organizational system may help to contextualize a visual scene for a visitor and so reduce the time to parse and identify its meaningful structure. Language can help set an interpretive framework and prime the identification of structural elements. So can knowledge of the desk owner's tasks. Yet without such help, the time it will take for a visitor to figure out the organization of the papers and related "stuff" on a desk, if it can be figured out at all, will depend on what the visitor has seen before and what he or she can infer from connections they see between the documents and other stuff on the desk. Because the time to recognize connections thus depends on factors we, as scientific measurers, typically know nothing about (i.e., the visitor's personal history), it becomes virtually impossible to predict how long it will take someone to see order in what at first looks like clutter.

I think it is wise to be skeptical of efforts to formalize the intuitive concepts of visual complexity and visual clutter. Yet it is still obviously true that visual layout can be made more or less cluttered with respect to tasks. Even if it is not possible to give a quantitative measure of visual complexity and clutter, it still may be possible to decide which structures are more or less cluttered relative to well defined tasks. This suggests that viewed from the framing assumptions of a task, visual clutter may be qualitatively assessed. For instance, Fig. 6.1b is less cluttered with respect to the task of font configuration because first, it is well modularized for the several subtasks involved. And second, it distributes the options present in each subtask in a manner that makes it easy for a user to read off and track the decisions they have already made and those that remain. It is easier to see, for example, that a choice of font style has been made already whereas a choice of font pitch has not. This has the further effect that users who are interrupted will find it easier to pick up where they left off, because their current work state will be more explicitly displayed (Kirsh, 1990).

The upshot of this is that good designs are cognitively efficient to the degree that they help users go about their tasks. They help them review where they are in their tasks and decide what to do next because they display the task-relevant features in a cognitively efficient manner. They should reduce error, increase speed, improve tolerance to interruption, and facilitate monitoring, evaluating, and deciding. See Fig. 6.3.

CUE STRUCTURE AND COGNITIVE WORKFLOW

One advantage of interpreting visual design as a structural language of affordances with its implicit reference to activity is that it emphasizes that good designs are good because they make it easier for learners to do their work. Designs cannot be evaluated for cognitive efficiency independently of what users of those designed environments need to do.

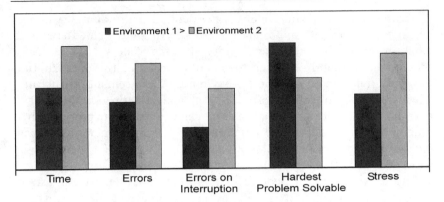

FIG. 6.3. Learning environments can be compared along several dimensions in addition to time and error. Of greatest interest are their tolerance to interruption, the hardest problem they allow a student of given ability to solve, and the stress they cause users while working in them.

The environments designed for e-learning are digital environments. They have properties that go well beyond those found in non-digital 2D layouts with stationary elements, such as books, charts, or whiteboards. Digitally enhanced environments use interactivity, reproducibility, and manipulability to drastically reduce the cost structure of many familiar activities. For instance, if someone is writing an essay in a word processor, he or she can readily alter the way things look or are presented. Documents can be searched more cheaply and in diverse ways. Various types of index files can be created by making digital shortcuts or copies. And it is possible to make changes faster, copy from arbitrary places and multiply paste, track changes and create version trajectories, send off copies while keeping the main copy at home, broadcast, and publish. Moreover, if documents are in digital form there are special applications, such as spell checking, autoformatting, and so on, that can be applied. All these functions are more costly if not impossible to do using paper documents. This increase in the range of activities possible in digital environments heightens the importance of understanding how people work in digital worlds and how to design the interactive elements they use.

To make the most of what is special about digital environments, designers need to deepen their analysis of affordance landscape. In Gibson's account (1966), affordances were opportunities for action. In his later writings, Gibson (1979) extended his interpretation of affordance well beyond the functional/dispositional properties of things (rooted in physically definable responses such as twisting or pulling) to the symbolic properties of things such as the meaning which stop signs, mail boxes, and other structures have, and whose identity is essentially cultural and symbolic. The suggestion that a mailbox affords letter posting, has seemed a reductio ad absurdum of the Gibsonian position to some readers. No one denies that humans respond adaptively to semantically and culturally laden stimuli. Our environment of action is obviously rich in semantic structures. The part of Gibson's later theory (1979) that alienates people is the claim that those semantic attributes can be perceived rather than processed by a different processing path, one which explicitly involves semantic retrieval, lexical priming, and so forth.

To avoid a battle over words, I will use the more neutral expression "cue structure" to refer to the richer field of task-relevant properties and structures in an environment that a designer can manipulate to help agents perform their tasks. This broader notion is meant to be wide enough to cover task-regulating attributes such as *artificial metrics* of closeness (inches, temperature readings, clocks, etc.) and *natural metrics* of closeness (fullness of a glass, loudness of a sizzle), which before I referred to as indicators. Competent agents constantly monitor such attributes as they perform their tasks. Cue structure also includes the interactive components of an environment such as navigational cues, which are displayed by visual means but which also carry a meaning. The meaning of these cues may be conventional, they may be inferred by association with similar cues whose meaning is known, or they may be learned by practice with similar cues.

For instance, road signs, links on a web site, annotations, section headings, and subheadings in a document are all familiar examples of visual cues which carry meaning. They typically carry information about what is outside one's immediate view, or, in the case of section headings, they carry metainformation about the semantic content of what is coming up in the section. One either knows what these cues mean just because one knows language, or one has learned what they mean in these sorts of contexts by experience. This latter type of learning is important. Knowledge of language is sufficient to know the literal meaning of a heading, but people require knowledge of the function that that language serves in these sorts of contexts to know that it tells them something important about the content of the next written section. The same holds for navigational links, annotations, and so on. In addition to having a literal content, they serve a functional role: commenting, signposting. These important aspects of visual cues do not seem to be affordances. They are similar to affordances in having functional roles, but their roles cannot be properly understood without knowing the meaning of the language they display.

For instance, the button labeled [Edit] has to be understood as offering editing possibilities to something near to it. The visual connection between the button and the file to which it refers helps us as users to understand the function of the button. But it will be a meaningless visual connection unless we also understand that the text nearby is a label for the file we can edit. This functional connection between button and file relies on an understanding of context that goes beyond understanding the function of the button. It requires that we know which file the button will interact with. Figure 6.4 shows the same concern, this time with a standard e-commerce button. Users have to know which item they are going to be pricing. They must appreciate that the "Check latest prices" button is linked to the sound card presented in the same visual region.

Visual cues such as proximity or grouping or coloring can combine with semantic cues to disambiguate the meaning and functionality of buttons, headings, labels, annotations, and so on. Whether people are aware of it or not, they rely on such cues to improve the way they interact with their environments. Visual cues help to structure the environment, and well-designed environments distribute such cues wisely.

A well designed cue structure can improve cognitive workflow because cues play such an important role in the coordination between agent and environment. If the environment is well designed, then users have an easier time of deciding what to do next and an easier time setting things up so that they can continue to keep their work activity under control. In working, they look, interpret, act, modify the environment, review, and start this perceive act review cycle over again. When the environment is set up well, this dynamic cycle is easier to maintain in a goal-oriented direction. The environment alerts the agent when an action has been taken or when it is successful, it exposes the actions that might be done or, in the ideal case, the actions that are best to do.

I define *cognitive workflow* as follows: Cognitive workflow is the physical and mental activity involved in keeping agent and environment appropriately coordinated to achieve the agent's goals (Kirsh, 2001). This includes all the movements and changes intentionally made to documents, windows, desktop elements, and all the other task-relevant structures that figure in getting things done in a particular space. It naturally includes attending to

Creative Sound Blaster Live! 5.1 Digital - sound card 20pk
Manufacturer: Creative
Specs: PCI, 5.1 channel surround, Microsoft Windows 95 OSR 2, Microsoft Windows 98/ME/2000, Microsoft Windows XP

compare

▸ Check latest prices

$19-$574
Add to my list

FIG. 6.4. The button-like appearance of "Check latest prices" helps users to know that it is a clickable element. However, it is the combination of the e-commerce context, the words on the button, and the visual design that helps users to figure out what clicking the button will do. Without a thoughtful visual presentation, users could easily be confused about which item they are pricing. For in fact, the name of the sound card being priced here is physically farther than the name of the next sound card that, although not shown here, is immediately below the button. To prevent confusion shading and layout make apparent which product a given button is tied to.

and interpreting the semantic aspects of cue structure as well as the nonsemantic aspects of affordance landscape. Cognitive workflow is about how agent and environment are causally and cognitively coupled, about how as a coordinated team, the system of agent and environment moves toward goal states. For instance, to prompt future activity agents sometimes write things down, sometimes they rely on prospective memory. Both are semantic cues that drive future action. If it were possible to track how a person comes to a decision by magically peeking into their minds, we would see them sometimes accessing internal memory and sometimes looking around and interpreting the contents of external 'memory.'

There is much more to cognitive workflow, however, than moving back and forth between internal and external memory. Not that this is trivial. By storing retrieval cues about where to look rather than storing full memory entries agents save resources and increase their power. Why remember when you can just look? But memory is only a fraction of cognition. It is dependent on prior interpretational activity, because what people remember depends on how they interpreted the situation they remember. How people interpret things is another aspect of cognitive coupling that cue structure can facilitate.

The connection between workflow and interpretation emerges from the constructive nature of action. People create structures in their environments that bias the way they interpret things. In the simplest case, this is achieved by writing down a language-based reminder or hint that activates an interpretive frame. But the more pervasive case is non-linguistic.

A useful example of how agents alter their environments to facilitate interpretation can be found in math when a student is trying to discover a rule that generates the sequence 2, 8, 18, 32, and 50. Most people try out conjectures on paper first, writing down differences and looking for patterns. Why is that? The goal is to find a good interpretation of the number sequence, a pattern. Usually this cannot be done without first creating additional structure to explore the interpretation space. Exploration, here, is part of the interpretation process because each time new number relations are exposed, the agent reconceptualizes the sequence.

How common is this sort of activity? How much of interpretive activity is based on an analogue of this active approach to discovering patterns and meaning? I believe it is pervasive.

Few questions are more central to interaction designers than the nature of exploration and active interpretation. Agents project structure (i.e., interpret their situation), they create structure (i.e., they act on their environments), and then on the basis of the two, they reproject or reinterpret. As designers, our job is to support this dialectic between projection and creation, between internal representation and externalizing structure better. We need to set up the environment so that users can build a better situational awareness of where they are in their activity. This concern with users' situational awareness is as much a matter of facilitating their metacognition as it is with facilitating first-order cognition. How is it being met in e-document design?

CUE STRUCTURE AND DIGITAL DOCUMENT DESIGN

Situational awareness may seem an odd topic to consider when looking at the structure of documents, especially digital documents. However, designers are always trying to improve the sense of presence readers have when working with large online materials. To put closure on this inquiry, I turn now to how the cue structure of paper and online newspapers have been designed to support situational awareness and metacognition.

Lessons derived from newspaper design are especially informative for e-learning designers because newspapers have successfully made the transfer from paper to online versions. Newspapers are like textbooks in that they cover a range of topics in varying degrees of depth. Both cover factual material. Both try to present the material in an interesting way that engages their readers, and newspapers now, especially online versions, typically contain a number of interactive components that enhance user experience. There is much to be learned by looking at the visual and interactive design of newspapers.

Two characteristics of newspapers deserve special comment. First, they contain a large number of visual elements, and second, these visual elements allow readers to plan and monitor their reading experience.

Visual Elements

In Fig. 6.5, we see a typical modern newspaper front page and a list of the specific visual elements being used to identify regions and attract eyes. Not all newspapers have as much visual complexity as found in this example. However, in every modern newspaper one will find most of the key elements identified here. This is in contrast with papers 50 years ago that were both simpler and textually heavier. See Fig. 6.6. Clearly, papers have undergone an important design revolution—a revolution that in many respects has anticipated the changes found in good writing for the web.

When one compares the two papers in Fig. 6.5 and Fig. 6.6, perhaps the most obvious difference, aside from the change from an eight-column to five-column format, is the huge increase in the number of visual features found in the paper in Fig. 6.5. In modern newspapers, there may be as many as 12 or 13 different types of visual attractors on the front page. These highlight specialized regions of the page or call out particular semantic elements such as pictures, captions, or bylines. This increase in the number of visual

FIG. 6.5. There is more visual complexity in this modern newspaper designed by Tim Harrower than in most. We can identify almost a dozen different types of visual attractors vying for the eye of the reader. Readers faced with decisions about what to read first are drawn by visual elements and then either scan or move on. Once a reader has scanned the beginning of a story, he or she must decide whether to dive deeper into the paper or check another story on the front page. How do readers decide?

elements is not merely a visual change. Modern newspapers also have types of semantic elements not found in earlier papers.

For instance, in Fig. 6.5 there is an index, a jump line, reverse type, illustrations, and other "infographics" as well as teasers. Some of these new features are prevalent because the cost of printing has fallen. No longer is it prohibitively expensive to publish several pictures on a single page, even color ones. Computer typesetting allows designers to use new graphic techniques without increasing cost significantly. Callouts can be added in

The Old York Times

HINDENBURG BURNS IN FIERY CRASH
21 DEAD, 64 ESCAPE, 12 MISSING

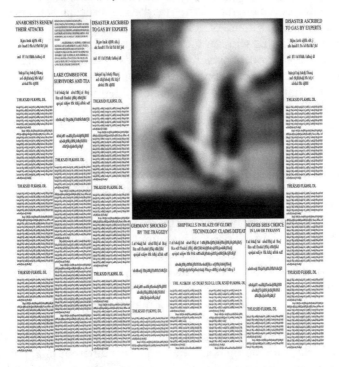

FIG. 6.6.   In this classic *New York Times,* the story of the Hindenburg disaster is told through long textual stories mostly unrelieved by images or other visual aids. The *New York Times* itself, at that time, was an eight column paper with several of the articles having multiple decks to give the gist of the contents of the long articles.

or around existing text and "wire frames" of the sort seen in Fig. 6.1b can be applied to regions, all at the last minute and without concern for cost. But some of these new features are found in newspapers because their readers have changes. Modern readers are more impatient, and they expect to get their information more visually through photos, charts, maps, diagrams, and callouts as well as through classical presentation of text.

One thing that newspapers can teach designers is that every semantic element ought to have an identifiable visual cue to help readers identify it. Font size, indentation, proximity to other elements, grouping, contrast, font style, and positioning: all of these affect the way readers take in material.

Some of these are more eye catching than others. Size is obviously a powerful attention getter, so much so that in newspapers, well-trained readers can interpret the importance of an event by the pica size of the headline alone.

Similarly, in textbooks, there are visually distinctive formats for titles, abstracts, headings, subheadings, graphics, captions, and page numbers. The topic sentence of a paragraph is not marked as a special sentence by anything as immediate as italics or bold font, but it is still indicated by being the only sentence starting with an indentation, or beginning after a few extra pixels of line separation, or by a change in font size (when appearing immediately after a heading). The concluding sentence too, although not marked by features that pop out, is nonetheless identifiable as the sentence immediately preceding the next paragraph.

Other semantic elements are marked by visual cues that are more prominent. Phrases or words of particular importance may be bolded or italicized, and callouts may appear in the margin or in different font type. Each of these visual techniques exercises some cue strength over a reader's eye such that what he or she does next, whether it be scan the big font headings, skim the italicized phrases, or leaf through subsequent pages to see how much there is to read, is a partial response to the cue structure presented.

Faced with this barrage of subtle manipulation, readers are faced with an almost continuous demand for metacognition. In books designed to be read linearly, this demand is less apparent. Readers have to follow the thread and understand how the current content makes sense given the context of what has come before. This may seem less a matter of visual design than good writing. Yet in newspapers, both paper and online varieties (see Fig. 6.7), magazines, and online textbooks in which there is always the opportunity to leave one's current reading point and jump to a different link, page, or image, readers are constantly making evaluations. To be efficient, readers need to plan how to read. They must monitor their reading for comprehension and the rate of return they are getting for their time. Given some (implicit) measure of this rate of return, they have to then decide whether to change to a new information source in the same newspaper, change to a new information environment, read in a different manner, perhaps skimming or spending more time on illustrations, or whether to stop reading altogether and do something else.

Just as with eye movement research, it is possible to develop a model based on Bayesian assumptions of maximum information to see if ordinary readers, even ones accused of little metacognition, can be deemed to be rational Bayesians in the way they move about a newspaper. I do not offer the equation here because it is an empirical matter just how accurately such a model predicts the visual and physical behavior of the average reader, and I have not tested the model experimentally. However, any trip on a New York or London subway in the early morning shows that decisions about when to

FIG. 6.7.   In the online version of the *New York Times* there are many more headlines and links to pages than are found in the paper version. The home page serves both as a traditional front page and also as an index, specifying more extensively the other pages and sections to be found in the current edition.

move deeper into a newspaper are constantly being made on the basis of reading and scanning the front page, and these decisions are clearly biased by the cue structure of the page. To be scientific, any such model must begin with a theory of user interests and goals because the maximally informative place to look depends on a reader's interests and the tasks he or she is trying to accomplish. This soon becomes even harder to estimate because interests and goals may change opportunistically, in response to unanticipated possibilities. However, this just reemphasizes that reading a complex document such as a newspaper is an activity in which interests interact with cue structure in a complex and dynamic manner.

The idea that distinctive visual elements exercise an attractive force over eyes and readers is even more apparent in the online versions of newspapers. In online newspapers, readers have to make their decision on less metadata because there are no decks or bylines augmenting headlines. Entry points or links to new text are clearly marked, but there are so many more of them present in online papers that there is greater need for the reader to decide whether to dive into a story or scan more headings before committing to any one article.

In the best e-newspapers, interactivity and extra multimedia are used to compensate for reduced metadata. In Fig. 6.8 one can see how this is accomplished via an interactive illustration. The topic here, home fires, is described well enough to situate the user in a relatively rich visual context, and then it is up to the user to choose which avenue of information to pursue. Clicking on a link leaves the house image in place while providing textual elaboration of the chosen topic.

In even better interactive illustrations, see Fig. 6.9, the trade-off between clutter and more metadata is altered by reducing the cost of displaying metadata. For instance, in many illustrations, mousing over a visual region or link provides a quick chunk of metadata, putting users in a better position to decide what to pursue in greater depth. This is the approach taken in Fig. 6.9 where mousing over topics in the timeline provides additional information.

The net effect of thoughtful interactivity and layout is that users have greater knowledge of where they are in local information space, and the actions and content that are nearby. The result is an improved situational awareness, a better metacognitive understanding of their activity space.

Road access: Homeowners should know the location of the closest fire department. What are the conditions of the roads and bridges leading to the property? Cul-de-sacs need a radius large enough – at least 45 feet – to accommodate a fire truck. Property and roadways should be clearly marked.

Source: National Interagency Fire Center, Firewise, MSNBC research.
Printable version

FIG. 6.8.   The cue structure of this interactive document is easier to identify and the behavior of users easier to track. There are three "pages," each with six to eight single paragraph descriptions.

FIG. 6.9. In this quartet of images taken from MSNBC's science section, Earth's timeline is shown in a compact manner. Clicking on an era, such as Cenozoic, opens a new tier of navigation while simultaneously changing the map of the earth. Mousing over the term "Global Shifts" overwrites the map with a description that calls attention to the shifts the user/student should notice. By having all information in a common frame users can click through eras and see geological changes in the same region. This helps the user note small differences in continent position, but when differences are large it is visually more effective to lay out frames in a side by side manner.

CONCLUSION

The thesis advanced here is that metacognition is a standard element of much, if not most, of everyday activity. People make decisions all the time concerning when to leave one area of exploration or reading or thinking and begin another. This sort of "reasoning" is rampant in reading newspapers and documents of all sorts. It is the norm of intelligent behavior and may even take place unconsciously. Much of this follows, I believe, from the tenets of situated and distributed cognition. The extra element I have been arguing for is that visual layout—whether of 3D learning environments or of documents—can have a significant effect on the ease with which people make these metacognitive decisions. Visual layout can affect work flow. Our goal as designers of e-learning environments, or more precisely as theoreticians of design, is to understand the principles that affect cognitive effort and metacognitive decision making and incorporate these into our environments.

The principles discussed here have all had to do with how agents' interaction with their environments can be made more coordinated and more efficient by shaping the cue structure of the environment they operate in. One reason metacognition is not fundamentally different in kind from cognition *simplicitur* is that both are concerned with managing the dynamic way in which agents project and create structure. This dynamic, which has much to do with cognitive work flow, can be influenced by cue structure because when cues are effectively distributed in an environment, they make it easier for agents to see what they can do next. Layout is one of the simplest aspects of cue structure. Another important aspect is interactivity. Designers of digital environments are acutely aware of the power of both visual layout and interactivity. My primary objective here has been to point out that this concern is justified and that with a deeper understanding of the way human agents are embedded in their environments, we may hope to inform better design.

ACKNOWLEDGMENTS

I thank Peter Gärdenfors, Petter Johansson, and the Lund University Cognitive Science program for helpful comments on ideas presented here.

REFERENCES

Agre, P. E., & Chapman, D. (1987). Pengi: An implementation of a theory of activity. In *Proceedings of the Sixth National Conference on Artificial Intelligence AAAI National Conference* (pp. 268–272). Morgan Kaufman.

Blake, A., & Yuille, Y. (Eds.). (1993). *Active vision*. Cambridge, MA: MIT Press.

Canetti, E. (1962). *Crowds and power*. London: Victor Gollancz.

Chaitin, G. J. (1975). Randomness and mathematical proof. *Scientific American, 232* (5), 47–52.

Clark, A. (1998). *Being there: putting brain, body, and world together again*. Cambridge, MA: MIT Press.

Gibson, J. J. (1966). *The senses considered as perceptual systems*. Boston: Houghton Mifflin.

Gibson, J. J. (1979). *The ecological approach to visual perception*. Boston: Houghton Mifflin.

Hartshorne, C., & Weiss, P. (Eds.). (1960). *C. S. Peirce: Collected papers*. Cambridge, MA: Belknap Press of Harvard University Press.

Hutchins, E. (1995). *Cognition in the wild*. Cambridge, MA: MIT Press.

Kirsh, D. (1990). When is information explicitly represented? In P. Hanson (Ed.), *Information, language and cognition: Vancouver studies in cognitive science* (pp. 340–365). Vancouver, British Columbia, Canada: UBC Press.

Kirsh, D. (1995). The intelligent use of space. *Artificial Intelligence, 73,* 31–68.

Kirsh, D. (1999). Distributed cognition, coordination and environment design. In *Proceedings of the European conference on Cognitive Science* (pp. 1–11).

Kirsh, D., & Maglio, P. (1995). On distinguishing epistemic from pragmatic action. *Cognitive Science, 18,* 513–549.

Li, M., & Vitanyi, P. (Eds.). (1997). *An introduction to kolmogorov complexity and its applications* (2nd ed.). Springer-Verlag.

Wittgenstein, L. (1953). *Philosophical investigations.* Oxford, England: Blackwell.

7

External Cognition, Innovative Technologies, and Effective Learning

Mike Scaife
Yvonne Rogers[1]
University of Sussex

Bruner (1972) once observed that "What a culture does to assist the development of the powers of mind of its members is, in effect, to provide amplification systems to which human beings, equipped with appropriate skills, can link themselves" (p. 53). Bruner's (1972) thesis was to develop an account of how a society should proceed in presenting the developing child with skills or beliefs or knowledge in "a form capable of being mastered by a beginner" (p. 53). This question, although posed more than 30 years ago, is highly relevant to much contemporary Information and Communication Technology (ICT) research. Further, Bruner's analysis is predicated on an important fact about the ways that humans operate in the world: They are highly resourceful at exploiting their environment to extend their cognitive capabilities, and they do this with a variety of strategies, tools, and representations. This, broadly speaking, is what we refer to as "external cognition." Understanding why and how this works in the case of rapidly evolving technologies such as ICT requires, we argue, a framework (or frameworks) that allow people to see technologies in as wide a context as possible and consequently, to better understand how and why we might make use of them in a

---

[1]Now at Indiana University

range of particular contexts: education, work, play, or leisure. In this respect, one needs to look at individual technologies both (a) as tokens of a wider type such as "tools" and (b) in terms of their specific properties or capabilities that might allow genuinely novel opportunities for learning. A result of this should be to derive some lessons for a more fruitful relation between research, design, and implementation in educational settings.

Here we are interested in developing a conceptual framework that can lead to a better understanding of the basis on which to design and use new technologies to support learning. Our focus is on the ways that technologies can allow new forms of representations—one not possible with existing media—and how these might be exploited for learning. This is not easily done simply by extrapolating from our understanding of existing media and technologies because not a great deal of generalizable information is known about the cognitive mechanisms that underpin learning from a wide variety of them, be they traditional (e.g., pictures) or novel (e.g., animations, multimedia, virtual reality; Scaife & Rogers, 1996). Thus, we proposed an emphasis on the need for an identification of the different kinds of cognitive benefits that particular representational formats and technologies may provide, what Scaife and Rogers (1996) call an analysis of "cognitive interactivity." In this chapter, we exemplify how such analysis can be used to help design learning environments by reference to research carried out by us at the INTERACT Laboratory. The examples will include a relatively mature technology, interactive multimedia (IMM), as well as two newer arrivals—virtual worlds with autonomous agents and mixed reality environments.

IMM

In terms of potential benefits for learners, IMM seems to offer much in the way of novel forms of representations (through its ability to combine graphics, animations, text, audio, video, etc.) and interactivity (by allowing the user to select, manipulate, and combine these representations). In particular, one of the major advantages offered for designing learning environments is IMM's capacity to develop novel ways of providing/viewing/ interacting with multiple representations. This is a significant feature because a common strategy in classroom teaching is to get students to interact with and use multiple representations (e.g., text, diagrams, pictures) when learning about a topic. For example, data may be shown as a table, graph, and histogram all depicting the same mathematical information in different formats. There is, here, an assumption that learning about a domain through multiple representations (different views on the same topic or concept) can engender different ideas while also helping learners constrain their interpretations. Furthermore, it is often argued that the more appropriately different representations are integrated by the learner, the more likely it is that "deeper" understanding will occur (Kaput, 1989).

A key research question this raises is what is the best way to coordinate different kinds of representations to support learning? One of the reasons why learners may find it difficult to integrate multiple representations is the fact that it requires additional work: They have to both interpret the individual representations and to translate between them (cf. Ainsworth, 1999; Cox, 1999; Narayanan & Hegarty, 2000; Rogers, 1999). Furthermore, the mappings between the representations may not be at all obvious to learners, making it confusing for them to try to switch between them. A key issue, therefore, when providing multiple representations for learning is to consider how to support better the translation process so that it is more obvious and explicit to the learner. This raises issues about what should be represented. For example, one strategy might be to use the representations to depict the same concept but at different levels of abstraction. This, perhaps, would lead to deeper understanding because deeper levels of description were being provided. An example of this, which we use in the system described following, is that of combining a "realistic" simulation of a domain with more abstract formalisms representing it. Used in this way, each representation can provide a different perspective but also map onto each other, guiding the learner to reflect on the relation between them. However, simply displaying representations at different levels of abstraction will not by itself enable the learner to understand the relation between them (Jones & Scaife, 2000; Rogers, 1999). What is also needed is a way of allowing the learner to actively explore the mappings.

To achieve some progress with this, we decided to apply a cognitive interactivity analysis (Scaife & Rogers, 1996). At the top level, the framework focuses on the properties of external representations in terms of their contributions to "computational off-loading": the extent to which different external representations reduce or increase the amount of cognitive effort required to understand or reason about what is being represented (and see Cheng, 1999; Larkin & Simon, 1987). High off-loading is where much of the effort is off-loaded onto the representation, requiring minimal effort on behalf of the learner for a given task. In our analysis, we identified several ways of achieving off-loading by manipulating the representational format (e.g., Cheng, Lowe, & Scaife, 2001; Rogers & Scaife, 1998). An apt example in the present context is that of rerepresentation—how different external representations that have the same abstract structure make problem solving easier or more difficult (see also Peterson, 1994; Zhang & Norman, 1994). These kinds of cognitive characterizations provide us with a starting point from which to begin to think about the value of using and combining different representations for different tasks. However, we need a more detailed analysis to decide, for example, on which combinations of representations to use to aid a given stage of learning. We now outline our own research to show how such decisions may be made.

INTERACTIVE ECOLOGY LEARNING (Ecoi): UNDERSTANDING DYNAMIC (eco)SYSTEMS

The chosen area for our research was that of understanding dynamic systems. Previous work has shown that children have considerable difficulty understanding how they work (e.g., Griffiths & Grant, 1985). Here we selected ecosystems as the example domain. Younger children encounter problems in learning about this using existing materials, particularly static diagrams in which the conventions of reading the food web's interrelation using the arrow links between nodes remains mysterious. Consequently, children are unable to reason about the food web as a whole and when asked to predict the knock-on effects of extinction of a species for others in the food web are unable to do so.

To us (Rogers and Scaife, 1998), therefore, the learning task seemed to be one of (a) explicating the meaning of the food-web links and (b) supporting integration of knowledge of the parts of the food web into a meaningful whole. We felt that the learner needed to understand what the diagram is about by mapping its structure to the world it represents. IMM seemed promising here because it has the capacity for providing a means by which multiple representations can be explicitly and dynamically linked with each other ("dynalinking"), a form of rerepresentational off-loading. This allows us to address the issue of the learner mapping between representations in ways that traditional media simply cannot. Thus, we designed Ecoi, an IMM system centered on a software prototype called "PondWorld," representing a simple pond ecosystem. The basic display was an animated simulation of the creatures in the pond and another, overlaid window showing some formalism of the ecosystem. It was aimed specifically at explaining food-web diagrams for 9- to 11-year-old children who were learning about basic ecosystem concepts in school. In terms of our framework, we wanted learning to be incremental, systematically decreasing the amount of off-loading by increasing the level of abstraction and task complexity as the learner progressed. Thus, the system was designed to be experienced as a succession of modules for each of which we chose forms of interactivity suitable for its degree of difficulty and the learning task. The modules are shown in Fig. 7.1.

Module 1: Learning Factual Knowledge

The level of computational off-loading in module one is high: There is little inferencing to do, and learners have only to interact with the animation by pointing, clicking, and listening to voices. The learning process supported in this module is obtaining factual knowledge: feeding relation between a set of organisms in the community. The animation shows fish predators eat-

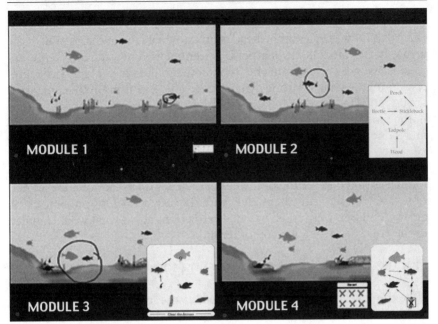

FIG. 7.1.   Finding out about PondWorld.

ing water beetles, water beetles eating tadpoles, and tadpoles consuming weeds. The child interacts with the animation by rolling the cursor over the organisms, which produces a loudspeaker icon. Clicking on this results in a "voice" from the creature telling the learner what it is and what it eats. The voices used were designed to vary in pitch, from low (top predator) to high (weeds)—a design idea based on a suggestion by the children during an in-formant design session (see Scaife, Rogers, Aldrich, & Davies, 1997). For example, clicking on the largest predator results in a deep voice: "I'm a perch, I eat beetles and tadpoles." By contrast, the primary food source says in a high-pitched, squeaky voice, "I'm a weed. I make my own food." The child's attention is further drawn to salient relations by having a red circle appear around feeding episodes, such as around a beetle eating a tadpole. After interacting with this module, a multiple choice quiz is presented on the screen allowing the learner to immediately test their knowledge of the feeding relations.

Module 2 "IntroWeb": Learning to Read the Diagram

Here the level of computational off-loading is still relatively high. The learning process supported in this module consists of understanding what the canonical notation (the arrow) used in food-web diagrams represents, that is, that the species at the head of an arrow eats the one at the tail of the arrow. In this module, the learner is presented with two adjacent representations: a food-web diagram and a concrete simulation of it. The two representations are coupled using dynalinking: The organisms in the animation are designed to behave in relation to the abstract feeding relations depicted in the food web. For example, clicking on the arrow link between the weed and tadpole in the food-web diagram results in the animation showing a token weed slowly being eaten by the tadpole. The learner has to select different feeding relations (as represented by the arrows) in the food-web formalism and observe the outcomes of their action in the concrete animation. After familiarizing themselves with the task by clicking on some of the arrows, children were asked to make predictions about what would happen in the pond before clicking on other links.

Module 3 "LinkWeb": Constructing the Diagram

Here the level of off-loading is reduced, as the learner has to consolidate and generalize knowledge from the previous module by constructing a food-web diagram in a new situation in which extra species are added. The child fills in the links by clicking on the organisms in the correct order (e.g., slime eaten by snail) on the diagram. Again, the purpose of dynalinking was to encourage the learner to make explicit links between the different levels of abstraction. Feedback is displayed in the form of colored arrows, which appear when the correct feeding relations have been linked. Children were asked to complete the whole diagram.

Module 4 "EraserWeb": Holistic Reasoning

The final module was designed to show the same two interlinked representations as in LinkWeb. This time, however, the learner was required to infer what would happen to the ecosystem when it is perturbed, that is, when one of the species is removed. The objective here was to get the learner to reason about the ecosystem as a whole (i.e., what the consequences will be for the other organisms) by reading off and interacting with the food-web diagram. An example perturbation is demonstrated initially through a narrated animation of what would happen to the ecosystem when the tadpoles are removed. The demonstration shows crosses placed sequentially on the organisms in the diagram to indicate the knock-on effects through the ecosystem as a consequence of tadpole extinction. At the same time, their concrete counterparts in the adjacent simulation are removed from the pond—the module again emphasizing the dynalinking between the two forms of representation. The child is then presented with two problems to solve by

themselves by working out which other organisms will die off as a consequence of one of the species being removed from PondWorld. To complete
this, the child is required to drag and drop crosses from an adjacent palette
onto the organisms they think will die in the food-web diagram, having verbally made predictions of what would happen first. Hence, the level of
off-loading is low: Even though the diagram provides the means by which to
reason about the ecosystem, the learner needs to know how to use it and to
reason correctly about which species will or will not be plausibly affected.

EVALUATING Eco1

The final version of Pondworld was tested with 9- to 10-year-old children
working in pairs to see whether it was effective for supporting learning in the
ways that we hypothesized. The children were allowed to interact with the
software with a minimum of intervention by the adult experimenter and
took from 25 to 45 min. Pairs were given a pretest and a posttest to assess
learning. The chief benchmark for success was that experience with the
software should result in a generalizable understanding of the abstract formalism of the food web such that the child will be able to reason better
about possible changes to the ecosystem purely on the basis of a diagram.
The formal testing, before and after using the system, utilized a different
food-web diagram to PondWorld to factor out the possible influence of rote
knowledge (or clever guesses) of species behavior. The children were asked
a series of questions about the different species tokens in the web such as (a)
"what does this one eat?," requiring that they read the arrows correctly; (b)
"what will happen if we take this one away?," requiring that they identify the
knock-on effects of removal in a simple way; and (c) "what produces its own
food?," a test of understanding how a food web layout usually places consumers and producers at different levels.

Overall, 11 pairs out of 14 (79%) showed statistically significant improvement and 3 pairs (21%) showed none. This was good evidence of improvement, but more revealing findings came from the detailed behavioral
observations during their experiences with PondWorld. We saw many instances of an "aha!" learning experience when the results of the animation
contradicted experience. For example, on the IntroWeb module, 1 pair's dialogue was as follows when discussing what would happen if they clicked on
link between species:

A: "Nothing will happen because the weed makes its own food" (initial
    prediction)
B: "Oh No! The tadpole's eaten the weed" (as a result of seeing the an-
    imation). And then a generalization to a previously misunderstood
    interaction with a simple three-item food chain seen in class

A: "Oh, so that's what that thing ... the arrows go up so the leaf gets
       eaten by the caterpillar and the caterpillar gets eaten by the bird."

By the time they had got to EraserWeb, most of the pairs were working
with the diagram by following the arrows, node by node, determining
whether the tokens for each of the species would die off as a consequence of
the weed being removed—indicating that they were understanding and using the diagram in the way it was supposed to be used. This contrasts sharply
with their inability in the pretest. As an example, one pair discussed the implications of an organism eating more than one other organism. The system
presents the scenario: The weeds have gone from the pond.

C: That (pointing to the tadpole) would die first because that eats the
       weed. And then one of those two would die (points to beetle and
       stickleback).
D: but that (pointing to the snail) eats weed as well.
C: That eats weed as well, so .... Yeah, but that eats slime as well, so
       that can survive on slime.

The apparent success of Ecoi would seem to demonstrate that our insistence on and methods for mapping between cognitive analysis and design
were well founded. We argued that the use of dynamically linked multiple
representations, abstraction tied to simulation, would facilitate the semantic task of understanding what the diagram links were about. We further argued that progressively increasing the level of abstraction would help to
integrate understanding into a more holistic domain model. Finally, we proposed that allowing the learner to actively manipulate the representation
would be important. All of these claims seem to have been supported in
what we observed. Indeed, the children actually performed on the posttests
at a level not expected of them until several more years of schooling had
been completed.

VIRTUAL WORLDS, VIRTUAL CHARACTERS

An IMM system such as Ecoi can, as we have shown, provide a rich environment in which new forms of representation can be offered to learners to give
them a different view of difficult problem spaces. However the kinds of
phenomenological experiences are limited when compared to more powerful three-dimensional (3D) virtual environments (VEs) that can offer opportunities for users for novel interactions with objects and navigation in
3D space. Many claims have been made about the benefits of interacting
with these kinds of VEs such as easier learning, better understanding, and
greater engagement (e.g., Allison, Wills, Bowman, Wineman, & Hodges,

1997; Psotka, 1995). More specifically, Wickens (1992) proposed that VEs encourage people to be more active in the way they interact with external representations through having to continuously choose their position and viewing perspective when moving through the virtual environment. In so doing, Wickens suggested that learning and retention of information can be increased. Whatever the general truth of such claims, it is the case that for our research, just as for the IMM example of the previous section, undertaking development of VEs necessitates posing specific questions about the particular properties of the media being implemented in relation to the task/goals under consideration. In this part of the chapter, we briefly describe an example of this from our own research (see Scaife & Rogers, 2001, for more details).

BUILDING A VIRTUAL THEATRE

The example project, the Virtual Puppet Theatre, had as its goal the creation of a virtual theatre for young (4–8 years old) children to support learning through playing (see Marshall, Rogers, & Scaife, 2002). Here, our aim was to provide young children with a means of extending their existing capacity for storytelling by providing them with a new set of tools that they could use to create, edit, direct, and act out plays in a virtual, imaginary setting. To do this, we created a child-friendly 3D world modeling a farm that allowed real-time interaction with and between believable life-like agents (virtual characters such as a farmer, sheep, or cow; see Fig. 7.2). The value of believable agents for storymaking has already been demonstrated, for example, by the Stanford Virtual Theatre and the Carnegie Mellon University (Mateas, 1997) Oz Project who developed the Woggle agent for microworlds. There is also increasing use of agents as assistants for children's learning in complex domains, for example, the Intellimedia project (Lester, Stone, & Stelling, 1999). For us, the value of using agents was first, that their behavioral characteristics could be scripted, for example, the response they exhibit when encountering another agent; and second, that they were autonomous, that is they would move and act by themselves. Thus, a simple story line could be set up and acted out by the agents on the basis of how their parameters were set. In the basic version of the virtual puppet theatre the child could, therefore, watch the story unfold as the agents encounter and interact with each other. However, such passive viewing was not particularly engaging for the children and does not provide much in the way of learning opportunities. For this reason, we built further facilities into the system that allowed the child far more interactivity.

One of our claims about the potential value of a virtual setting over and above a physical one is that it can provide an extensive range of novel supports for children to be creative. We started from a particular point of view on the

FIG. 7.2.   A scene from the virtual theatre showing a low-status cow and a high-status farmer.

possible differences between play in a physical (real world) and virtual environment. During the normal course of improvisational play, the child is dealing with ephemeral actions/interactions: They occur and are gone, and the child has no time to reflect on them. Using our (Scaife & Rogers, 1996) ideas on externalization, we argued that by contrast a virtual theatre can be structured to assist development of a number of different skills. For example, autonomous agents offer the possibility of characters, inside play, which are not ephemeral (in the child's imagination). They offer the potential for the child to "read" the motivations and intentions of the characters in situations, which are still playful. Providing avatar facilities, allowing them to view the world through the eyes of individual characters, is of particular interest here. The cognitive benefits of all this, we hypothesized, was that reading of agents will be a useful means for exposing the child to situations in which such decentering skills can be polished (cf. Piaget, 1972).

The scripting for the agents was based on a dramatic scenario of them trying to achieve certain simple goals: The farmer wished to have the animals neatly in their stables/pens; some animals wished to stray and others could act to either help or hinder the farmer. Goals were mediated through setting parameters for the states of the agents. The first was "status" (high or low), which determined how dominant or submissive the agent was in the interaction. The second, "attitude" (positive or negative) characterized the strategy of each, for example, cajoling versus herding for the farmer, fleeing versus confronting for the cow (see Fig. 7.2). These parameters changed as a function of the continuing interaction: They were not fixed. Thus, the basic model for the world was quite simple, but the combinatorial possibilities ensured that up to 10 min of varied interaction was possible between any two characters for a single run.

However, we wished to specifically promote the child's reflection on and consequent understanding of the different roles involved in story development and enactment. This is achievable by having the virtual theatre provide a variety of editing tools to build up/change agents' personality traits and behavior. For example, we provided a touchscreen interface that showed a number of icons portraying, for example, happy or sad expressions. Selecting an icon set the starting state for the agent in question for the next run of the scenario. Another facility allowed the child to stop the action and to record voices for the character. These clips then become attached to the particular status/attitude combination that the agent was demonstrating at the time of recording and would be played whenever the state was revisited during the scenario. Having such interactivities available allows, therefore, a continuum between the situation of just observing, as when children watch agents behave within the 3D world, and ones in which they manipulate the situation in a more direct fashion. The child could thus move between

- Spectating: The child observes the agents act in the virtual environment.
- Acting: The child joins the stage as an avatar and acts together with the agents.
- Directing: The child can make choices in terms of the agents' character or appearance and edit elements in a story line.

EVALUATION OF THE VIRTUAL PUPPET THEATRE

We have carried out an extensive evaluation of the virtual theatre (Marshall et al., 2002). A main finding was that the children's ability to read unambiguously what the agents are "up to" within the dramatic scenario described previously is not clear-cut. In observing mode, they do not seem to read the intentions and behaviors of the agents with much accuracy. This seems, however, to be at least partly due to their reduced interest—they have expectations derived from playing computer games that seem to determine what they perceive, for example, the farmer is often glossed as trying to kill the cow. However, once there is a greater degree of involvement (interactivity) such as taking an avatar view or being involved in recording, they pay far more attention, and the legibility of the characters increases markedly. This, however, has a strong age effect. Younger children (4 or 5 years) disregarded the status/attitude cues in deciding what sound each character should make. For example, when the farmer was in the state low-status, positive attitude, one 5-year-old chose to record as a sound file "I'm mad because of you! [angry tone]" and as a sound for the cow, also in a low-positive state after being taken back to its pen by the farmer, "I won't stay in my kennel [defiantly]." However, even if young children showed little sensitivity to the expressive elements of the improvisational scenario, this provides evidence that they were able to grasp the basic narrative and to some extent play with it.

Older children, however, exhibited a much greater sensitivity to the scenario. For example, an 8-year-old girl, when asked to provide a sound for the cow in low-positive, recorded "Do I have to? Will I still get my supper if I stay out here? I promise I really will be really good Mr. Farmer. Please." Thus, older children are sensitive to status differences. The same girl also demonstrated an understanding of character viewpoint, deducing that the sound made by the farmer when standing alone must be a monologue: "I think he must be talking to himself because he can't be talking to the cow," and "I'm glad Daisy's gone back in her pen now. She's a good girl and she shall get her supper."

The children seemed to greatly enjoy their encounters with the virtual puppet theatre and its characters once it was sufficiently interactive. The great successes of the project seems to lie in the demonstration of the power of agent worlds to engage children in playful interactions and of the value of providing tools for externalization to develop their understanding of motives and intentions.

MIXED REALITY ENVIRONMENTS (MREs)

Both the virtual puppet theatre and Ecoi were projects that explicitly focused on the power of representing things in a novel way in a virtual form. However, a different set of challenges and possibilities are offered by more recent advances in the design of interactive technologies, namely, MREs. Drascic and Milgram (1996) offered one description of them: "Between the extremes of real life and Virtual Reality lies the spectrum of Mixed Reality, in which views of the real world are combined in some proportion with views of a virtual environment" (p. 123). A good example of this is the work at the Nottingham Mixed Reality Laboratory (2001) where a poet was immersed in a virtual environment to control a virtual representation of himself and see a video view of the audience displayed within the world looking out from the stage. From a theoretical point of view, we consider a potential distinction for such MREs as being that between (a) a real world where spaces and artifacts are acted on by conventional physical actions and where the user's understanding is, therefore, in terms of general causal models of the world, and (b) a virtual world where a different and as yet little-understood set of causal models are applied and action may be arbitrarily coupled to the properties of the perceived world. However, the scope of MREs as sketched out previously is already insufficient. We now also have the possibility of extending the ontological profusion of worlds and objects to include in our MREs artifacts that might appear like regular physical objects but that have embedded intelligence of some sort: ubiquitous computing devices (Weiser, 1993). This raises the question of how people will deal with MREs that combine real, virtual, and ubiquitous forms. Such environments provide a challenge for understanding how we—as users—might appropriate them but also offer possibilities for learning in new ways and just as important, learning about new things. Thus, in the last of our three examples, we focus on the possibilities of MREs.

CONCEPTUALIZING MREs

The kinds of example ICT that the reader has already encountered in this chapter, IMM and VEs, have been glossed in terms of learning by using much conventional psychological terminology and concepts. However, in thinking about MREs, we need to take a different tack. Understanding what children, for example, will make of an MRE—and making design decisions about how such environments can be best configured—requires a high level of description in terms of a framework, at least initially. In the INTERACT Laboratory, we began by conceptualizing the issue in terms of "experiences": What is the phenomenology of being in and interacting with an MRE? How can we describe this or design for it? We have begun, as a heuristic ploy, to develop a taxonomy for describing a mixed reality experience in terms of "transforms": changes in the state of the world (Rogers, Scaife, Gabrielli, Smith, & Harris, 2002). People encounter and represent transforms between states of the world routinely in everyday life, for example, in perception (e.g., seeing an object disappear/reappear or changing one's viewpoint), in action (e.g., when the purpose of a gesture changes), and in cognition (as when we rerepresent and reinterpret the state of the world). Dealing with transforms will involve the user in some implicit or explicit theory of what causes changes of states, and this is something that we can investigate.

In an MRE, we can have real, virtual, and digitally enhanced objects or spaces, and we can design experiences that can cross between them, for example, action with a physical device, such as a wand, could result in an effect in a virtual space such as a projected display. We have decided to use the term *digital* (D) to refer to actions/activities/effects involving virtual or digitally enhanced artifacts. For the remainder we use *physical* (P) as a cover-all term. It is important to note that in using D and P as labels, we are referring to the mechanism that potentiates the transform. Thus, a "D action" (such as using a painting program on a display screen) inevitably involves some degree of P action on the part of the user, but it is the (D) mechanism that allows this that is crucial for us.

THE CHROMARIUM:
AN MRE FOR EXPERIMENTATION (2002)

To try out these conceptual distinctions we designed an MRE for young children as part of our contribution to the Equator Project (Rogers et al., 2002a). This was called the Chromarium (a space where color may be contained, observed, and experimented on). The goal here was to create a mixed reality space that enables children to experiment and play with color mixing across different media and representations. Thus, we designed a series of color-mixing tasks that could utilize either P or D actions and have their outputs in either P or D forms. This 2×2 design therefore gave us four classes of activity/transform types. For example, the P→P transform, with action and effect of the same kind, was mixing paints in pots. The D→P transform, with action and effect of different kinds, used interaction with an animation on a computer screen used to cause the differently colored blades on a small physical model windmill to rotate (mixing their colors).

Pairs of children, aged 6, took part in the Chromarium study. They were told that they would be mixing colors in fun and unusual ways and were allowed to explore the activities as they liked. To illustrate how the Chromarium was implemented, we described one example, the P→D transform. Here we used Radio Frequency (RF) technology to enable physical actions to trigger a virtual effect (RF tags are devices that can be hidden in objects, broadcasting their presence and thus recognizable to a suitable reader). Two colored blocks having a different color displayed on each face were built, each with an RF tag inside. The children could select blocks and place them on a table surface where they were detected by the tag reader concealed beneath the table. An animation (written in Macromedia Director, Version 8, 2001) mirroring the colors would appear projected onto a wall showing the effect of mixing the selected colors accompanied by a variety of sounds (Fig. 7.3).

We wanted children to both experience and reflect on their interactions, allowing some insight into their conceptualizations of these environments. The results from the children's explorations were quite complex. They en-

FIG. 7.3.   Children exploring the physical-digital transforming in the chromarium.

joyed activating the various transform types and were able to collaboratively discover creative ways of using the mixed reality setups for the activity of color mixing. They also made a variety of experiments into and reflections on the novel causality of the MRE. For the P→D transform, the example described previously, the children began by placing the blocks in towers to see whether anything would happen (we had not designed for this combination). They also pressed the blocks down hard on the table surface as if trying to amplify or speed up the feedback from the animation. Some of the children tried out different exploratory behaviors to discover how the block faces were read. They tried to put the blocks against the computer screen that was behind them or against the image projected on the wall to see if "any effect was coming out." They also tried to see if they could select a block's face for the animation by orienting it toward the area projected on the wall.

Activities performed in the mixed conditions, P→D and D→P, turned out to be the most effective for prompting children to provide causal explanations about the mechanism enabling the transforms. Their understanding of the causality involved in these transforms seemed to be affected by the fact that their actions produced effects in a different space. When we asked the children to explain where the effects (animations) of the physical manipulation of the blocks came from, they said things such as "the effect is coming from the computer's screen over there, and it arrives here by means of electricity." Another child pointing, first at the table under which the tag reader was concealed, then to the projected image, then to the computer, said "… connect, connect, connect … wire … it is connected under here [table] and goes all the way up to there!" [PC behind him]. Thus, children seemed to understand that there were causal links between distant objects and their actions, but their explanations were often an idiosyncratic mix of magical thought with bits of previous knowledge. For the D→P condition, some children did not believe that they could control in the virtual space the effect obtained in the physical world. A 6-year-old girl, for example, said that the spinning of the physical windmill was caused by the wind coming in from a window (even though no open window was available to justify this). Other children, however, were much more likely to seek contingent reasons for causal relations. For example, one pair looked under the table to discover which device was causing an effect and how the different bits of kit were connected to each other.

THE HUNTING OF THE SNARK: AN MRE FOR EXPLORATION AND IMAGINATION (2002)

The Chromarium was a first attempt to design MREs for the specific purposes of examining children's causal models of the new technologies and to see how these might be adapted for science experimentation. The Hunting of the Snark project has a wider brief, being aimed at enabling young children (8–10 years old) to create and be part of novel mixed reality experiences both indoors and, eventually, outdoors (Rogers et al., 2002b). This MRE is named as a nod to the Lewis Carroll story poem in which a group of people describe their encounters with an elusive, never really found, fantasy creature, the Snark. In our MRE, groups of children are given the task of finding out about a Snark: its form, likes/dislikes, personality, and so forth. The hunt made use of a search space—to look for things to help them find out more about the creature—and a separate set of other spaces, each instantiating a different MRE, as areas to go and look for it. The searching for clues was done using a handheld computer or "snooper" that allowed the children to move around a room and discover hidden objects. The snooper was sensitive to X-Y location in the room and could show a variety of visualizations on its screen as an aid to discovery. The objects that the children discovered could be used to enter or activate a space in which the Snark might be. Here we describe one example of such a space: "the well."

Initially, the children use the snooper to find "food" for the Snark. These are plastic food facsimiles (e.g., tomato, onion, piece of chicken) with an RF tag embedded inside each. The children take the food to the well, a place where the Snark is known to sometimes be. The well is, in essence, a horizontal screen allowing back projection so that visualizations may be projected on to it. At the well (Fig. 7.4) we provided a feeding device, a slot, where food could be posted into the (virtual) water that could be seen rippling at its surface. As the children approached the well, there was a sound of snoring coming from it. They could then rouse the Snark by gestures (interpreted through a gesture recognition system) and feed it by dropping food through the slot (with appropriate visualization of food dropping, sound of a splash, etc.). The result of these actions was to trigger different visualizations on the screen. For example, if the Snark was vegetarian (we could change its nature), vegetables would be received with a sight of an appreciative mouth and the sound of happy feeding noises. Feeding it meat would result in disgusted noises and an angry mouth. Once the food was all gone, the Snark would appear to swirl in the well and disappear through a tunnel in its side, cuing the next search for clues and discovery.

We used fairly abstract and changeable visualizations and sound effects to maximize the imaginative potential of the MRE. The children were told that they had to discover as much about the Snark as possible during the hunt, and this would be difficult if a highly specific and unchanging creature was provided. We gave them a "camera" to capture information, explaining that this would capture sound as well as visuals. It was basically a vibrating physical toy to which we added a "lens" and capture button. The camera worked by sending a signal to the software infrastructure when the

FIG. 7.4.   The "Well" showing a happy feeding expression.

button was pressed, allowing the system to store the current state of the Snark (what the children could see/hear of it at that point). At the end of the hunt, they could "download" what had been taken with the camera and see/hear it again. This procedure instantly reminded them of their experiences with the Snark, enabling them to reflect on what it was like, what it was doing, and so forth.

We have, here, only described the well, but there are several other activities in place involving the use of a range of technologies such as wearable computing and GPS devices. The children who have tried out the prototype system have been highly engaged and were fascinated by their MRE experiences (Rogers et al., 2002b). For the well, they had no difficulty understanding what they needed to do with the physical food tokens they had collected, that is, to transform them into "electronic" food for the Snark to eat, and they found the effects of their actions, the Snark liking or disliking certain foods, to be compelling and instantly recognizable. The children would reflect on these preferences, often based on their own experiences. For example, one child said the Snark didn't like onions was because it made it cry—as was true for the child.

In the Chromarium, we tried to conceptualize the activities in terms of transform types. For Snark, a key additional concept is that of "traversals"— experiencing things that cross the boundaries between physical and virtual spaces. Thus, the food objects in the well are physically present one moment and virtual food objects the next: They cross an ontological boundary. There is surely much potential here for the imaginative design of a new generation of learning environments.

CLOSING THOUGHTS

We began with a reminder of Bruner's (1972) insight into the value of technologies as amplifiers for bringing learners into the culture. In this chapter, we have encountered a richness in terms of ICT that must place it firmly among the ranks of such amplifiers with its potential to improve learning and understanding of the world. Our emphasis throughout has been that it is an extremely good idea to go about realizing this potential by first putting in place a theoretical framework that allows one to map between the possibilities afforded by technology and the kinds of skills or learning or other experiences one wishes for the child. Such a mapping will necessarily be context dependent, varying with the particular technology (what it might or might not do) and the goals for which we might use it. We summarize our own experiences in this regard as well as the lessons of the exercise.

For IMM we were able to focus on the ways in which dynalinking could "bring to life" the conventions and semantics inherent in a particular class of abstractions. With PondWorld, we hoped that the interactivity provided by the program would be effective in allowing students to go beyond the information given (Bruner & Anglin, 1973) to generate hypotheses to fill in the gaps in their understanding. However, we needed the cognitive interactivity framework to be able to design the specific modules: choosing an appropriate interactivity to gradually reduce the degree of computational off-loading. In this case, the evidence is quite clear that there was an increased ability to handle abstraction and to use the abstraction to make inferences about the represented domain.

The virtual world (agent/3D) technology offers a different set of potential properties to IMM, in particular, new kinds of objects to interact with. Again, in designing the system, we looked for a form of externalization that is consistent with our emphasis on the value of external cognition and the system's ability to do something that is difficult or impossible to do in the everyday world. For the virtual puppet theatre, we were able to use the capacity to interact with the autonomous agents as a platform for bringing out children's often implicit ideas about the motives and intentions of others and various editing facilities to allow the child to "step back" from the immediate action, promoting reflection and perhaps the development of narrative skills. This is, potentially, a highly creative process enabling children to do something relatively novel and one with a potentially substantial learning benefit as well.

The final class of technologies we looked at, the MREs, presented a less clear picture in the search for a mapping between cognitive analysis, technological capability, and learning advantages. One reason for this is that some of the basic elements of the MRE are still very much under development, for example, the various wireless technologies. Another is that one cannot clearly formulate cognitive analyses of optimal use in learning contexts until we have a better idea as to how children might appropriate the technology in the first place. Thus some of our research effort has been about discovering the ways children interact with and form causal explanations for the new experiences available in an MRE. The preliminary investigations reported here have shown that children's play and creativity as well as the their attempts at scientific investigation can be well supported by digitally augmented objects that children are free to manipulate in a 3D space as representational or pragmatic devices. Of particular relevance in this context is how children's creativity appears to be enhanced when their physical activity in the everyday world leads to rich multimedia effects in a digital space.

In this chapter, we have tried to show how cognitive interactivity might be a valuable conceptual tool, certainly for designing IMM and virtual world applications. We have also discussed an initial set of taxonomic devices for MREs, that of transforms and traversals, in an effort to capture and design for a new kind of experience for the user. It is these kinds of development that are needed to drive the design of effective learning environments.

ACKNOWLEDGMENTS

The authors gratefully acknowledge support for the research cited here from (a) the ESRC Cognitive Engineering Programme, Award No. L127251033 for the Ecoi project; (b) The EU i3 ESE Programme, Project EP 29335 for the Virtual Theatre project; and (c) The EPSRC for the Equator project, Award No. GR/N15986/01. Finally, thanks to the children, schools, and parents in East Sussex, United Kingdom for their help.

REFERENCES

Ainsworth, S. (1999). The functions of multiple representations. *Computers & Education, 33,* 131–152.

Allison, D., Wills, B., Bowman, D., Wineman, J., & Hodges, L. (1997). The virtual reality gorilla exhibit. *IEEE Computer Graphics and Applications, 17,* 30–38.

Bruner, J. S. (1972). *The relevance of education.* Middlesex, England: Hardmonsworth.

Bruner, J. S., & Anglin, J. M. (1973). *Beyond the information given: Studies in the psychology of knowing.* London: Allen & Unwin.

Cheng, P. (1999). Interactive law encoding diagrams for learning and instruction. *Learning and Instruction, 9,* 309–325.

Cheng, P., Lowe, R., & Scaife, M. (2001). Cognitive science approaches to understanding diagrammatic representations. *Artificial Intelligence Review, 15,* 79–94.

Cox, R. (1999). Representation construction, externalised cognition and individual differences. *Learning and Instruction, 9,* 343–363.

Drascic, D., & Milgram, P. (1996). Perceptual issues in augmented reality. In M. T. Bolas, S. S. Fisher, & J. O. Merritt (Eds.), *SPIE Volume 2653: Stereoscopic displays and virtual reality systems III.* San Jose, California, USA, 123–134.

Equator Project. Retrieved October 10, 2001 from www.equator.ac.uk

Griffiths, A. K., & Grant, B. A. (1985). High school student's understanding of food webs: Identification of a learning hierarchy and related misconceptions. *Journal of Research in Science Teaching, 22,* 421–436.

Jones, S., & Scaife, M. (2000). Animated diagrams: An investigation into the cognitive effects of using animation to illustrate dynamic processes. In M. Anderson & P. Cheng (Eds.), Theory and applications of diagrams. *Lecture Notes in Artificial Intelligence, 1889,* 231–244.

Kaput, J. J. (1989). Linking representations in the symbol systems of algebra. In S. Wagner & C. Kieran (Eds.), *Research issues in the learning and teaching of algebra* (pp. 167–195). Hillsdale, NJ: Lawrence Erlbaum Associates.

Larkin, J. H., & Simon, H. A. (1987). Why a diagram is (sometimes) worth ten thousand words. *Cognitive Science, 11,* 65–100.

Lester, J., Stone, B., & Stelling, G. (1999). Lifelike pedagogical agents for mixed-initiative problem solving in constructivist learning environments. *User Modelling and User-Adapted Interaction, 9,* 1–44.

Marshall, P., Rogers, Y., & Scaife, M. (2002). The value of a virtual environment for learning about narrative. *ACM SIGGROUP Bulletin, 23*(2), 14–15.

Mateas, M. (1997). An Oz-Centric Technical Report CMU-CD-97-156. School of Computer Science, Carnegie Mellon University, Pittsburgh, PA.

Mixed Reality Laboratory. (2001). Retrieved October 11, 2001 from www.mrl.nott.ac.uk/projects/performances.html

Narayanan, N. H., & Hegarty, M. (2000). Communicating dynamic behaviors: Are interactive multimedia presentations better than static mixed-mode presentations. *Proceedings of the 1st International Conference on the Theory and Applications of Diagrams*, Springer-Verlag, pp. 178–193.

Oz Project. Retrieved September 5, 2000, from www-2.cs.cmu.edu/afs/cs.cmu.edu/project/oz/

Peterson, D. (1994). Re-representation and emergent information in three cases of problem solving. In T. H. Dartnall (Ed.), *Artificial Intelligence and Creativity* (pp. 81–92). Dordricht: Honer.

Piaget, J. (1972). *The child and reality*. Paris: Editions Denoel.

Psotka, J. (1995). Immersive tutoring systems: Virtual reality and education and training. *Instructional Science, 23*, 405–431.

Rogers, Y. (1999). What is different about interactive graphical representations? *Learning and Instruction, 9*, 419–425.

Rogers, Y., & Scaife, M. (1998). How can interactive multimedia facilitate learning? In J. Lee (Ed.), *Proceedings of First International Workshop on Intelligence and Multimodality in Multimedia Interfaces* [CD-ROM]. Menlo Park, CA: AAAI Press.

Rogers, Y., Scaife, M., Gabrielli, S., Smith, H., & Harris, E. (2002a). A conceptual framework for mixed reality environments: Designing novel learning activities for young children. *Presence: Teleoperators and Virtual Environments, 11*, 677–686.

Rogers, Y., Scaife, M., Harris, E., Phelps, T., Price, S., Smith, H., Muller, H., Randall, C., Moss, A., Taylor, I., Siznton, D., O'Malley, C., Corke, G., & Gabrielli, S. (2002b). Things aren't what they seem to be: Innovation through technology inspiration. In *Proc. Dis '2002, Designing Interactive Systems Conference*, AMC, pp. 373–379.

Scaife, M., & Rogers, Y. (1996). External cognition: How do graphical representations work? *International Journal of Human–Computer Studies, 45*, 185–213.

Scaife, M., & Rogers, Y. (2001). Informing the design of a virtual environment to support learning in children. *International Journal of Human–Computer Studies, 55*, 115–143.

Scaife, M., Rogers, Y., Aldrich, F., & Davies, M. (1997). Designing for or designing with? Informant design for interactive learning environments. In S. Pemberton (Ed.), *Proceedings of CHI'97* (pp. 343–350). New York: ACM Press.

Virtual Theatre Project. Retrieved September 5, 2001 from www.ksl.stanford.edu/projects/cait/

Weiser, M. (1993). Ubiquitous computing. *Computer, 26*, 71–77.

Wickens, C. (1992). Virtual reality and education. In *Proceedings of IEEE International Conference on Systems, Man, and Cybernetics*, 842–847.

Zhang, J., & Norman, D. A. (1994). Representations in distributed cognitive tasks. *Cognitive Science, 18*, 87–122.

8

Seeing Through the Screen: Human Reasoning and the Development of Representational Technologies

Jonas Ivarsson
Roger Säljö
Gothenburg University

Material artifacts play a prominent role in most social practices. Humans learn and develop not only in a world of social relationships but also in a world of things. In spite of the ubiquity of physical objects in all that we do, most theoretical accounts of learning and development downplay or even disregard the fundamental manner in which our actions, insights, and modes of knowing are dependent on familiarity with and use of things. By failing to consider the role of such resources in human activities, most theoretical perspectives simultaneously downplay the role of artifacts in the cumulation of knowledge and skills in society at large.

In addition to the centrality of tools in most human practices in general, a large portion of the objects that figure in children's activities (e.g., various kinds of toys, games, books, computer software) in many societies is specifically manufactured with the ambition of developing cognitive and communicative skills of various kinds.

In a sociocultural perspective (Vygotsky, 1986; Wertsch, 1998), artifacts can be seen as objectifications of human intentions and insights. "What the child learns to see, to touch, to move around, to throw is a range of artifacts that already has a human significance for even the very young child" as Wartofsky (1983, p. 13) put it. As children relate to these objects in social practices, caregivers will provide guidance where the signifying functions of artifacts are central. In guided participation (Rogoff, 1990) children thus appropriate socioculturally prominent interpretations of the world around them through the use of artifacts. They learn about such diverse matters as techniques for counting, writing, and drawing, about gender roles, and how to compete in various kinds of games. Cultural psychologists and socio-cultural theorists argue that cognitive development is not universal but will depend on the specific social practices and the tools and technologies that children are exposed to and learn to use as mediational means (Cole, 1996; Leont'ev, 1978; Vygotsky, 1986).

In a technologically complex society, children develop skills in using a range of symbolic artifacts. These symbolic tools are intimately related to physical tools. In fact, it is in most cases not easy to make a distinction of this kind. Written language and counting systems are obvious examples of symbolic systems that are implemented by means of physical objects. How-ever, there is a wealth of artifacts that embody symbolic systems and nota-tions including maps, graphs, charts, drawings, and tables, to mention some examples. In a historical perspective, the trend seems to be fairly clear; people are exposed to an increasing number of such artifacts, and they are expected to be competent users of them at an early age. As we ex-amine further in this chapter, such intellectual tools must be seen as medi-ating perceptual activity. Human's very seeing and understanding of the world are in a fascinating sense related to the development of symbolic and technological systems.

In what follows, we explore two issues in the context of children's use of the particular kinds of representational tools that are built into information technology. First, how can we understand the relations between these cul-tural artifacts and the cognitive development of children? Second, how will the very nature of human cognitive and communicative development itself be affected or modified by social and technological development? The for-mer question has been investigated in a number of studies taking both cul-tural and historical factors into account (e.g., Greeno & Hall, 1997; Roth & McGinn, 1998; Säljö, 1996). In contrast, the second question of the very na-ture of the interplay between developmental trajectories of individuals and the introduction of new artifacts/social practices in society has received lit-tle attention. In the following, we consider both questions by means of an exploratory case study of the introduction of a certain kind of digital repre-sentation to a number of young children (aged between 6 and 11 years) growing up in the digital age. What we attend to is the nature of reasoning they engage in the context of digital representations and how this reasoning is coordinated with the technology at hand.

REPRESENTATIONS AND SCIENTIFIC REASONING

Issues of the relation between children's reasoning, scientific concepts, and visual representations are very general and have been investigated from different theoretical positions. The immediate background of this research, however, can be found in two earlier studies by Schoultz, Säljö, and Wyndhamn (2001) and Ivarsson, Schoultz, and Säljö (2002). The common interest in these two studies was to analyze children's reasoning in the area of elementary astronomy. Both studies were conducted to critically dialogue with the research findings in the tradition of studying "conceptual change" within a cognitivist tradition. In the cognitivist studies, children (from 5 years and up) are typically interviewed about their understandings of the shape of the earth and elementary concepts such as gravity. The results generally show that children have various "mental models" of the earth as flat, hollow, and so on and that they often claim that people can fall off the earth or that they can only live on top of it (Nussbaum, 1979; Nussbaum & Novak, 1976; Vosniadou, 1994; Vosniadou & Brewer, 1992).

As much of the earlier research that we wanted to dialogue with had used the structured interview, in the Piagetian tradition of the *méthode-clinique* (Piaget, 1929) to gather data, this method was largely maintained in our previous studies (Schoultz et al., 2001; Ivarsson et al., 2002), although with some significant modifications. One of these modifications concerned the analytical attitude in relation to the empirical material. Instead of regarding the interview situation as a privileged context in which the mind can be tapped of its conceptual content, the interviews were analyzed as concrete social and discursive encounters. A second modification concerned the resources made available to the participants. The children in these studies were given the possibility to reason about elementary astronomy with the support of well-known artifacts such as a globe (Schoultz et al., 2001) and a map (Ivarsson et al., 2002), respectively. The studies showed how a globe or a map supports the reasoning of even very young children to accomplish rather complicated accounts in which sophisticated knowledge about the shape of the earth and gravity was introduced. Contrary to the earlier research (e.g., Sneider & Pulos, 1983), these two studies contained no reports of children saying that one could fall off the earth, a fact that was attributed to the familiarity with and physical presence of the representational objects. Also, there were no suggestions that the shape of the earth was flat or had any other form. Thus, these artifacts seem to serve as quite efficient prosthetic devices for reasoning if one is interested in studying how children are able to use fairly abstract explanations and approximate scientifically acceptable accounts.

From such culturally established artifacts as globes and maps, this study takes the step to the digital medium and representations of a related but at the same time less familiar kind. In a modern society, children will meet a plethora of visual representations in many walks of life in movies, games, books, toys, and so on. The cognitive socialization needed to handle these new, rich, and dynamic representations must be very different from the one that was valid, say, 50 years ago or so. This is the general issue that underlies the observations we report in what follows. Two specific questions are addressed. First, what happens to children's reasoning when confronted with an unfamiliar and dynamic representation? Second, what discursive strategies and resources will children use in their argumentations? These are, of course, very generic questions, and we only exemplify some aspects of them. To simplify the understanding, we keep to the same context as in the studies just mentioned: children's reasoning about gravity and the shape of the earth.

Before turning to the empirical material, we briefly articulate a theoretical framework suitable for the kind of analysis we present.

PERCEPTION, REPRESENTATION, AND ACTION

A fascinating theory of the nature of visual representation and one that is firmly grounded in an attempt to take human practices as a starting point has been developed by the philosopher Wartofsky (1979). Traditionally, philosophers and psychologists have studied and conceived perception as a biological capacity and as a characteristic of the species. Consequently, even though the contents of perception obviously have varied historically, its structures and modes have been understood as ahistorical and determined by humans' visual system as a biological entity. Wartofsky (1979) sketched an alternative view of perception and knowledge more in general, which he referred to as a "historical epistemology." Wartofsky's general argument is that the forms or modes of perception, their very structures, are historically variant; they change historically in accordance with changes in our social or cultural practices.

Following this line of reasoning, several reinterpretations of human perception are necessary. For example, seeing is understood not primarily as a physiological act but as a social and cultural activity. Furthermore, Wartofsky (1979) argued that "the specific feature of perception as a mode of action is that it is mediated by representation" (p. 189). This notion of mediation is compatible with the one developed in the Vygotskian tradition (Vygotsky, 1978, 1986; Wertsch, 1998). As an interesting contribution and maybe even extension of this tradition, however, we view Wartofsky's (1979) insistence on the idea that "it is by the variation in *modes of representation* [italics added] that perception itself comes to be related to historical changes in other forms of human practice, and in particular, to social and technological practice" (p. 189).

To clarify Wartofsky's (1979) notion of a historical epistemology, such a position can be contrasted with Piaget's (1972) genetic epistemology and his theory of developmental stages. An illustrative example connected to the previous discussion of representations comes from Piaget and Inhelder (1969) in their analyses of how children construct representations of the world through drawings of their own. Through the works of Luquet,[1] Piaget and Inhelder (1969) claimed that "until about eight or nine a child's drawing is essentially realistic in intention, though the subject begins by drawing what he *knows* about a person or an object long before he can draw what he actually *sees*" (p. 64). This stage is referred to as "intellectual realism" in which the drawing depicts the conceptual attributes of the model without concern for the visual perspective of the observer. An illustration of this intellectual realism is that in the drawing of a child; "a face seen in profile will have a second eye because a man has two eyes" (Piaget & Inhelder, 1969, p. 64). At about 8 or 9 years of age, "intellectual realism" is allegedly succeeded by "visual realism," and "the drawing now represents only what is visible from one particular perspective. A profile now has only one eye, etc., as would be seen from the side, and the concealed parts of objects are no longer visibly represented" (Piaget & Inhelder, 1969, p. 65).

It is exactly this kind of theory of visual perception that is called into question by Wartofsky (1979) in his argumentation for a historical epistemology. According to Wartofsky (1979), such argumentation builds on an anomalous, 17th-century mechanist model of perception that is known as geometrical optics:

> What I take to be anomalous here are precisely the mechanist feature of the model which confuses a particular theory of geometrical optics—i.e. a theory of the transmission, reflection and refraction of light, especially through lenses—with a theory of vision, and in particular, with a theory of visual *perception*. (Wartofsky, 1979, p. 192)

This difference between a scientific theory of optics and vision as part of human practices is important in a sociocultural perspective. Wartofsky (1979) further argued that both the theory of geometrical optics and the theory of perspective drawing are recent historical developments, which have now become an integral part of humans' visual understanding, or of our visual "common sense." The visual realism that Piaget and Inhelder (1969) referred to is not a universal realism that the child simply acquires; it is a sociohistorically derived model of representation according to which we view objects. However, by carrying on unaware of the relations between developments in science and changes in common sense and "thereby taking

---

[1]G. H. Luquet (1927) as cited in Piaget and Inhelder (1969).

today's common sense to be the universal and unchanging common sense of the species, such philosophy of perception," according to Wartofsky (1979), "remains blissfully ignorant of its own historical limits, and the historical datedness of its models" (p. 192).

There is no reason to doubt the empirical observations reported by Piaget and Inhelder (1969), but their theory of "stages" fails to acknowledge any historical or cultural dimensions and transformations that impact on how humans perceive the world. It is precisely because of this ignorance, to paraphrase Wartofsky (1979), that Piaget and Inhelder (1969) reported how these stages "attest to a remarkable convergence with the evolution of the spontaneous geometry of the child" (p. 66). The solution to this problem—following Wartofsky (1979) and, we claim, Vygotsky (1986)—is to refer the change from intellectual realism to visual realism to a socioculturally learned mode of representation that came with the introduction of perspective drawing.

According to Wartofsky (1979), the manners in which representations are arranged, the so-called modes of representation, mediate people's perceptions. Thus, in such a conception, seeing is understood as guided by our culturally adopted modes of representation that have emerged over time in the context of various human practices. However, not all modes become canonical (i.e., culturally accepted and dominant). The establishment of what Wartofsky (1979) called "canons of representation" must be understood as a historical act, which involves the adoption and acceptance of certain interpretative rules for what counts as a relevant and accurate representation in the context of a particular medium. A visual representation becomes a "conventionally adopted specification, which looks 'right,' or is a 'proper' representation, by virtue of our acceptance of a certain 'vocabulary of forms' " (Wartofsky, 1979, p. 181). Thus, the theory of perspective drawing cannot be seen as an unequivocal premise for a true visual realism that objectively represents the world. Rather, this theory suggests and endorses a particular "vocabulary," and one that has been made canonical in most parts of the Western world. Yet, and this is important, for the individual, its rules and conventions have to be learned through a process of cognitive socialization.

For the individual, familiarity with relevant canons of visual representation is necessary to perform certain actions and to see certain things. Knowledge is intrinsic to the way humans represent things, and this conceptualization makes Wartofsky's theorizing (1979, 1983) highly relevant for the study of learning in educational settings (and elsewhere). Wartofsky's (1979) argument calls for an awareness of the existence of different canons of representation in various practices and the possible conflicts between them. This position seems even more important to consider in present-day society with an increasing exposure to new media and the new modes of representation that are introduced, for instance, through the use of computers in instructional settings. For, as suggested by Healy and Hoyles (1999) and many others, something interesting has happened to visual representations as they have become integrated with digital technology:

> Images now can be externalized through computer constructions, rendering more explicit previously hidden properties and structures. A visual image can be made open to inspection, an object of reflection, which can serve as a building block in an argument—something more concrete rather than transitory and fleeting. Once constructed on the computer, images are manipulable: They can be debugged, reconstructed, transformed, separated or combined together, following sets of procedures with something like the reproducibility and rigor previously limited to symbolic representation. (Healy & Hoyles, 1999, p. 59)

Healy and Hoyles (1999) further argued that given these developments, the role of visual representations in schools must be explored to reach a better understanding of the potentials of the new media and technologies for teaching and learning. It should also be pointed out that researchers, as well as educators, need to know more about how children relate such pictorial and graphic displays and how they manage to incorporate these into their argumentation when "talking science" (Lemke, 1990). This is the issue we explore.

RESEARCH DESIGN

This work should be seen as exploratory. It connects to the earlier research (Schoultz et al., 2001, Ivarsson et al., 2002) mentioned previously about children's understanding of gravity and the shape of the earth through the interest in studying the tool-dependent nature of human cognition and communication. Our ambition is to compare some features of children's reasoning in the context of multimodal digital representations with their reasoning when supported by other forms of representations. What is in focus in this line of research is the interest in children's familiarity with the canons of representations that such multimodal and dynamic digital resources embody.

Participants and Analysis

Interviews were held in a Swedish school during regular school days. Participation was voluntary, and in all, 19 children took part. However, in this analysis, excerpts from four children are included, and we use these as exemplars illustrating variations in children's reasoning. These children were aged 6 (preschool) to 11 (fifth grade). The interviews were carried out in the same manner as in the case of the studies by Schoultz et al. (2001) and

Ivarsson et al. (2002). The purpose was not to find out what the children knew in any general sense. Rather, the idea was to explore the interrelation between their reasoning and the use of some multimodal representations. The interview sessions started with a brief, introductory discussion during which a digital, three-dimensional atlas was used. The children were asked about the meaning of the different colors and whether they recognized any countries. As about half of the children were immigrants, mostly from the Middle East, these discussions often involved the location of a specific country and how one would travel to get there. Other children talked about holiday travels or relatives living on a different continent. After these initial discussions, the interviewer (Jonas Ivarsson) changed to a program specifically designed for this study. The sessions lasted between 10 and 20 min and were audio recorded. All recordings were later transcribed in full.

The Graphical Representation

As a basis for the main part of the interviews, a specially designed program had been constructed using Macromedia Director (Director, 1998). The program mainly consisted of a large picture of the earth, which was a composite of many satellite images without clouds. There was no geopolitical information (see Fig. 8.1). This image was a two-dimensional version of the atlas initially used in the interviews. On the left side of the screen there was also a panel containing various icons. With the help of these icons, different objects could be placed on the earth: a boy, a girl, an airplane, and a rocket ship. These two-dimensional figures could be moved with the mouse, and they had been assigned different behaviors with reference to how they should orient.

The issue that was scrutinized in this study concerns the children's reasoning in the context of the movements of the object representing an air-

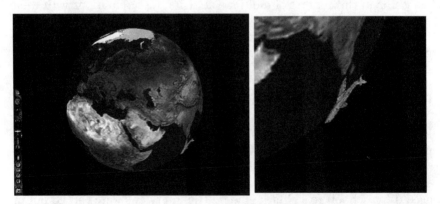

FIG. 8.1.   The constructed program with the discussed airplane.

plane. This object had been selected because it was believed that it would prove a more challenging topic when discussing gravity and the shape of the earth than that of people living on different parts of the earth. The plane was always oriented with its underside toward the center of the screen, thus representing gravity. In the interviews, the interviewer controlled the computer program. The plane was first located in the Northern hemisphere and later moved towards the Far East and India. The figure was kept close to the edge of the earth, and the children were asked if it would be possible to travel in the manner suggested by the representation (see enlargement in Fig. 8.1).

RESULTS

The general impression from the analysis of the interviews is the increasing difficulties the children had when reasoning about gravity and the shape of the earth in this context in comparison to what was found in the two earlier studies (Schoultz et al., 2001; Ivarsson et al., 2002) using a globe and a map, respectively. For instance, when the interviews were based on such familiar artifacts, no single child accepted the claim that it would be possible to fall off the earth. Instead, these artifacts seemed to function as cognitive prostheses, making even young children able to participate in complicated discussions about gravity, as we have already mentioned. In this study, however, the representational technology did not function in this transparent manner for the children. Even though this program could be described as more powerful than a traditional, static artifact such as the globe and the map in the sense that it incorporates and visualizes information dynamically, several children had trouble coordinating what they saw with what they already knew. To illustrate this point, we focus the analysis on one particular issue: how the orientation of the plane on the screen should be understood.

In the following sections, we show how the children picked out certain visual characteristics as significant for their reasoning. More specifically, we illustrate how the term *upside down* was used to signal something problematic with this particular representation. We selected four excerpts to illustrate three different ways of reasoning. This grouping is an analytical construction based on the manners in which the graphical representation was incorporated into the argumentation. Our point is to illustrate the kinds of difficulties children had in identifying the modes of representation that are relevant for this particular artifact.

In the first excerpt,[2] Eric, who is about 6 years of age, reasons about airplanes and whether they can travel upside down or not (see Table 8.1).

---

[2] The transcriptions were made in accordance with Sacks, Schegloff, and Jefferson (1974).

In this interview, as in some others, the fact that the sky is not represented in the computer program constitutes a problem. Eric knows that planes travel in the sky and not in space. He makes a remark about this, and in lines 115 to 118 (Table 8.1), the sky is negotiated. Having established this common point of departure, the interviewer then restates his question somewhat more specifically: "what about here, then? Could one go like this?" Eric's response is a prompt "N:o" with an added justification that the "plane falls down on the ground." This pattern, consisting of a short answer to the question plus a justifying account, is very common in the interviews. It is interesting to note that even at his young age, Eric knows that one can be held accountable for one's claims, and that one therefore has to supply a contextually relevant explanation to the claim made. On a more general level, this illustrates that Eric is familiar with one of the most elementary elements of scientific reasoning. Eric's argument that "the plane falls down on the ground" is open to interpretation, and the interviewer tries to clarify through a suggestion that the plane would fall "down into the water." Simultaneously, the interviewer (in line 121) moves the figure of the plane up on the screen and toward the Indian Ocean. This act can be seen as a form of guidance or offer to render Eric's answer a scientifically acceptable one. Eric does not acknowledge this alternative interpretation and tries to clarify his position by saying that if the plane were upside down, then it would fall "straight down." Here again he introduces an argumentative resource by using the *if-then* structure. After that, the interviewer asks "What's down there, then?," and Eric's response (line 130) implies that it would fall to the "ground."

In this brief exchange, Eric makes two important qualifications in the context of this particular representation. He first introduces the missing sky, and later he adds ground to the scene. Taken together with the plane, these three symbols constitute one of the most common ways of portraying an airplane: as flying in the sky high above the ground. In this sense, one could say that Eric is trying to reconcile what he sees with what he knows about how to represent flying airplanes. Or, alternatively, his argumentation can be interpreted as an attempt to re-create the canon of representation (Wartofsky, 1979) that he is familiar with. This manner of representing, however, is challenged by the images presented by the computer program. Eric accounts for what he sees on the screen as a plane flying "upside down." Thus, the rotation of the represented plane is not taken as something that is relative to the surface of the depicted globe (which would be the expected interpretation if one considers gravity); it is taken as a plane flying upside down.

In the second excerpt (see Table 8.2), Isaac confirms the interviewer's suggestion that it is possible to fly around the globe. Nevertheless, he objects to the way this is represented by the computer program.

In this discussion, the notion of the plane being upside down is again introduced by the child. Isaac is clear about the fact that planes can travel all

TABLE 8.1
Excerpt 1: Eric (Preschool)

111	I:	Does it look like this if we fly here ((moves the plane clockwise, starting from the Northern Hemisphere)) do you think?
112	Eric:	(1.1) No:
113	I:	Round like this-
114	Eric:	Then- then you are- then you see the sky, you don't see the sky when you are up in space=
115	I:	=Oh no so you have to travel about here ((moves the plane closer to the edge)) perhaps
116	Eric:	M:
117	I:	Ye:s (1.2) at the edge like that
118	Eric:	M:
119	I:	Y:es (4.1) but what about here, then? Could one go like this? ((seemingly flying upside down, see Fig. 8.1))
120	Eric:	N:o 'cos then- 'cos then the plane falls down on the ground=
121	I:	=>Do you think it falls down here< down into the water or? ((moves the plane in a northerly direction, toward the Indian Ocean))
122	Eric:	(0.6) No
123	I:	Or where would it go then?=
124	Eric:	=Well if it would have flown in wate:↑r
125	I:	Yes
126	Eric:	And it would've been upside-do:wn it would've fallen straight down
127	I:	Aha (0.4) down here ((moves the plane to the bottom of the screen))
128	Eric:	M:
129	I:	What's down there then?
130	Eric:	(1.5) Grou:nd!
131	I:	Is there ground there?
132	Eric:	M:

TABLE 8.2
Excerpt 2: Isaac (Fifth Grade)

73	I:	Can one fly around the whole earth
74	Isaac:	Yes
75	I:	Would it be possible to fly like this ((moves the plane clockwise, starting from the Northern Hemisphere and ending up like Fig. 8.1))
76	Isaac:	M: (0.5) but you don't fly upside-down but you can fly around the earth
77	I:	Yes (2.4) but if- if it is like this (0.4) does it fly upside-down then=
78	Isaac:	=>No:<
79	I:	(1.6) But the way it is in the picture then?
80	Isaac:	(1.4) There it flies upside-down but I don't think that it would do that for real
81	I:	No (8.5) if we go like this ((following the curvature of the globe))
81	Isaac:	M:
83	I:	Does it start to tu↑rn then do you think
84	Isaac:	(2.1) °No I don't think so°
85	I:	(1.4) Isn't it possible that the plane fo↑llows the earth
86	Isaac:	(2.2) >I don't know< I've never travelled in a plane myself so
87	I:	No:↓ no then it's a bit hard to know (3.1) but do you think that it could fall off here?
88	Isaac:	No I don't

over the earth, but what he sees on the screen with the plane appearing up-side down puzzles him (Table 8.2, line 76). This excerpt illustrates a conflict between what is known and what is seen, a condition that Isaac is able to ex-press very eloquently himself by saying "there [in the picture] it flies upside-down but I don't think that it would do that for real" (line 80). Although Isaac is struggling with how to interpret the picture, the interviewer never really invites him to talk about the premises for the representation in this case. Instead, the interviewer keeps the representation of the plane as the topical focus, and from within such a frame of reference, it is hard to resolve the conflict.

A very similar kind of argumentation is found in the discussion with Helen in Table 8.3. The main difference, in comparison with the previous excerpt, is that Helen manages to explicitly express some of the logic of the representation.

Like Eric and Isaac, Helen spontaneously introduces the term upside down and signals her reactions to the image by saying "you can't fly upside-down." As is the case with Isaac in Excerpt 2, she obviously has problems connecting what she knows with what she sees on the screen. When the interviewer picks up on her remark, she argues against the claim that the plane really is upside down and says that she thinks that it is not. Next, the interviewer shifts the focus from the represented to the representation itself by explicitly referring to appearance: "why does it look like this, then?" This change of topical focus from the represented to the representation seems to be enough for Helen to come up with the answer that the appearance is due

TABLE 8.3
Excerpt 3: Helen (Second Grade)

103	I:	If one travels in a plane like this (0.6) around the earth (2.6) would it be possible to fly here then? ((see Fig. 8.1))
104	Helen:	(3.1) You can't fly upside-down
105	I:	(1.0) No: can you go upside-down or does it go upside-down when it's going like this?
106	Helen:	(1.5) No:
107	I:	(1.0) So it doesn't?
108	Helen:	(1.0) I don't think so
109	I:	No: (0.9) why does it look like this then?
110	Helen:	(1.4) Only because (0.8) it's rou:nd
111	I:	Yes that's right (0.7) so it only looks this way perhaps=
112	Helen:	=Yes
113	I:	(0.5) Yes
114	Helen:	But perhaps it really flies straight=
115	I:	=It actually travels straight yes that's right (2.1) so then it couldn't fall off like this ((moves the plane away from the earth))
116	Helen:	No

to the curvature of the earth: "only because it's round." She then further re-
solves the conflict by stating that "perhaps it really flies straight."

A third kind of argumentation can be found in the fourth and final excerpt (see Table 8.4). There, the representation enters the discussion somewhat differently in comparison with the other examples in the sense that it
does not appear as problematic to the child. This time, the term upside down
is introduced by the interviewer as an attempt to challenge the reasoning of
the child.

Compared to the earlier excerpts, Oscar has very few objections to the images presented to him. Even though the underlying rationale for the questions
is the supposed problems with gravity, Oscar does not seem to share these pre-

TABLE 8.4

Excerpt 4: Oscar (Fourth Grade)

40	I:	Can one travel with aeroplanes all over (0.2) the earth?
41	Oscar:	>Yes<
42	I:	(1.9) Would it be possible to go like this then? ((moves the plane clockwise, starting from the Northern Hemisphere))
43	Oscar:	Ye:s
44	I:	(2.7) How about here (0.7) what happens then? (0.8) ((as in Fig. 8.1)) would it be like this?=
45	Oscar:	=He's flying over the water
46	I:	Flying over the water (1.7) are you supposed to fly like this (0.4) when you are in (1.0) southern Africa?
47	Oscar:	(2.5) Yes
48	I:	(2.5) One isn't upside-down there then?
49	Oscar:	(1.2) Upside-down? (1.2) No: I can't see that
50	I:	(3.5) You only fly like this (4.5) ((completes a full circle and starts on a second lap)) but if I come here (0.2) again ((as in Fig. 8.1)) (1.2) you wouldn't fall here then?
51	Oscar:	(0.2) No
52	I:	(1.7) Why wouldn't you do that
53	Oscar:	Because eh: (1.6) we:ll as I said before, that they think that the earth is flat so you can't- "we will fall down"- they thought a long time ago

mises. Oscar still tries to make the questions as meaningful as he can. In line 44 (Table 8.4), he gets the rather vague question "how about here, what happens then?" This is very close to a leading question because it suggests that something should happen when the plane is in that particular position. Oscar responds by saying that the plane is "flying over the water" (line 45), and through this, he denies that there is anything remarkable in the picture. Oscar responds to the next question (line 46) with a hesitant "yes." Realizing that Oscar handles the representation seemingly without problems, the interviewer then changes tactics in his questioning. The interviewer's next question—"one isn't upside-down there, then?"—is much more straightforward and focuses on the represented phenomenon as he uses the indefinite pronoun *one* together with the adverb *there*. Oscar opposes the implied proposition, and the particular manner in which he does this is very interesting. At first, he seems baffled, as he repeats the word "Upside-down" with a questioning intonation, but then he adds, "no I can't see that." Oscar's wording, in our opinion, is quite revealing: "Upside-down? No I can't see that." Oscar's problem with this question seems to be that he cannot understand why it is asked in this particular manner. Because the interview implies an asymmetrical power relation set within the school context, Oscar is obligated to take the questions as relevant and not arbitrary. By introducing his own perspective in the answer, Oscar simultaneously denies that the plane would be upside down and implies that there may be other interpretations as well (e.g., the perspective implicated by the interviewer and that he cannot identify).

An important element of the utterance in line 49 (Table 8.4) is the use of the word *see*. In Swedish, the word (*se*) does not share the same close connotations of "knowing" or "understanding" as does the English term and in this situation; it should be interpreted in the literal, that is, visual sense of the word. In the two earlier excerpts, the children's previous knowledge came into conflict with their reading of the visual representation. They obviously saw something—a plane seemingly upside down—which they initially found somewhat confusing. In contrast, Oscar says he "can't see" how the plane could be upside down. It is tempting to explain this difference by saying that Oscar has a better theoretical grasp of phenomena that relate to gravity. However, such an explanation risks being circular and begs the question of exactly why Oscar does not see the plane as being upside down. In the following section, our discussion focuses specifically on these differences in reasoning and their relation to culturally adopted modes of representation.

DISCUSSION

If a representation, as suggested by Wartofsky (1979), is seen as a form of specification, then a certain set of adopted rules may be regarded as intrinsic to any representation—but only as long as one remembers that "representing is something that we *do*, and that nothing *is* a representation excerpt insofar as we construct or construe it as one" (p. xxi). Thus, it is important to keep in mind that any representation may refer to several practices, and the relevant interpretations of a representation between these may differ. This line of reasoning becomes clearer if illustrated by the case of the earth and its various representations.

When the earth is talked about as an astronomical body, which is one of the many ways we as humans can discuss our planet, a number of details are made relevant: the spherical shape, certain rules of gravity, and the somewhat strange fact that this massive body seems to "float freely" in space. If the particular representation of a globe is used in such an astronomical discussion, the spherical shape is physically present and does not have to be added. The concept of gravity, however, is not directly represented by the globe, and to explain various observations (such as that airplanes will not fall off the globe), the concept will have to be invoked or at least recognized by the speakers as a relevant premise. If, instead, the very same globe is used in a history class while discussing the journeys of Columbus or the first attempts to sail around the globe, gravity will most likely not be an issue at all. In this case, the spherical shape of the earth, the location of different continents, and the navigational problems of finding passages will probably appear as the relevant features to focus on. Thus, the globe affords a range of different perspectives and discursive practices that focus on different features.

When representations are embodied in a digital medium, the possibilities of incorporating conceptual distinctions increase significantly. Things that cannot be represented on a flat sheet of paper or through a mechanical construction can come alive in several modalities simultaneously, for instance, through visual, aural, tactile, and proprioceptive[3] displays or any combination of these (Biocca & Delaney, 1995). The representation used in this study differed from a globe in several respects. It was a two-dimensional image presented on a flat screen, but it was also interactively fixed (because it was a projection from a single viewpoint). On the other hand, it did model events on the basis of the concept of gravity through the dynamic orientation of movable objects. This whole configuration embodies a mode of representation that turned out to be quite challenging for some of the children who had to struggle with what they saw. Previously, we have shown three analytically distinctive forms of reasoning that are illustrated in the four excerpts. We argue that these differences in reasoning are related to differences in perception of the graphical representation. We recapitulate some of the observations and add some theoretical interpretations.

---

[3]The human proprioceptive system registers the motion and position of both individual limbs and the body as a whole. The most easily recognized proprioceptive display would probably be the roller coaster or other forms of theme park attractions.

In the first case, Eric brought in what he saw as the missing elements of the image, that is, "sky" and "ground," to arrive at a picture of a plane over which he had some conceptual control. Through his reasoning, he actively construed a mode of representation that was not physically present, a mode illustrated by Fig. 8.2[4] (which is a drawing by a child taken from a different context). If one considers the manner in which Eric considers these added elements necessary for illustrating how airplanes fly, the isolated airplane presented on the screen (see Fig. 8.1) could be understood as upside down.

One important thing to realize in this context is that Eric was working very hard to make the discussion intelligible, in part by adding thematically relevant elements that had not been mentioned by the interviewer. Furthermore, it should be noted that it was not only the interviewer who contributed with modes of reasoning that were theoretical in character. Eric's seeing was also theoretically informed, although by an alternative mode of representation. Eric displayed skills in reasoning, indicative of familiarity with a particular kind of scientific argumentation, through the use of an *if–then* structure and by realizing that he would be held accountable for his claims. What Eric did not seem able to do—at least not in this discussion—was to go beyond his adopted frame of reference and realize some critical features of how this particular representation was designed. Unlike the inter-

FIG. 8.2.   Child's drawing of planes.

[4]Note that this illustration is taken from a different context. The drawing was done by Daniel Meyers, Grade 6, and can be found at http://quest.arc.nasa.gov/aero/events/regimes/contest/Daniel-Mun-SS.jpeg

viewer, Eric was not simultaneously managing different canons of representation; however, we do not discuss this further here.

Turning to the talk with Isaac and Helen (Excerpts 2 and 3), these discussions differed from Eric's line of reasoning mainly because they focused on a conflict between what they saw and what they knew. To Piaget (Piaget & Inhelder, 1969), these excerpts would represent an intermediary or perhaps unaccounted for stage between intellectual realism and visual realism. However, by following the argumentation of Wartofsky (1979), it seems reasonable to assume that Isaac and Helen struggled with two alternative and radically different canons of representation at the same time. Both children noted and commented with some surprise on the fact that the plane appeared upside down. By further considering and discussing how airplanes fly, they were able to bracket their initial, visual interpretation of an airplane apparently flying upside down and reinterpret this appearance in line with a mode of representation premised on gravity. To take the next step of explicitly formulating this, however, both children seemed to need some mild communicative support, and as it turned out, only the discussion with Helen resulted in an explicit verbal resolution of the conflict between what was seen and what was known. Helen's coming to this conclusion must be construed as an interactive achievement, and it illustrates how reasoning with the support of others may take people further in their understanding of a given representation.

The practice of representing objects as following the spherical earth is a relatively recent one. It is also less frequent than the canon of linear perspectivity discussed earlier. Nevertheless, Oscar (Excerpt 4), representing the third way of reasoning, displayed a familiarity with this new representation, the same mode of representation that Eric never really dealt with and that Isaac and Helen had only started to apprehend. Compared with the three other children, Oscar had the inverse problem when talking about the orientation of the plane. To him, upside down did not seem a fitting description of what the image portrayed. On the contrary, he seemed so attuned to the mode of representation where gravity is visualized in a particular manner that he did not see how the plane could be described as upside down. Most likely, even Oscar could be instructed to see the plane as upside down, but he did not seem to consider this relevant in a discussion premised on the notion of gravity and the movement of objects around the earth.

On a general level, the development of reasoning and human knowing schematically visible in the four excerpts can be understood as related to the constant adjustment of human perception to evolving technologies. When human knowledge is transformed and given a material shape through externalizations in the shape of various symbolic representations, such resources will serve as active elements in the cognitive socialization of future generations of learners. Through this duality inherent to material objects embodying specific conceptual structurings, the insights and perspectives that have emerged through sociocultural evolution will live on in society. Thus, objects are not simply out there in the world. Rather, they are instructive and actively contribute to sustaining specific manners of reasoning and perceiving. In some cases, they will even be naturalized and assumed to perfectly match what they represent in a mirror-like fashion. However, the important point to keep in mind is that our modes of knowing are continuously transformed as technologies contribute to the reconfiguration of our practices.

CONCLUSION

The overall aim of this study was to explore some of the relations between representational technologies, perception, cognition, and human action. The evolution of digital technology has opened up new possibilities for visual expression, and when these representations enter the classroom, pupils will face the problem of coming to grips with the conceptual premises of these representational tools. The question is how children disambiguate and manage to make productive use of such tools for understanding in the learning environment.

The point of our study was to contribute to a better understanding of the potentials of the new technology for teaching and learning. To address this issue, an unfamiliar and dynamic representation was introduced to a group of young pupils. The analysis focused on the scientific reasoning that took place in the context of such an artifact and what discursive strategies and resources the children used in their argumentations. By grounding our analysis in the theoretical position suggested by Wartofsky (1979), we have attempted to illustrate how the pupils, to grasp the graphical environment, made use of distinctions and perspectives that are indicative of specific canons of representation. The results suggest that perception and understanding are closely interlinked with these cultural modes of action. Furthermore, it is through the successive adoption of these modes that cognitive development itself becomes related to social and technological change.

ACKNOWLEDGMENTS

The research reported here has been funded by the Knowledge Foundation (KK-foundation) and the Swedish Research Council.

REFERENCES

Biocca, F., & Delaney, B. (1995). Immersive virtual reality technology. In F. Biocca & M. R. Levy (Eds.), *Communication in the age of virtual reality* (pp. 57–124). Hillsdale, NJ: Lawrence Erlbaum Associates.

Cole, M. (1996). *Cultural psychology: A once and future discipline.* Cambridge, MA: Belknap Press of Harvard University Press.

Director. (Version 7). (1998). San Francisco: Macromedia, Inc.

Greeno, J. G., & Hall, R. (1997, January). Practicing representation. Learning with and about representational forms. *Phi Delta Kappan,* 361–367.

Healy, L., & Hoyles, C. (1999). Visual and symbolic reasoning in mathematics: Making connections with computers? *Mathematical Thinking and Learning, 1,* 59–84.

Ivarsson, J., Schoultz, J., & Säljö, R. (2002). Map reading versus mind reading: Revisiting children's understanding of the shape of the earth. In M. Limón & L. Mason (Eds.), *Reconsidering conceptual change. Issues in theory and practice* (pp. 77–99). Amsterdam: Kluwer.

Lemke, J. L. (1990). *Talking science: Language, learning, and values.* Norwood, NJ: Ablex.

Leont'ev, A. N. (1978). *Activity, consciousness, and personality.* Englewood Cliffs, NJ: Prentice Hall.

Nussbaum, J. (1979). Children's conceptions of the earth as a cosmic body: A cross age study. *Science Education, 63,* 83–93.

Nussbaum, J., & Novak, J. (1976). An assessment of children's concepts of the earth utilizing structured interviews. *Science Education, 60*(4), 535–550.

Piaget, J. (1929). *The child's conception of the world.* London: Paladin.

Piaget, J. (1972). *The principles of genetic epistemology.* London: Routledge & Kegan Paul.

Piaget, J., & Inhelder, B. (1969). *The psychology of the child.* London: Routledge & Kegan Paul.

Rogoff, B. (1990). *Apprenticeship in thinking: Cognitive development in social context.* New York: Oxford University Press.

Roth, W.-M., & McGinn, M. K. (1998). Inscriptions: Toward a theory of representing as social practice. *Review of Educational Research, 68,* 35–59.

Sacks, H., Schegloff, E. A., & Jefferson, G. (1974). A simplest systematics for the organisation of turn-taking for conversation. *Language, 50,* 696–735.

Säljö, R. (1996). Mental and physical artifacts in cognitive practices. In P. Reimann & H. Spada (Eds.), *Learning in humans and machines: Towards an interdisciplinary learning science* (1st ed., pp. 83–96). Oxford, England: Pergamon.

Schoultz, J., Säljö, R., & Wyndhamn, J. (2001). Heavenly talk. Discourse, artifacts, and children's understanding of elementary astronomy. *Human Development, 44,* 103–118.

Sneider, C., & Pulos, S. (1983). Children's cosmographies: Understanding the earth's shape and gravity. *Science Education, 67*(2), 205–221.

Vosniadou, S. (1994). Capturing and modelling the process of conceptual change. *Learning and Instruction, 4*(1), 45–69.

Vosniadou, S., & Brewer, W. F. (1992). Mental models of the earth: A study of conceptual change in childhood. *Cognitive Psychology, 24*(4), 535–585.

Vygotsky, L. S. (1978). *Mind in society: The development of higher psychological processes.* Cambridge, MA: Harvard University Press.

Vygotsky, L. S. (1986). *Thought and language.* Cambridge, MA: The MIT Press.

Wartofsky, M. W. (1979). *Models. Representation and the scientific understanding.* Dordrecht, The Netherlands: Reidel.

Wartofsky, M. W. (1983). From genetic epistemology to historical epistemology: Kant, Marx, and Piaget. In L. S. Liben (Ed.), *Piaget and the foundations of knowledge* (pp. 1–17). Hillsdale, NJ: Lawrence Erlbaum Associates.

Wertsch, J. V. (1998). *Mind as action.* New York: Oxford University Press.

9

WISE Design for Lifelong Learning—Pivotal Cases

Marcia C. Linn
University of California at Berkeley

Lifelong science learners revisit their ideas and have the potential to develop more normative and coherent accounts of scientific phenomena throughout their lives. After completing science courses, most learners use scientific ideas in everyday contexts such as making health decisions, selecting energy-efficient solutions to problems, or voting on scientific-related policies. To extend the impact of science instruction, I call in this chapter for including an important class of examples called pivotal cases, and I offer criteria to help designers create new pivotal cases.

To illustrate how well-designed examples promote knowledge integration, I analyze the spontaneous examples students develop in longitudinal case studies. Research studies that have compared courses with and without pivotal cases have shown how examples can take advantage of the interpretive, cultural, and deliberate character of the learner. Pivotal cases form the focal point for knowledge integration to help learners interpret new information. Pivotal cases offer compelling comparisons that reveal the power of scientific inquiry, connect to the cultural beliefs of learners, and stimulate learners to deliberately seek more cohesive accounts of scientific phenomena.

Students come to science class with a complex, varied set of spontaneous ideas about the scientific phenomena they study. For example, when students study thermodynamics and specifically, insulation and conduction, they articulate images of conductors as people found on buses, wires that transmit electricity, and materials that transmit heat or cold. When asked about insulators, students often refer to television commercials showing home insulation materials, advertisements for outdoor clothing, and depictions of sound-absorbing walls. In class, students conjecture that insulators accelerate, divert, slow, or stop heat. Most students hold multiple, conflicting ideas, some of which are cued by specific contexts.

Linn and Hsi (2000) reported on longitudinal case studies following students from middle school through high school. Linn and Hsi have shown that students spontaneously develop a repertoire of ideas about scientific phenomena as they interpret the world around them, act on cultural beliefs, and deliberately make sense of new situations. Science instruction helps students connect, examine, sort out, and apply their ideas to a broad range of scientific problems by adding new, instructed ideas and by supporting activities that lead to more cohesive accounts of science. This process, called *knowledge integration* (Linn, 1995; Linn, Davis, & Bell, 2004; Linn, Songer, & Eylon, 1996), depends on both adding powerful examples and enabling students to grapple with their full repertoire of ideas to form a more coherent perspective on the scientific domain. In this chapter, I discuss *pivotal cases*, a class of scientific examples that when added to the mix of ideas used by the students to make sense of complex scientific situations, promote knowledge integration.

Other writings have discussed aspects of instruction that help students sort out their instructed and spontaneous ideas. Designers can take advantage of activities that promote knowledge integration such as reflection, peer collaboration, and autonomous work when they create projects using the Web-based Inquiry Science Environment (WISE) (The Web-based Science Inquiry Environment, 2004). WISE (see Fig. 9.1) guides students to carry out projects about scientific phenomena by sorting out their ideas, comparing alternatives, and critiquing views of others (Linn, Clark, & Slotta, 2003; Linn & Slotta, 2000). WISE frees teachers to monitor student progress, point out issues of concern to the class, and tutor small groups (Linn et al., 2003).

Pivotal cases, when added to the repertoire of ideas held by a student, promote linking, connecting, and organizing of ideas. Pivotal cases promote knowledge integration by taking advantage of the interpretive, cultural, and deliberate nature of the learner (Linn, 2002). The *interpretive nature* of the learner refers to the way individuals make sense of new material in light of their initial ideas (Linn et al., 1996). The *cultural nature* of the learner refers to the propensity of students to rely on societal images of science and scientists when they reason about science. For some, this means feeling marginalized from the scientific enterprise or assuming that science only makes sense to experts. The *deliberate nature* of the learner refers to the decisions individuals make about selecting science experiences and persisting in scientific problem solving. Many students decide to switch out of science or avoid sustained reasoning due to frustration or boredom.

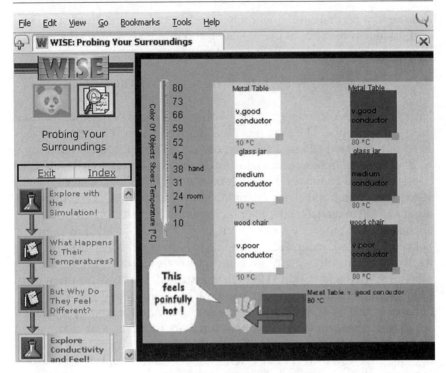

FIG. 9.1. Web-based Inquiry Science Environment (WISE) activity on thermal equilibrium (see also http://wise.berkeley.edu).

Examples that support the interpretive, cultural, and deliberate nature of the learner make science knowledge durable, extensible, and reconstructable. Durable cases support the interpretive process by coalescing spontaneous ideas around a focal point for knowledge integration. Extensible cases allow students to test their cultural beliefs in new situations. Reconstructable cases support the deliberate nature of the learner by enabling students to reformulate their own ideas and reinvent ideas they have forgotten. In this chapter, I describe research on pivotal cases to help curriculum designers, including teachers, create pivotal cases for new topics.

To develop an understanding of pivotal cases, I begin this chapter by looking at the role of examples in instruction on complex topics. In the next section, I analyze the spontaneous cases generated by two students to make sense of insulation and conduction during their eighth-grade science course and report on how these cases contribute to the understanding of high school science. In the third section, I describe compelling comparisons between traditional instruction and instruction with pivotal cases and characterize how pivotal cases might improve student learning. In the final section, I identify features of pivotal cases and discuss how pivotal cases can help achieve the goals of science courses.

EXAMPLES IN THE SCIENCE CURRICULUM

Designers choose science examples with varied levels of abstraction, conflict, and relevance. The examples used in textbooks and classroom demonstrations undergo little trial and refinement with the intended audience.

Psychological research has illustrated the difficulties that result from poorly designed examples. Research on the Luchins (Luchins & Luchins, 1959) Water Jar problem, for example, shows that students can learn procedures and fail to reanalyze their appropriateness. Students in this case rigidly applied a multistep process when a single-step process would have worked. Schoenfeld (1986) extended this finding to mathematics instruction, showing that students often apply procedures without reflecting on their appropriateness. Reif and Larkin (1991) demonstrated that students often learn to manipulate formulas without insight. Chi (1996) found that many students read texts without pausing to reflect and monitor comprehension.

Considerable research shows that students interpret new information based on past experience and on their cultural beliefs about science knowledge (e.g., Dewey, 1901; Lave & Wenger, 1990; Linn et al., 1996), yet examples often seem designed to transmit information rather than encourage productive interpretation. Clement (1993) analyzed the prototypic text example for Newton's first law—asking students to imagine a car driving on an icy road. Many students in the United States have difficulty connecting this example because they have not experienced icy roads and lack driving licenses. Clement showed the advantage of "bridging analogies" to help students connect scientific ideas to more familiar situations they encounter in their lives. To help students understand Newton's first law, for example, instructors might ask students to compare a ball rolling on mud, grass, and pavement.

ABSTRACT EXAMPLES

Textbook examples often communicate abstractions such as molecular models, free body diagrams, or formulas that students find inaccessible. Linn et al. (1996) demonstrated that in chemistry, molecular models, including ball and stick diagrams, distill expert knowledge of molecules but confuse students who conclude that each individual molecule had the properties of the whole, such as color, viscosity, and a boiling point. Lewis (1991) reported on examples illustrating heat and temperature for middle school students that rely on electron microscope photographs—a technology unfamiliar to all but experts. When texts describe conduction in terms of kinetic theory or explain acceleration using algebraic expressions, students have difficulty applying these ideas beyond the context of instruction (diSessa, 2000; Halloun & Hestenes, 1985).

For mathematics, Stigler and Hiebert (1999) analyzed the cases typically used in American texts and those used in Japan and Germany. Stigler and Hiebert reported that American examples are both more abstract and less connected to student ideas. They argued that the American texts discourage reasoning, whereas instruction in Germany and Japan supports sustained investigation.

Abstract examples deter students from connecting science ideas to new contexts because all contexts differ from the instructed case. Psychological research analyzing the impact of instruction on transfer to new contexts has consistently shown the difficulty that students face when trying to transfer a concept from one context to another (Bransford, 1979; Gik & Holyoak, 1980; Kuhn, 1993). Researchers including Kintsch (1998), Bruner (1979), and Stigler and Hiebert (1999) have all argued that finding problems at the right level of complexity such that they both encourage students to generate alternative solutions and help students distinguish among those solutions have advantages for lifelong learning. More generally, these researchers have illustrated a tendency on the part of students to succumb to an "illusion of comprehension" when examples fail to test their understanding. Students who engage as both experimenters and critics learn more than those who perform only one of these functions (Linn, 1995).

DISCREPANT EVENTS

Some designers, inspired by the Piagetian view of the learner as assimilating and accommodating to new ideas, have created discrepant events to enhance learning (Piaget, 1970). Teachers or texts often show photographs of man-eating plants, demonstrate that a metal pin can float on water, or use a burning candle to move a boiled egg inside a milk bottle. Instead of creating a new, cohesive perspective, students confronted with these examples often instead just add the new idea to their repertoire. Students even distinguish science-class ideas from everyday experience, remarking, for example, that "objects may remain in motion in science class but they come to rest on the playground" (Linn & Hsi, 2000).

ACCESSIBLE EXAMPLES

Designers who endorse the concrete and formal operations view of the learner from Piagetian theory (Inhelder & Piaget, 1958) seek concrete, accessible examples. These researchers complain that current courses with abstract examples and fleeting coverage of too many topics result in fragile knowledge. Researchers have called for concrete, complex, authentic, personally relevant, and familiar examples. These examples succeed best when students make predictions, test their ideas, and generate connections.

The Cognition and Technology Group at Vanderbilt (1997) showed the advantage of anchoring mathematics problems in a realistic situation such as a rescue mission and offering students a challenge based on the anchoring situation. Linn and Hsi (2000) showed the benefit of asking students to predict, test, and reconcile their ideas but also reported that some concrete examples, such as the benefit of sweaters as insulators, backfire when students conclude that sweaters warm people up. To place examples in more complex contexts, educators in mathematics (Cobb & Bowers, 1999; Lampert & Blunk, 1998), computer science (Linn & Clancy, 1992), business, and other fields cite similar strengths for authentic case studies.

Researchers from a behaviorist perspective have frequently argued against complex cases and problems and for a more controlled instructional setting that prevents students from going down wrong paths or elaborating flawed ideas. Anderson and Schunn (2000) called for tasks that pinpoint the underlying elements or production rules for a problem solution and direct attention to central aspects of the domain. Anderson and Schunn advocated examples that combine these elements in promising patterns that they called "chunks." Anderson and Schunn carefully analyzed tasks to ensure that they exercise appropriate chunks. To help students generalize their knowledge, Anderson and Schunn advocated teaching the chunk in multiple contexts so students distinguish contextual effects from the central aspects of the chunk. Anderson and Schunn (2000) criticized less well-specified approaches such as "insight, learning with understanding, and transfer, which are part of the free lunch myth" (p. 2).

Design of accessible, relevant examples can take advantage of research on human learning and memory. Research on working memory has identified symbolic, episodic, visual, verbal, kinesthetic, and other aspects of memory and shown the advantage of relying on several forms of memory (Baddeley & Longman, 1978). Consistent with this work, examples that connect varied representations could enhance science learning by stimulating a more complete and nuanced interpretation of the scientific phenomena.

Visual representations and animations, when they provide feedback on conjectures, seem especially valuable for learning of complex material but are difficult to design effectively (Hegarty, Quilici, Narayanan, Holmqvist, & Moreno, 1999). Too often science courses fail to test visual or animated representations and end up offering unproductive representations such as the molecular models studies by Linn et al. (1996) or the programming visualizations studies by Grillmeyer (2000). Multiple representations of ideas succeed when they encourage learners to revisit connections, raise useful questions about the concept they illustrate, and point out salient features.

Memory research has also reinforced the idea that examples can encourage students to deliberately reconsider their ideas. Bjork (1999), Kintsch (1998), and others have shown that when students encounter verbally presented information that seems straightforward and logical, they recall less than when the information takes more effort to understand. For example, when an outline aligns perfectly with a text, it helps learners immediately; an outline that aligns poorly with the text elicits more interpretation and ultimately enhances long-term recall (Kintsch, 1998). Similarly, students learn material such as foreign language vocabulary better when they practice, perform an intervening task that results in some forgetting, and then practice some more than when they only practice (Bjork, 1994). In both of these examples, the successful condition involves a deliberate process of making connections in spite of some difficulties.

In summary, designers often create abstract, discrepant, or relevant examples that fail to help students interpret complex phenomena, may reinforce unproductive cultural beliefs, and deter sustained, deliberate activities in science. Research on promising examples has shown the need for design studies (Linn, 2000) to refine speculations about what works.

PAT AND ASHLEY STUDY INSULATION AND CONDUCTION

Pat and Ashley illustrate how students use spontaneously developed cases to interpret questions about insulation and conduction. These longitudinal examples come from a larger study (Linn & Hsi, 2000); gender-central names were chosen because males and females performed similarly throughout the longitudinal interviews.

These students participated in a physical science course described by Linn and Hsi (2000) that engages students in making predictions, conducting experiments about heating and cooling, constructing principles to explain the results, carrying out projects, and modeling heat flow. During the 10-week unit, students study the direction of heat flow, thermal equilibrium, insulation, conduction, and the distinction between heat and temperature. They encourage a range of examples and have the opportunity to work with these examples in multiple contexts. The course has undergone numerous cycles of trial and refinement. The emergent course helps students gain deep, enduring understanding of these concepts. Students who studied the curriculum outperformed their peers who studied a traditional course when tested in high school (Linn & Hsi, 2000).

In the interviews, both Pat (see Fig. 9.2 and Linn & Hsi, 2000) and Ashley (see Fig. 9.3) spontaneously generate multiple connections and

[Interviewer] *What if you had to keep a drink cold or something, would you rather have aluminum foil or wool [or Styrofoam]?*

> [Pat] Well, I was thinking that wool keeps people hot. I don't know about wrapping a drink in it.

What is it that the wool does to keep something hot?

> The fibers. I don't know.

Interview 3—after heating and cooling instruction

What would you wrap a frozen candy bar in to keep it cold for your lunch?

> The metal. ...Because I think the metal would keep the cold in um better than something like um a napkin or something because there's little holes in the fiber and the heat energy would come into the candy bar and then make it heat up.

So I pick up this piece of metal and it feels cold to me. Why?

> It's because your hand is hotter than um at first it feels cold and then your hand will warm it up. It's like if you were outside and you walked into where it's cold, you'll feel colder than actually, you got all used to it.

But when I touch the wood, it doesn't feel cold. What's going on there?

> Um I don't know maybe there's like fibers and there's like little tiny tiny holes in wood and so maybe the heat energy goes through your hand and it doesn't stay in it or something.

So metal's a good conductor. What does it do?

> They hold the temperature in and they don't have little holes in it and so the heat energy won't go out of, or go in at all.

Interview 4—after experimenting with insulators

So what is it that the Styrofoam would do that the metal couldn't do?

> Well it just like keeps the air in because ... all the little holes. And so the air goes into the little holes and stays there.

But there's no holes in the aluminum.

> I know. I don't get it. That's like the heat energy would want to go to the aluminum because it like takes the—attracts the heat energy. And it would just stay there and not be in whatever you had in there.

Interview 5

But if they are the same temperature, why do they feel different?

> Because the wood has those little holes of air in it. And they just--it feels different. It's not a conductor. [holes] .....They keep air ...I'm not really sure. The air does something. Makes it like not go in. Makes heat energy not go.

High school—years after instruction

But if you wrapped it in you were saying plastic wrap or bubble wrap, what would be different about that?

> Because of the air pocket. ...There's something with how the air is an insulator. If you have like um, let's say the Styrofoam wrap, that's really porous. So then the air kind of holds in the little holes and then it insulates against heat energy coming in.

FIG. 9.2. Pat's responses to interviews in middle school while studying science and in high school.

continuously reinterpret their knowledge during their eighth-grade physical science class and in subsequent interviews conducted when they are in high school. Pat uses a spontaneously developed case based on holes in materials to develop more and more normative notions about insulation and conduction; this case helps Pat sort out fruitful and unproductive ideas. Ashley spontaneously devises several cases including the notion of an insulator as a barrier that keeps an object at a constant temperature. The barrier model impedes knowledge integration for Ashley. Comparing the knowledge integration of Pat and Ashley reveals how good examples can take advantage of the interpretive, cultural and deliberate nature of the learner.

Pat initially focuses on the nature of materials that insulate or conduct, saying at the pretest that "the fibers" in wool help it keep something hot. Pat revisits and connects other ideas to the fiber notion at each interview in interviews carried out at regular intervals during eighth-grade instruction. When considering ways to keep a frozen candy bar cold, Pat speculated that "little holes in the fiber" mean that "heat energy would come into" a frozen candy bar. Pat distinguishes the fibers in material like wool from "metal" that "would keep the cold in better." These non-normative notions align with the view held by many middle school students that wool warms things up so would not keep a frozen candy bar cold.

When explaining why metal feels colder than wood in a classroom, Pat explains that "your hand is hotter" and observes, for metal, "at first it feels cold and then your hand will warm it up." For wood, Pat again connects to the notion of holes and fibers and says "like fibers and there's like little tiny holes in wood so maybe heat energy goes through your hand and it doesn't stay in or something."

Pat uses an assortment of inquiry skills to test ideas about fibers and holes. Pat compares the fibers and holes in different materials including metal, Styrofoam, wood, wool, and napkins and uses these distinctions to reason about heat flow. Pat incorporates an instructed idea—that your hand is warmer than wood or metal at room temperature—to revisit the holes and fibers idea and hypothesizes that heat flows out of your hand into the wood but does not stay in the wood because of the holes.

Later in this interview, Pat defines metals as conductors because they, "hold the temperature in and they don't have little holes ... so the heat energy won't go out." To construct this explanation about why metal will keep something cold, Pat combines an understanding of scientific inquiry as requiring a mechanism—here represented by an analysis of the materials that insulate or conduct—with the instructed ideas that some materials slow the rate of heat flow and that metal is a conductor. Although non-normative, the resulting argument reflects a deliberate commitment to inquiry and coherence that serves Pat well as the course continues.

[INTERVIEWER]   *Like what is it that makes it keep your soda cold?*

    [ASHLEY]   The metal that keeps the cold in . . . They use metal for conductors. . . . Like in wires, they have copper . . . rubber or plastic is not a good conductor. Because that is what they put around it. [Distinguishes outside and inside of an object.]

And why is Styrofoam a good insulator?

    Well the heat and the cold can't really get through very well . . . if you have a cooler made of Styrofoam, it really doesn't feel that cold on the outside . . . If you have like a metal cooler . . . You can feel the cold on the outside . . .

So if you want to keep something hot, it is good to have something that conducts heat and if . . .

    Well, yeah, I mean, yeah, it would keep it hot, 'cause, um, the aluminum would get hot, too, but then it wouldn't go anywhere....

Interview 3—after heating and cooling instruction

Why do you think that the metal feels hotter than the wood?

    . . . a lot of the heat energy goes into the wood and most of it stays on the outside of the metal so you feel it more on the outside, but there's just as much heat energy in both of them.

[To keep ????? Candy bar cold?]

    Um probably foil . . . keep the cold in there so it doesn't go out.

What about things like wool?

    I think it would keep an object warm, I don't know if it will keep an object cold.

And what about Styrofoam wrapped around the bar?

    Yeah . . . a Styrofoam cup keeps stuff, keeps drinks cold.

What would be better, foil, wool...?

    I think the foil because I use the foil a lot.... Keeping the heat energy out so a lot of it can't get in, more can't get in.

So why do you think that the metal is doing . . . ?

    . . . like on a hot day, and you have a metal bar in your backyard, and when you touch it it feels a lot hotter than when you feel like a piece of wood that's been out. So I think that the heat energy stays more on the outside of the metal so you feel it more than, there's a lot more heat energy—there's the same amount of heat energy but it's circulating inside so you don't feel it as much on the wood. And Styrofoam . . . I don't think it feels that . . . it keeps the heat energy in more.

Interview 4—after insulation and conduction experiments

What if instead of a hot casserole in the cooler, we put a half gallon of ice cream in there?

    . . . the same thing is going to happen. The amount of heat energy in the ice cream will stay inside . . . The heat energy to heat it up or make it softer will not be able to get in . . . the air outside will not be able to get in. The heat energy that is inside won't be able to get out.

Can heat energy from the outside get in?

    No. It can warm the foil up, but it can press against the ice cream, but it won't be able to get in.

FIG. 9.3.

What would keep things cold better? The wool or the foil?

Um, I thought the foil earlier, but now wool is thicker. It is thicker so it will take longer for the heat energy to get into the inside.

I wonder if it makes a difference whether you are keeping a cold thing cold or a hot thing hot?

It might, but I think one thing could work for both. If it holds the heat energy in, it should be able to keep it out.

Interview 5—after posttest

You said Styrofoam . . .

. . . the Styrofoam in the coke lab worked the best to keep the heat energy inside of an object and or keep heat energy from going in . . . it would keep it in and it wouldn't let it out. It wouldn't, it wouldn't let heat energy go into it.

. . . aluminum foil . . .

Well aluminum foil is a good conductor . . . so the heat energy will leave faster than a good insulator will

And wool and Styrofoam. . .

they're both um good insulators. So it'll keep the heat energy in or keep it out.

Any idea which is better?

I think Styrofoam because it's, that was the first one in our lab that works best.

High School—years after instruction

So say I took this can-cold can of soda out of the refrigerator

. . . leave it as it is. Um..I-I used to . . . put a tin foil around my Coke but . . .the only time I've ever studied that was in 8th grade and you know tin foil was really important . . . I think wool or-or a blanket worked as-about as effectively as tin foil did. Which I never knew. I always thought that tin foil would hold it in. But I guess tin foil would've uh...conducted the coldness away from it.

What does a conductor do?

. . . an insulator contains the heat or the coolness into an area . . . the conductor does the opposite of letting it free of heat.

So if you were to wrap it in . . . wool?

. . . the coolness would be held in to a point as . . .But I think the warmth of the wool would eventually, you know, counteract it-make it warmer . . . I think that wool has a natural warming temperature as far as surround-trapping heat energy into the wool and not letting it um...flow away. It keeps the heat inside.

do insulators work for cold things only or warm things only?

...the cooler . . . keeping the heat energy from the outside from passing through to . . . the Cokes . . . not letting the heat energy come in.

. . . this spectrum of a good insulator to a good conductor. [Put] the materials . . . on this spectrum.

. . . metal would be a good conductor . . .I just remember- . . . Styrofoam was for coffee or Coke . . . Styrofoam would be a good insulator because on a cold day, putting coffee in a Styrofoam cup it would uh- the heat would not be able to go through the Styrofoam as easily as say without it....I'd put paper on the conductor . . . I would put Saran Wrap in the insulator . . . if you put stuff in the refrigerator , you close it up . . . So the air from the refrigerator doesn't get to the food . . . Blocking is an insulator and a conductor is not.

FIG. 9.3.   Ashley's responses to interviews in middle school while studying science and in high school.

After experimenting with metal and Styrofoam, Pat revisits this argument and incorporates the finding that Styrofoam insulates because "it just keeps the air ... in all the little holes." When asked to extend this to aluminum, Pat says, "I don't get it." Then Pat considers a new mechanism to explain the role of metal, saying it "attracts the heat."

After the posttest, Pat combines all these ideas—again relying on impressive inquiry skills—to articulate a new, normative argument to explain why wood and metal feel different but have the same temperature. In a stunning series of connections, Pat says, "the wood has those little holes of air in it ... it's not a conductor ... the air does something. Makes it not go in. Makes heat energy not go."

In high school, Pat revisits this argument, struggles to recall details, and uses inquiry skills to explain a novel problem—how bubble wrap works. Pat says, "The air kind of holds in the little holes and then it insulates against heat energy coming in."

For Pat, the fibers and holes model is a pivotal case. It connects a broad range of observations, instructed ideas, and experiments and forms a focal point for knowledge integration. This case engages Pat's inquiry skills, provides a mechanism for insulation, guides analysis of an assortment of materials, and evokes a deliberate approach to knowledge integration. More details from these interviews appear in Fig. 9.2.

Pat's trajectory contrasts with Ashley's trajectory as shown in Fig. 9.3. Ashley also spontaneously develops ideas about insulation and conduction and uses them to connect both class and personal ideas. Ashley, at the first interview, says metal keeps drinks cold because it "keeps the cold in" and that Styrofoam is a good insulator because "the heat and cold can't get through very well." Ashley connects these views to experiences with coolers, arguing, "If you have a Styrofoam cooler it really doesn't feel that cold on the outside." Ashley then says, "If you have a metal cooler you can feel the cold on the outside." When asked to explain these differences, Ashley says metal can keep things cold or hot because, "it would get too hot but it wouldn't go anywhere."

Ashley develops both the idea that insulators keep heat energy out and the idea that metals feel hotter because the heat is more on the surface in subsequent interviews. Ashley also combines the instructed energy conservation idea with observations of wood and metal at thermal equilibrium, saying "a lot of the heat energy goes into the wood and most of it stays on the outside of the metal ... but there is just as much heat energy in both of them." Ashley does not connect the instructed ideas about heat flow to this account and instead speaks of both heat and cold flow.

After experimenting with insulation and conduction, Ashley elaborates on a notion of an insulator as a barrier that keeps heat energy in or out. Ashley remarks, when discussing ice cream in a cooler, "the heat energy to heat it up or make it soft will not be able to get in." Ashley connects the barrier model to barriers that prevent airflow, saying, "the air outside will not be able to get in" and also points out that, "the heat energy that is inside won't be able to get out."

In comparing wool with foil as insulators, Ashley generates a new criteria, thickness, and says wool would be better because "it is thicker so it would take longer for the heat energy to get inside." Note also that in this response, after doing class experiments, Ashley depicts insulators as slowing but not stopping heat from getting inside. Ashley also concludes that insulators and conductors work for both hot and cold things, saying, "if it holds the heat energy in it should keep it out." In these responses, Ashley consistently uses instructed ideas about heat energy and results of experiments conducted in class. Ashley also uses inquiry skills to generalize the role of insulators to both hot and cold objects.

In the final middle school interview, Ashley reiterates the idea that insulators keep heat energy in and "wouldn't let it out." Ashley also sorts out insulators and conductors saying wool and Styrofoam are insulators and foil is a conductor. To distinguish wool and Styrofoam, Ashley prefers Styrofoam because "that was the first one in our lab that works best." Here Ashley, compared to Pat, has multiple foci for knowledge and uses idiosyncratic reasons such as which material was tested first.

Ashley makes progress in understanding insulation and conduction and in recognizing the direction of heat flow during middle school but does not form a coherent argument. Ashley retains a barrier model as well as a material-based model for insulation.

In high school, Ashley recalls being surprised by the properties of foil and initially reiterates her view of foil as "conducting the coldness away" and of wool as having "a natural warming temperature." Ashley describes a picnic cooler as "keeping the heat energy from … passing through … and keeping the coolness temperature." These responses represent some connections between a materials perspective and an insulators as barriers perspective. The instructed heat energy idea remains in Ashley's repertoire, but Ashley also reconnects to ideas about cold.

When Ashley is asked to place a set of objects along a continuum from insulators to conductors, the centrality of the barrier idea becomes clear. Ashley prefers to sort materials into insulators or conductors rather than placing them in relative positions to each other. Ashley asserts, "Blocking is an insulator and a conductor is not." This notion of insulator as a barrier overshadows the focus on the nature of individual materials. Furthermore, Ashley uses inquiry skills of comparison and experimentation to connect to an idea about preventing airflow developed earlier. Ashley remarks, for example, that Saran Wrap® is an insulator because it is used "so the air from the refrigerator does not get to the food." Ashley marshals an assortment of observations and connections to support the barrier idea. Ashley connects to materials using descriptive criteria, such as the "Naturally warming temperature of wool," to warrant assertions.

Both Pat and Ashley use rich examples to organize their ideas about insulation and conduction. Pat's holes case leads to a coherent account—fitting the ideal for a pivotal case. Pat connects instructed ideas to the case and uses inquiry skills to make sense of new situations. Ashley's barrier case does not promote coherence. Rather than extending instructed ideas, this case appears to interfere with recall and to privilege descriptive warrants for connections. The barrier case also interferes with the generative process and ultimately overshadows results from experiments with insulators. Ideally, instruction would give every student the opportunity to develop or appropriate pivotal cases that productively engage their inquiry skills. Rather than relying on students to spontaneously devise promising cases, designers can create pivotal cases that apply broadly.

COMPARISON STUDIES OF PIVOTAL CASES

To investigate pivotal cases, design study has proven useful (Hoadley & Linn, 2004; Linn, 2000). Design studies involve iterative refinement of a complex educational program and feature both multiple methodologies for gathering information in the complex settings where education takes place and the design of compelling comparisons that contrast alternative ways of solving specific problems within the broader context of the instruction.

Spontaneous Pivotal Cases

Design of powerful pivotal cases can result from analysis of the cases students develop spontaneously. Pat, in making sense of insulation and conduction, generates a focus on fibers and eventually on the holes between those fibers and regularly revisits this notion from eighth grade through high school to come up with an account of insulation and conduction based on the interaction between air and holes. Pat develops a highly generative and extensible account of how holes might make "air not go" and thereby enhance the insulation property of materials. This case has tremendous advantages. It leads to pro-normative knowledge—by connecting to related ideas about thermal equilibrium and heat flow. The case also has limitations, leading to confusion about materials such as asbestos and hard plastic. It nonetheless provides a good set of criteria for distinguishing among materials such as bubble wrap and supports use of the inquiry skills of comparison and analysis to reach more coherent ideas about the role of air pockets in insulation.

In the longitudinal sample, few students came up with such unique and useful pivotal cases. Many students devised cases that interfered with coherent understanding. Ashley's view of insulation and conduction as mutually exclusive categories stood in the way of interpreting insulation as a continuum. The barrier model inhibited knowledge integration for many students by focusing attention on stopping heat flow.

The absorption model, mentioned briefly by Ashley and Pat and embraced by others, suggests that heat flows until the insulator is full. Some students assume that the insulator loses its effectiveness when filled, whereas others imagine insulators as storing heat indefinitely and keeping it away from another object. Both these views inhibit knowledge integration, although many who initially hold the absorption model eventually embrace the heat flow model and refine their ideas about absorption to fit the new view.

Comparing the spontaneous cases developed by students reveals that some, such as the holes model, support the interpretive character of the learning and help students generate pro-normative views. Pat reformulated the holes model and made it more and more the focal point for knowledge integration. Pat reconstructed the holes idea numerous times, moving from a decidedly non-normative account of holes to a very sophisticated view. Pat could also extend the holes idea to new contexts and situations, looking for the existence of holes in new materials.

Cases like the holes model take advantage of the interpretive, cultural, and deliberate nature of the learner to help students gain a more normative account of insulation and conduction. Others such as the barrier model stay in the repertoire but limit the interpretive process and constrain reasoning. Ashley could not extend the barrier model to the continuum between insulation and conduction. In addition, the barrier model could not be reconstructed to incorporate examples showing that heat flows in all materials but at different rates. Ashley had these additional ideas about heat flow and the continuum in the repertoire of ideas but could not find a focus for connecting them. These findings suggest that students might benefit if designers created cases that when added to the mix of ideas formed a durable focus for knowledge integration, could be readily extended to new situations, and could be reconstructed using inquiry skills to increase the coherence of ideas.

Designed Cases

To study pivotal cases, the Computers as Learning Partners (CLP) research partnership has followed an iterative design process. The designer creates initial ideas for cases based on interviews with students such as Pat and Ashley. The research group formulates a possible pivotal case, tests it in classrooms, and revises it until it benefits a large number of students.

In response to students' difficulties with insulation and conduction, Lewis (1991) and Foley (2000) have designed the heat bars software simulation to illustrate the rate of heat flow in different materials (see Fig. 9.4). After a number of design and refinement cycles, Lewis tested heat bars in pilot studies and eventually in whole classroom studies.

Heat bars responds to the absorption and barrier model by enabling students to compare materials and view the rates of heat flow in each material. Heat bars animates the variation in rate of heat flow, helping students distinguish among materials and suggesting an elaboration of the barrier model. Heat bars also helps reinterpret the absorption model by demonstrating that heat flows through an object and keeps flowing through it after the object has reached the same temperature as the heat source. Heat bars enables students to use their inquiry skills to test the rates of heat flow in different materials. Classroom observations have revealed that students perform multiple tests and repeat tests they have done earlier as their understanding of the topic expands.

To test the effectiveness of heat bars, Lewis (1991) carries out a compelling comparison study where, of the six classes studying thermodynamics in a single school, half used the heat bars simulation for about 30 min, and half did not. All the classes were taught by the same teacher. Lewis (1991) compared pretest and posttest performance and found an impact for heat bars, especially on questions about heat flow. On the posttest, students in the heat bars condition were almost one standard deviation more successful than

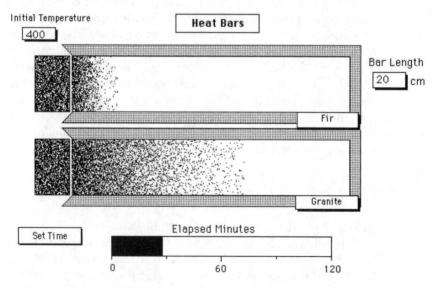

FIG. 9.4.   Heat bars software (see also http.//www.clp.berkeley.edu).

those in the non-heat-bars condition on questions about heat flow. Performance on the overall posttest controlled for initial performance was also significantly better. This compelling comparison illustrates the power of the heat bars pivotal case on a posttest administered over 6 weeks later.

To illustrate the durability of pivotal cases, Clark (2000) reported on a student called Cedar who reflects on the heat bars animation. Cedar starts middle school with many of the same ideas expressed by Pat and Ashley. Cedar initially expects Styrofoam to be poor at keeping things hot or cold and describes aluminum foil as good for keeping things hot and excellent for keeping things cold. When asked about insulators, Cedar mentions home insulation materials advertised on television and explains, "It's compact, and it would keep like heat in or cold in." During instruction, Cedar expects foil and Styrofoam to help keep a frozen candy bar cold but also thinks that Styrofoam might be better because it "would trap the cold or heat energy in."

Later, after experimenting with heat bars, Cedar distinguishes insulation and conduction and often describes insulators as "able to keep the heat in, heat energy in, or out." Cedar continues to mention keeping "cold in." However, to explain these observations, Cedar relies on the heat bars simulation. Cedar distinguishes materials based on the rate of heat flow and specifically refers to experiments with varied materials. In addition, Cedar explains how hear bars helps him understand by drawing "a picture in your mind instead of having all those words." Cedar, like other students, places great importance on the visual aspects of heat bars but also articulates the value of experimenting and comparing multiple materials.

Like other students, Cedar trusts the heat bars simulation and explains how the simulation provided a mechanism for everyday experience saying, "Well I knew that heat traveled through objects like copper faster than others but I really wasn't sure why. But when we did the experiment, it showed the heat going through quick and it would shade it in." Cedar continues to hold both normative and non-normative ideas about insulation and conduction, but following experience with heat bars, Cedar starts to organize ideas about insulation and conduction around rate of heat flow.

During the longitudinal interviews in high school, Cedar forms a more and more normative view of insulation and conduction and abandons the notion of cold or cold energy. Cedar also connects the middle school science ideas to ideas introduced in high school chemistry saying, "heat energy … the faster the molecules move around the hotter it gets." To explain cooling, Cedar links heat energy and molecular motion by saying, "heat energy would be taken away and the molecules would be slowed down." Cedar describes interactions between warmer and colder objects in language similar to the words used for heat bars earlier saying metal is "a better conductor, and the heat energy it can escape and go through the object faster than wood." Cedar also speculates about heat energy and insulation at the molecular level, saying, "I guess the molecules are so close together so that the heat energy can go through quickly and like in Styrofoam, I guess they're like further apart of something so that is has a harder time traveling through it."

In reflecting on middle school science, Cedar recalls the processes and ideas but is sketchy on the details. For example, Cedar says, "there was an experiment about how time effects the rate of giving off energy" and mentions that the computers could display graphs. For Cedar, middle school science connected to cultural beliefs about science and expanded the strategies for science learning. Cedar explains the benefits of "using different experiments to kind of work things out ... trying things several different ways instead of just looking at it one way." Cedar articulates the benefits of experiments, visualizations, and discussions with a laboratory partner saying, "you can use your hands and go to work instead of all just trying to visualize it in your head ... sometimes if one of us didn't understand it and the other did, we could try to explain it or try to get through it together, instead of trying to struggle by yourself."

Cedar illustrates the complexity of knowledge integration. Cedar starts with a mix of ideas, adds normative ideas, retains non-normative ideas, and regularly organizes ideas in new ways. Middle school science including the heat bars pivotal case provides Cedar with a foundation that connects to high school instruction. The heat flow model becomes the focal point for forming more and more normative ideas about thermodynamics. Cedar uses inquiry skills supported by the heat bars animation to test alternatives and reconstruct notions about insulation.

Foley (2000) extended research on the heat bars pivotal case, testing the impact of models involving color and other mechanisms for depicting heat sources. Foley replicated the Lewis (1991) results but found no benefit for other variations in instruction, revealing the design challenges facing those eager to create pivotal cases.

Clark (2000) extended the heat bars example to address the difficulties students face when studying thermal equilibrium. When comparing the feel and thermometer temperature of varied materials at thermal equilibrium, students have difficulty resolving seemingly contradictory information. Clark created an animation of heat flow in a hand when it touched metal and wood objects at different surrounding temperatures based on heat bars and embedded it in the WISE software (see Fig. 9.1). The hand animation showed that when wood and metal were at room temperature, heat would flow faster from the hand to metal than from the hand to wood, explaining why objects at the same temperature might feel different. The animation also demonstrated that when wood and metal were touched on a playground on a very hot day, the metal would feel hotter rather than cooler. The hand animation combined the benefits of the heat bars heat flow model with the comparison of different surrounds—a room temperature surround and a hot day surround—to sustain inquiry skills and focus knowledge integration. Compelling comparison studies comparing classes with and without the animation demonstrated a significant impact of the hand animation on thermal equilibrium understanding (Clark, 2000).

Studies of other science topics including light, the rock cycle, and mechanical design reveal similar benefits for design studies leading to pivotal cases. Study of student ideas about light have revealed a persistent confusion between visual acuity and the physics of light propagation. When students researched the nature of light, they located a Web site illustrating night goggles (Linn & Hsi, 2000). In the "How Far Does Light Go?" WISE activity, Bell (1998, 2004) contrasted classes using the night goggles pivotal case combined with SenseMaker (Bell, 1997) software to classes not using the case and showed that the case led to significant gains in understanding of how far light goes.

The Geo3D (Kali, Orion, & Gorni, 1998) animation of geological formations had an impact on students' understanding of the rock cycle as shown in a compelling comparison study (Kali, Orion, & Eylon, 2003). Kali, Orion, and Gorni engaged students' inquiry skills to explore the layers of the earth.

The Display Object (Osborn & Agogino, 1993) software enables students learning mechanical design to explore the cross-sections and rotations of complex objects. Research demonstrated the impact of Display Objects as a pivotal case to help students understand the spatial rotation of objects in a graphical communication course (Hsi, Linn, & Bell, 1997).

These pivotal cases all resulted from a process of iterative refinement. Each case has involved analysis of students' existing ideas and the difficulties that students have faced in developing a robust and coherent account of a complex science or mathematics topic. All the cases have taken advantage of technology to support student inquiry by providing an animation, simulation, or representation of a phenomenon that students might find difficult to visualize. All the cases have enabled students to perform multiple investigations with the software and get powerful feedback on their ideas. These cases have been typically introduced in less than half an hour of classroom instruction, yet they provide students with the opportunity to conduct multiple experiments and to rethink the ideas from the experiments after the class is over. These cases have provided powerful mini-investigations and have drawn on a variety of relevant inquiry skills.

Pivotal cases in these studies can be described as durable, extensible, and reconstructable: durable because they remain the focal point of knowledge integration for activities in varied contexts, extensible because learners can apply them successfully in numerous contexts, and reconstructable because learners can use inquiring procedures to reformulate them to account for new information and to recollect them when new, relevant problems arise.

DISCUSSION

Pivotal cases offer promise as a class of examples designed to promote knowledge integration. When judiciously designed, pivotal cases can improve the impact of science courses.

Case studies of Pat, Ashley, and Cedar reveal how spontaneous and pivotal cases contribute to student understanding. Cases form the focal point for knowledge integration about insulation and conduction. For Pat, the focus on holes and fibers generated cohesive, normative ideas. For Ashley, the focus on barriers led to unproductive conjectures. Introducing the heat bars pivotal case helped Cedar clarify the complex relation between how objects feel when touched and their temperature as indicated by a thermometer.

Compelling comparison studies demonstrate that pivotal cases, when introduced into an effective educational program such as WISE that includes support for knowledge integration, have a demonstrable effect on student learning both initially and longitudinally (Bell & Linn, 2000; Linn & Slotta, 2000). The programs that utilized pivotal cases also featured peer-to-peer discussion, opportunities to reflect, and supports for organizing information (see Linn et al., 2003). Even when all of these features are in place, compelling comparison studies reveal that adding pivotal cases to the instruction has a significant effect on initial and lifelong learning.

Criteria for Pivotal Cases

Research on pivotal cases suggests a set of criteria that designers can use to create new pivotal cases and researchers can test with compelling comparison studies. Pivotal cases illustrate complex science concepts crucial to the success of scientific endeavors and help students understand these concepts, build connections between these concepts and related phenomena, and generate new connections in the future. By studying new cases based on the criteria, research groups can help designers create better cases and can also refine the criteria.

Create Compelling Comparisons.   Pivotal cases create compelling comparisons by distinguishing two or more situations that showcase the focal point for knowledge integration such as heat flow, the hand as a temperature detector, or the eye as a light detector. Bridging analogies advocated by Clement (1993) offer students similar comparisons between multiple examples. By contrasting two situations that differ on a crucial dimension, pivotal cases invite students to test their ideas about the dimension.

Cases such as the molecular models in chemistry that do not offer students a compelling comparison may mislead students about the focal point for knowledge integration as was shown by Linn et al. (1996). This case directed attention to the elements of a single molecule rather than to the features of a group of molecules. The case also drew attention away from the particulate nature of matter—an idea that many students find difficult.

Pivotal cases strip away irrelevant dimensions. Heat bars compares heat flow in different materials and underspecifies other context issues so the crucial distinction of rate of heat flow in different materials can predominate. The case leaves open questions about the thickness of the material, the insulation around the bars, and the nature of the dots that appear to be flowing. The unresolved dimensions entice learners to use inquiry skills to explore the topic.

Place Inquiry in Accessible, Culturally Relevant Contexts. Pivotal cases feature contexts and scientific analyses relevant to the learner. Heat bars depicts thermal phenomena at a macroscopic level, relying on heat flow rather than molecular-kinetic theory. This grain size for analysis makes the science inspectable and testable. The heat flow idea also lays the groundwork for a microscopic view as illustrated in the longitudinal interviews with Cedar.

Pivotal cases place science in contexts that connect to problems students might encounter in solving everyday problems, in reading news accounts of current scientific breakthroughs, or in subsequent science classes to promote knowledge integration. Pivotal cases can help explain dilemmas students will encounter outside of science class by a judicious selection of context effects. By connecting to contexts students are likely to encounter in the future, pivotal cases enable students to test and elaborate their ideas. As the longitudinal interviews have suggested, students find the heat bars example generative and have used it to explain how dishes feel when they are still warm in the dishwasher, to understand the design of colors, and to analyze labels on outdoor clothing. In contrast, the car on a icy road example is less likely to connect to experiences of students and may, as a result, discourage inquiry.

Pivotal cases make inquiry skills accessible to students by showcasing natural comparisons between different conditions and supporting sustained inquiry. Heat bars showcases comparisons between materials and enables students to perform multiple experiments. Comparisons of visual acuity at night and during the day showcase the limitations of the eye as a detector and encourage personal experiments under additional conditions.

Pivotal cases engage students in mini-investigations—relatively short cycles of inquiry and reflection. By enabling students to engage in inquiry around a complex scientific concept that can form the focus for knowledge integration such as rate of heat flow, pivotal cases allow students to repeatedly ask the relevant question for the topic and to test their ideas about alternative accounts of the concept in new contexts.

Pat and Ashley illustrate how well-chosen pivotal cases can engage students in mini-investigations. When Ashley compared metal and wood in a cold room as well as metal and wood on a hot day on the playground, this natural experiment provides feedback and prompts reflection on the relation between thermal equilibrium and insulation and conduction. Ashley's exploration of the properties of thermoses resulted in another mini-investigation. The thermos example raises questions about the shell, which might be made out of metal, and the internal material, which is often Styrofoam. Comparing varied thermoses allowed Ashley to perform a thought experiment about the metal shell. Comparing the mini-investigations of Pat and Ashley reveals that Pat used more rigorous standards for evidence than Ashley. Pivotal cases can engage the cultural beliefs about scientific inquiry held by the learner (Bell & Linn, 2002).

By engaging in inquiry around an accessible case, students learn inquiry processes they can reuse to reconstruct their understanding in the future. Cedar and other students in the longitudinal sample often reconstructed their ideas when asked about insulation and conduction. These students can use cases to reflect on the inquiry process and reconstruct their understanding if they become confused.

Provide Feedback to Support Pre-Normative Self-Monitoring.   Pivotal cases focus knowledge integration in a pro-normative direction by encouraging students to make predictions or create artifacts and then providing feedback on these productions. Opportunities or prompts that encourage reflection increase the likelihood that students will evaluate their own learning practices. Students often get little feedback on their reasoning as they learn and have difficulty monitoring their own progress. When science courses emphasize abstract representations such as the periodic table or Newton's Laws, students may lack the ability to determine whether or not they are making progress. Research has shown that students who have the opportunity and feedback to monitor their progress allocate their intellectual energy more efficiently than those who just follow directions and complete assignments (White & Frederiksen, 1998). Programs that provide opportunities for comprehension monitoring and encourage students to continuously assess their understanding have shown considerable benefit for science (Chi, 1996).

The spontaneous cases developed by Pat and Ashley illustrate the value of pro-normative reflection. The holes case eventually moved Pat's thinking in a pro-normative direction by enabling an account of insulators as trapping air and slowing heat flow. Pat actively monitored progress, often wondering if connections made sense based on additional observations. In contrast, Ashley's barrier model for insulation and conduction elicited new, non-normative ideas in the high school interview. Ashley had difficulty getting feedback on the barrier model and compared to Pat was less likely to seek coherence among ideas. Other students studied by Linn and Hsi (2000) and Clark (2000) have followed similar patterns.

Designed pivotal cases can include feedback that helps students monitor their progress and that nudges students in a pro-normative direction. These cases offer students additional benefits when combined with instruction that requires predictions, experimentation, and reflection. Heat bars allows students to make predictions about materials and test them with the animation. Clark's (2000) hand animation provides feedback on how heat flows between the hand and objects in various contexts. Similarly, Display Object and Geo3D allow predicting and testing of ideas about the spatial composition of geological forms and complex three-dimensional objects. All of these pivotal cases take advantage of technology to provide feedback and prompt students for self-monitoring.

Researchers have also created instruction with pivotal cases that provides feedback and encourages reflection without using technology. Case, Griffin, and Kelly (1999) used a number line representation and specific activities to test predictions about addition and subtraction on the number line. Teachers worked with small groups of first-grade, at-risk students to elicit predictions, reflection, and self monitoring. The number line representation was designed much like other pivotal cases. After study of the spontaneous ideas of the students, Case et al. designed instruction in line with developmental theory, created a series of examples using the number line to respond to student ideas, tested the ideas by engaging students in making predictions and revising their ideas, and revised instruction until it was effective. Case et al. demonstrated, in a longitudinal, compelling comparison study, that instruction using inquiry and self-monitoring with the number line cases dramatically enhances performance of first graders and carries through to subsequent years.

Palinscar and Brown (1984) used a similar approach to identify a method to help students whose spontaneous ideas about interpreting text focus on word decoding rather than meaning making. Palinscar and Brown designed small-group activities to introduce inquiry about the text by engaging students in summarizing, asking questions, and clarifying difficulties. Initially, the approach was introduced in student–teacher interactions. Eventually, the approach was used in peer-to-peer interactions. Palinscar and Brown found in a compelling comparison study that at-risk students who previously had considerable difficulty with comprehension not only gain comprehension skills but gain insight into their own learning.

Pivotal cases can encourage the deliberative character of the learner by providing students with information about their progress in understanding science and encouraging self-monitoring. Cases designed to provide feedback ensure that when students reflect and monitor their progress, they are likely to make connections to relevant material and develop a more robust and coherent view of the phenomena. By encouraging pro-normative reflection, pivotal cases help students recognize the value of linking and connecting ideas. They also help students recognize that ideas from science class can apply to new situations.

Ideally, curriculum designers would construct pivotal cases for the curriculum that, when viewed as a group, revealed connections across different complex scientific concepts. For examples, the night goggles and sunglasses pivotal case in the WISE "How Far Does Light Go?" example raises questions about the eye as a source of evidence about light much as the hand animation for thermal equilibrium raises questions about the sense of touch as a source of evidence about heat flow. These connections among topics have the potential of spurring students to develop self-initiated ways to monitor their progress.

Enable Narrative Accounts of Science.   Pivotal cases help convert complex scientific information from varied sources including text, visuals, animations, models, movies, and formulas into a narrative. Narratives that connect multiple examples into a story with the mechanism of the pivotal case as the focal point pull together diverse representations and strengthen understanding. Narratives such as personal accounts of success, parables, or anecdotes have considerable persuasive appeal. Narrative can increase the interest in science while at the same time combining sources that increase the likelihood of recalling complex information.

Pivotal cases encourage stories that depend on and reveal the coherence of science. Both Pat and Ashley extended their ideas about holes and barriers into more and more comprehensive stories. The holes story gained coherence over time, and the barrier story encountered obstacles. Students discussing heat bars including Cedar extended their ideas into a story about the relative rate of heat flow in materials and about the materials that they had studied. Heat bars stories take heat flow as the focal point and often drop references to the software animation. Narratives convert a visual and animated account of the topic into a linked and connected story.

Creating a narrative to link science experiences requires an iterative process in which students make conjectures and test them against alternatives. Science courses with fleeting coverage of numerous topics fail to provide opportunity or resources for sustained efforts to create powerful narratives. Many textbook examples, especially those designed to contradict common ideas—such as floating a pin on water to contradict the notion that metal sinks—lead students to separate their ideas rather than connect them.

Ensuring that science narratives rely on valid evidence, incorporate a broad range of sources, and undergo revision based on new information generally depends on the discourse community created in the classroom. Scientific discourse serves an important role in solidifying and challenging narratives. Scientific communities engage in a series of practices including seminars, meetings, and reviews of research reports to refine their narratives. By enabling learners to develop narratives and discuss them with peers, science courses can encourage knowledge integration. The interviews reported for Pat, Ashley, and Cedar demonstrate the power of narrative. These students often struggled to tell coherent stories and frequently identified flaws in their own reasoning in the process of constructing a narrative.

These results resonate with the success of curriculum materials featuring case studies or case-based reasoning. Case studies use a narrative format to present a complex case (Kolodner, 1993; Linn & Clancy, 1992). Using case studies, students contrast alternatives and generate coherent solutions. Computer programming case studies, for example, provide a narrative account of a complex problem. Linn and Clancy (1992) studied the programming language PASCAL and found that understanding a complex example and solving problems using that example was enhanced by a narrative account of how an expert had solved the same problem. The narrative featured discussion of trade-offs between alternative solutions, illustrations of common patterns in programming, and discussion of mechanisms for diagnosing flaws and debugging solutions.

Kolodner (1993) argued that complex case studies use narrative to engage students in problems of appropriate complexity and encourage them to form connections among ideas. Kolodner argued that narrative case studies in which students analyze alternative sources embed knowledge in situations students have experienced. Students learn to interrogate the knowledge presented in the case and are better prepared to use it in new problems. Kolodner pointed out that cases emphasize concrete instances rather than abstractions and are particularly useful for domains in which theory is weak and in which decomposition of a problem is either impossible or unhelpful. Cases such as those used by Linn and Clancy (1992) and Kolodner (1993) have represented the most complex end of a continuum of methods for presenting narrative accounts of scientific problems.

Pivotal cases and the mini-investigations they support provide opportunities to develop coherent narratives and test them against alternatives. Learning environments such as WISE support a series of activities using formats such as the inquiry map (see Fig. 9.1). With support from a technology like WISE, teachers can devote their energies to guiding students in forming coherent and normative narratives.

Goals of Science Courses and Pivotal Cases

Standards documents, curriculum frameworks, and textbooks break down goals for science courses roughly into three categories: concepts such as insulation or conduction, inquiry such as experimentation or analysis, and lifelong learning such as preparation for future courses or for personal science dilemmas. The trajectories of Pat and Ashley suggest that pivotal cases, when added to effective science courses, could contribute to all these goals.

Precollege science standards and textbooks emphasize concepts—often listing concepts for each grade level or course. The intended level of understanding or degree of sophistication is often left to textbook authors or assessment designers. Creating pivotal cases to illustrate concepts would enhance connections among existing and instructed ideas.

Science courses generally have the goal of communicating inquiry—some aspects of scientific investigation, methodology, epistemology, or experimentation. Inquiry in standards documents typically involves generating ideas, comparing alternatives, reflecting on progress, critiquing experiments, collaborating with peers, convincing others of the validity of results, and evaluating the rigor of an investigation. The mini-investigations supported by pivotal cases can help students link science concepts and inquiry in sustained projects.

Many standards documents distinguish inquiry from concept learning. Recent research has suggested that this distinction overly simplifies the situation and prevents full-fledged knowledge integration (e.g., Greeno, 1989; Lave & Wenger, 1990; Linn et al., 1996). For example, researchers have shown that students who control variables in one context fail to control variables when conducting investigations in other contexts. Students would not organize an unfair footrace (Linn, Clement, & Pulos, 1983) but might neglect variables they believe they understand when testing cookie recipes (e.g., Tschirgi, 1980). Thus, students appear to act pragmatically rather than testing all their conjectures (e.g., Linn, Clements, & Pulos, 1983). Pivotal cases can connect concepts and inquiry and reveal the nature of scientific investigation.

Furthermore, students need a nuanced understanding of inquiry linked to the discipline. Students need to appreciate the specific methodologies appropriate to the field to engage in inquiry. Exploring the fossil record, for example, demands a different set of methodologies than studying insulation. Only by carrying out projects in several topic areas can students develop this comprehensive understanding of inquiry. Pivotal cases that illustrate the methods and findings in the discipline can advance this type of understanding.

Instructional programs generally aspire to engage students in autonomous projects, but these often involve following recipes rather than conducting investigations. Effective inquiry problems also need to provide feedback to students so that they can evaluate their investigation. Designing pivotal cases that provide clues about the investigation can encourage critiques, connections to related situations, and insight into the epistemological underpinnings of science. Too often students conclude that science is a relatively linear process of hypothesizing, gaining results, and coming up with the next hypothesis because of their impoverished inquiry experiences. Bell (1998) engaged students in researching how far light goes by contrasting their visual acuity with feedback from light detectors. Contrasting night goggles and sunglasses provided a pivotal case that coalesced these experiences for most students (e.g., Bell & Linn, 2002).

A third goal of science courses concerns lifelong learning. Ultimately, students who achieve coherent understanding have a greater likelihood of revisiting their ideas and generating new ideas. Lamentably, standardized tests that feature long lists of multiple-choice problems send a misleading message about the ideal form of instruction to achieve scientific understanding. These tests tempt textbook authors and teachers to provide drills on information at the same grain size and level of connection as found on the test. Research contradicts this notion, showing that even when courses neglect a good portion of the topics, students who gain coherent understanding of complex cases still do as well or better as those prepared with a more complete coverage but less emphasis on coherence (Cobb & Bowers, 1999; Shymansky & Kyle, 1992; Walker & Schaffarzik, 1974).

Coherent understanding enables learners to interrogate their own understanding. Many expert computer scientists, mathematicians, and scientists have described a reconstructive process used to recall previously studied material. Experts might carry out a thought experiment or test to infer a principle such as the commutative property in algebra. Reconstructing understanding using an incomplete memory of a concept and some inquiry steps occurs frequently and enhances the ability of experts to recall complex information and make sense of complex situations. This process can be supported by pivotal cases that make reconstruction of ideas relatively easy.

Scientists also achieve coherent understanding when they identify and resolve controversies. The current precollege curriculum offers few examples of controversy—fewer than one page in every hundred in a typical science text addresses a controversy (Champagne, 1998). The Science Controversies On-Line Partnerships in Education (Science Controversies On-Line Partnerships in Education, 2004) project has shown that using pivotal cases and debates to introduce controversy in science class increases students' understanding of the epistemological underpinnings of science (Bell & Linn, 2002; Linn, 2000). Controversy projects can also help students learn generalizable communication processes because they construct arguments and discuss them with peers (Hoadley & Linn, 2000; Linn, 2000).

diSessa and Minstrell (1998) advocated benchmark lessons to help students connect new ideas to existing views and sort out the alternatives. In this approach, the class considers an example that resembles a pivotal case such as how much liquid a 400 g block of wood and a 400 g block of metal will displace. Students generate a set of alternative outcomes, discuss their ideas, make predictions, conduct a class demonstration, and revisit their ideas. In the case of density, the teacher might have students compare objects with the same volume and unequal mass as well as objects with unequal volume and equal mass. diSessa and Minstrell's benchmark lessons as well as the Japanese instruction featuring discussions of alternative principles to explain a phenomena also show how instruction can help students sift through a repertoire of views, critique each others' ideas, and develop coherent ideas (Clark, 2000).

CONCLUSIONS

Pivotal cases can strengthen science courses by helping students recognize similar situations and by encouraging students to use inquiry skills to test the connections. When combined with powerful supports for knowledge integration in environments such as WISE, pivotal cases dispose learners toward connecting a novel situation to existing, instructed ideas and enable learners to test the adequacy of their connections by using relevant inquiry skills. Well-designed pivotal cases propel students into a lifelong quest for more complete understanding of science.

Research up to now suggests the following criteria for the design of pivotal cases:

- Create compelling comparisons.
- Place inquiry in accessible, culturally relevant contexts.
- Provide feedback to support pro-normative self-monitoring.
- Enable narrative accounts of science.

Curriculum designers and educational researchers are invited to create and test new pivotal cases to extend our understanding of what makes a good example for science instruction. Future work should not only apply the criteria for pivotal cases proposed here but also test these criteria and suggest elaborations and improvement to them.

Research has suggested that pivotal cases take advantage of the interpretive, cultural, and deliberate nature of the learner. To engage the interpretive nature of the learner, pivotal cases offer compelling comparisons that draw attention to crucial variables. They allow learners to inspect the impact of the variable and to hold examples up against alternatives. By interpreting pivotal cases in relation to their existing ideas, students incorporate a naturally controlled experiment and reconsider related perspectives. Compared to more abstract examples, pivotal cases connect to more of the ideas held by the learner. Compared to examples with only a single case—such as the temperature of wood and metal in the classroom—pivotal cases encourage reorganization of ideas.

To engage the cultural nature of the learner, pivotal cases illustrate a naturally occurring experiment that captures the epistemological underpinnings of the discipline. By presenting contrasting cases and encouraging students to see an explanation, pivotal cases reinforce the notion that science experiences make sense. By making a comparison accessible to all learners, pivotal cases suggest that citizens can participate in science rather than just memorize scientific information.

To engage the deliberate nature of the learner, pivotal cases support an iterative process of reconsidering and reformulating scientific information. Pivotal cases spur students to make connections and seek criteria to explain their perspectives. Pivotal cases have the potential of connecting to new experiences and motivating students to think about science after their science classes end. Thus, when Pat and Ashley responded to questions in high school, they have added everyday examples to their accounts of insulation and conduction in the intervening years.

Pivotal cases support knowledge integration by connecting to the interpretive, cultural, and deliberate nature of the learner and by adding durable, extensible, and reconstructable ideas to the mix of views students bring to science class. Pivotal cases point learners in a pro-normative direction by offering a durable focus for knowledge integration. Pivotal cases, compared to examples designed to transmit knowledge, encourage the extension of scientific ideas by leaving some context questions unanswered and some dimensions open for exploration. Pivotal cases enable the reconstruction of scientific understanding by supporting students as they create narratives and incorporate additional information into the narrative. By providing feedback and encouraging self monitoring, pivotal cases allow students to both extend and reconstruct their ideas in a more normative direction.

Students need cases that showcase potential links to related contexts, draw attention to salient aspects of the scientific phenomena, and leave irrelevant details underspecified. Science instruction that provides learners with an inviting puzzle and entices them to keep seeking the missing pieces will ultimately result in lifelong science learning.

ACKNOWLEDGMENTS

This material is based on work supported by the National Science Foundation under Grants 9873180, 9805420, 0087832, and 9720384. Any opinions, findings, and conclusions or recommendations expressed in this material are those of the author and do not necessarily reflect the views of the National Science Foundation.

This material was partially prepared while Marcia Linn was a Fellow at the Center for advanced Study in the Behavioral Sciences with support from the Spencer Foundation.

I gratefully acknowledge helpful discussions of these ideas with members of the Web-based Inquiry Science Environment group and members of the memory group at the Center for Advanced Study in the Behavioral Sciences. Special thanks go to Robert Bjork, Douglas Clark, Richard Duschl, Batsheva Eylon, and Ference Marton for stimulating discussions.

I appreciate help in production of this manuscript from David Crowell, Scott Hsu, Deanna Knickerbocker, and Lisa Safley.

REFERENCES

Anderson, J. R., & Schunn, C. D. (2000). Implications of the ACT-R learning theory: No magic bullets. In R. Glaser (Ed.), *Advances in instructional psychology: Educational design and cognitive science, Vol. 5* (pp. 1–33). Mahwah, NJ: Lawrence Erlbaum Associates.

Baddeley, A. D., & Longman, D. J. A. (1978). The influence of length and frequency of training session on the rate of learning to type. *Ergonomics, 21,* 627–635.

Bell, P. (1997). *SenseMaker* (computer software). Berkeley, CA: University of California, Berkeley.

Bell, P. (1998). *Designing for students' conceptual change in science using argumentation and classroom debate.* Unpublished doctoral dissertation, University of California, Berkeley.

Bell, P. (2004). Promoting students' arguments construction and collaborative debate in the science classroom. In. M. C. Linn, E. A. Davis, & P. Bell (Eds.), *Internet Environments for Science Education* (pp. 115–144). Mahwah, NJ: Lawrence Erlbaum Associates.

Bell, P., & Linn, M. C. (2000). Scientific arguments as learning artifacts: Designing for learning from the web with KIE. *International Journal of Science Education, 22,* 797–817.

Bell, P., & Linn, M. C. (2002). Beliefs about science: How does science instruction contribute? In B. K. Hofer & P. R. Pintrich (Eds.), *Personal epistemology: The psychology of beliefs about knowledge and knowing* (pp. 321–346). Mahwah, NJ: Lawrence Erlbaum Associates.

Bell, P., Hoadley, C. M., & Linn, M. C. (2004) Design-based research in education. In M. C. Linn, E. A. Davis, & P. Bell (Eds.), *Internet environments for science education* (pp. 73–88). Mahwah, NJ: Lawrence Erlbaum Associates.

Bjork, R. A. (1994). Memory and metamemory considerations in the training of human beings. In J. Metcalfe & A. Shimamura (Eds.), *Metacognition: Knowing about knowing* (pp. 185–205). Cambridge, MA: MIT Press.

Bjork, R. A. (1999). Assessing our own competence: Heuristics and illusions. In D. Gopher & A. Koriat (Eds.), *Attention and performance XVII. Cognitive regulation of performance: Interaction of theory and application* (pp. 435–459). Cambridge, MA: MIT Press.

Bransford, J. D. (1979). *Human cognition: Learning, understanding, and remembering.* Belmont, CA: Wadsworth.

Bruner, J. S. (1979). *On knowing: Essays for the left hand.* Cambridge, MA: Belknap Press of Harvard University Press.

Case, R., Griffin, S., & Kelly, W. (1999). Socioeconomic gradients in mathematical ability and their responsiveness to intervention during early childhood. In D. P. Keating & C. Hertzman (Eds.), *Developmental health and the wealth of nations: Social, biological, and educational dynamics.* New York: Guilford.

Champagne, A. (1998, February). *Attributes of debates among the science literate.* Paper presented at the American Association for the Advancement of Science (AAAS) Annual Meeting, Philadelphia, PA.

Chi, M. T. H. (1996). Constructing self-explanations and scaffolded explanations in tutoring. *Applied Cognitive Psychology, 10,* 33–49.

Clark, D. (2000). *Scaffolding knowledge integration through curricular depth.* Unpublished doctoral dissertation, University of California, Berkeley.

Clement, J. (1993). Using bridging analogies and anchoring intuitions to deal with students' preconceptions in physics. *Journal of Research in Science Teaching, 30,* 1241–1257.

Cobb, P., & Bowers, J. (1999). Cognitive and situated learning perspectives in theory and practice. *Educational Researcher, 28*(2), 4–15.

Cognition and Technology Group at Vanderbilt. (1997). *The Jasper Project: Lessons in curriculum, instruction, assessment, and professional development.* Mahwah, NJ: Lawrence Erlbaum Associates.

Dewey, J. (1901). *Psychology and social practice.* Chicago: University of Chicago Press.

diSessa, A. A. (2000). *Changing minds.* Cambridge, MA: MIT Press.

diSessa, A. A., & Minstrell, J. (1998). Cultivating conceptual change with benchmark lessons. In J. G. Greeno & S. Goldman (Eds.), *Thinking practices* (pp. 155–187). Mahwah, NJ: Lawrence Erlbaum Associates.

Foley, B. (2000). *Visualization tools: Models, representations and knowledge integration.* Unpublished doctoral dissertation, University of California, Berkeley.

Gik, M. L., & Holyoak, K. J. (1980). Analogical problem solving. *Cognitive Psychology, 12,* 306–355.

Greeno, J. G. (1989). Situations, mental models, and generative knowledge. In D. Klahr & K. Kotovsky (Eds.), *Complex information processing: The impact of Herbert A. Simon.* Hillsdale, NJ: Lawrence Erlbaum Associates.

Grillmeyer, O. (2000). *Functional composition, recursion, and applicative operators: An exploration into the more difficult areas of functional programming.* Unpublished doctoral dissertation, University of California, Berkeley.

Hegarty, M., Quilici, J., Narayanan, N. H., Holmqvist, S., & Moreno, R. (1999). Multimedia instruction: Lesson from evaluation of a theory-based design. *Journal of Educational Multimedia and Hypermedia, 8,* 119–150.

Halloun, I. A., & Hestenes, D. (1985). The initial knowledge state of college physics students. *American Journal of Physics, 53,* 1043–1056.

Hoadley, C. M., & Linn, M. C. (2000). Teaching science through on-line peer discussions: SpeakEasy in the knowledge integration environment. *International Journal of Science Education, 22,* 839–857.

Hsi, S., Linn, M. C., & Bell, P. (1997). The role of spatial reasoning in engineering and the design of spatial instruction. *Journal of Engineering Education, 86,* 151–158.

Inhelder, B., & Piaget, J. (1958). *The growth of logical thinking from childhood to adolescence; An essay on the construction of formal operational structures.* New York: Basic Books.

Kali, Y., Orion, N., & Eylon, B.-S. (2003). Effect of knowledge integration activities on students' perception of the earth's crust as a cyclic system. *Journal of Research in Science Teaching, 40,* 545–565.

Kali, Y., Orion, N., & Gorni, C. (1998). Geo3D Software for assisting high school students in the spatial perception of geological structures [computer software]. Rehovot, Israel: Weizmann Institute of Science.

Kintsch, W. (1998). *Comprehension: A paradigm for cognition.* Cambridge, MA: MIT Press.

Kolodner, J. (1993). *Case-based reasoning.* San Mateo, CA: Morgan Kaufmann Publishers, Inc.

Kuhn, D. (1993). Science as argument: Implications for teaching and learning scientific thinking. *Science Education, 77,* 319–337.

Lampert, M., & Blunk, M. L. (1998). *Talking mathematics in school: Studies of teaching and learning.* New York: Cambridge University Press.

Lave, J., & Wenger, E. (1990). *Situated learning: Legitimate peripheral participation.* Cambridge, England: Cambridge University Press.

Lewis, E. L. (1991). *The process of scientific knowledge acquisition among middle school students learning thermodynamics.* Unpublished doctoral dissertation, University of California, Berkeley.

Linn, M. C. (1995). Designing computer learning environments for engineering and computer science: The scaffolded knowledge integration framework. *Journal of Science Education and Technology, 4,* 103–126.

Linn, M. C. (2000). Designing the knowledge integration environment: The partnership inquiry process. *International Journal of Science Education, 22,* 781–796.

Linn, M. C. (2002). Science education: Preparing lifelong learners. In N. J. Smelser & P. B. Baltes (Eds.), *International encyclopedia of the social and behavioral sciences* (Vol. 3). New York: Pergamon.

Linn, M. C., & Clancy, M. J. (1992). The case for case studies of programming problems. *Communications of the ACM, 35*(3), 121–132.

Linn, M. C., Clark, D., & Slotta, J. D. (2003). WISE design for knowledge integration. *Science Education, 87,* 517–538.

Linn, M. C., Clement, C., & Pulos, S. (1983). Is it formal if it's not physics? *Journal of Research in Science Teaching, 20,* 755–770.

Linn, M. C., Davis, E. A., & Bell, P. (Eds.). (2004). *Internet environments for science education.* Mahwah, NJ: Lawrence Erlbaum Associates.

Linn. M. C., & Hsi, S. (2000). *Computers, teachers, peers: Science learning partners.* Mahwah, NJ: Lawrence Erlbaum Associates.

Linn, M. C., & Slotta, J. D. (2000). WISE science. *Educational Leadership, 29–32.*

Linn, M. C., Songer, N. B., & Eylon, B. (1996). Shifts and convergences in science learning and instruction. In R. Clafee & D. Berliner (Eds.), *Handbook of educational psychology* (pp. 438–490). Riverside, NJ: Macmillan.

Luchins, A. S., & Luchins, E. H. (1959). *Rigidity of behaviour: A variational approach to the effect of einstellung.* Eugene: University of Oregon Books.

Osborn, J., & Agogino, A. (1993). Display Object [computer software]. Berkeley, CA: University of California, Berkeley.

Palinscar, A. S., & Brown, A. L. (1984). Reciprocal teaching of comprehension-fostering and comprehension-monitoring activities. *Cognition and Instruction, 1,* 117–175.

Piaget, J. (1970). *Structuralism.* Cambridge, MA: Harvard University Press.

Reif, F., & Larkin, J. H. (1991). Cognition in scientific and everyday domains: Comparison and learning implications. *Journal of Research in Science Teaching, 28,* 733–760.

Science Controversies On-Line Partnerships in Education (SCOPE). (2004). Retrieved August 30, 2004 from http://scope.educ.washington.edu

Schoenfeld, A. H. (1986). On having and using geometric knowledge. In J. Hiebert (Ed.), *Conceptual and procedural knowledge: The case of mathematics* (pp. 225–263). Hillsdale, NJ: Lawrence Erlbaum Associates.

Shymansky, J. A., & Kyle, W. C., Jr. (1992). Establishing a research agenda: Critical issues of science curriculum reform. *Journal of Research in Science Teaching, 29,* 749–778.

Stigler, J. W., & Hiebert, J. (1999). *The teaching gap: Best ideas from the world's teachers for improving education in the classroom.* New York: Free Press.

Tschirgi, J. E. (1980). Sensible reasoning: A hypothesis about hypotheses. *Child Development, 51,* 1–10.

The Web-based Inquiry Science Environment (WISE). (2004). Retrieved August 30, 2004 from http://wise.berkeley.edu

Walker, D. F., & Schaffarzik, J. (1974). Comparing curricula. *Review of Educational research, 44,* 83–111.

White, B. Y., & Frederiksen, J. R. (1998). Inquiry, modeling, and metacognition: Making science accessible to all students. *Cognition and Instruction, 16,* 3–118.

10

Determinants of Discovery Learning in a Complex Simulation Learning Environment

Ton de Jong
University of Twente

Jos Beishuizen
Leiden University

Casper Hulshof
University of Twente

Frans Prins
Leiden University

Hedderik van Rijn
University of Amsterdam

Maarten van Someren
University of Amsterdam

Marcel Veenman
Leiden University

Pascal Wilhelm
Leiden University

Nowadays, there is a strong emphasis on learning environments in which students are seen as active and self-directed constructors of knowledge.

257

Discovery learning is a form of learning that fits well in this approach. In discovery learning, learners use inductive processes to generate hypotheses and design experiments to validate these hypotheses. A type of learning environment that is specifically suited for discovery learning is (computer-based) simulation. In simulation environments, learners can change values of (input) variables and observe the consequences on values of (output) variables. These basic activities can be used for the inductive and for the validation aspects of discovery learning. The actual discovery processes of learners are determined by a number of factors that are partly outside the learner (e.g., the complexity of the domain) and partly internal to the learner. As internal determinants of discovery learning, we distinguish prior domain knowledge, generic (model) knowledge, discovery skills, and intelligence and general metacognitive skills. In a number of studies, we have examined the effects of these determinants on discovery behavior. This was done in the context of a simulation learning environment on the physics topic of geometrical optics. This chapter summarizes the theoretical background of the research program, the overall setup of the studies, the design of the learning environment, the tests that were developed to measure the determinants, and the overall findings of the program.

The major purpose of this chapter is to outline research and design issues that we encountered in a research program on discovery learning in science. By taking discovery learning as a topic, the research program focused on knowledge acquisition, knowledge representation, and knowledge restructuring taking place at the "edge" of an individual's personal knowledge base. More specifically, we clarify the major determinants of discovery learning to identify which factors influence discovery learning processes. In the program that comprises four different projects, we used an interactive simulation learning environment on the physics topic of geometrical optics. We start this chapter by specifying discovery learning, as this is the pivot concept in our research program; we specify our main research questions, which concern the determinants of discovery learning; then we detail the characteristics of the domain used in our studies, that is, geometrical optics, and give a description of the learning environment that was used. In the next section, we present the research methods and techniques used in the different studies within the program. In doing this, we also indicate design decisions for the learning environment that were taken to enable data collection. Finally, we present the main results from the program.

DISCOVERY LEARNING

In the process of knowledge development in complex domains, three stages can be distinguished: (a) the cognitive stage, (b) the associative stage, and (c) the autonomous stage. These stages are described by one of the most advanced and comprehensive theories for knowledge acquisition: Anderson's (1993) ACT–R theory. As a number of authors (e.g., Glaser & Bassok, 1989) have noticed, Anderson's theory concentrates on knowledge acquisition in "procedural domains" (e.g., learning how to find a geometry proof). In these domains, algorithmic prescriptions for task accomplishments are available. The expert serves as a model of performance attainable along a training path of gradual changes in performance through each of the mentioned stages. In "conceptual domains" (e.g., physics topics such as dynamics), however, the first stage of expertise development can better be described as a series of qualitative restructurings of knowledge representations. In this process, the initial knowledge structure is weak. Gradually, however, fragments of knowledge are connected in organized structures by means of combining knowledge fragments (chunking), inferring analogy relations, and transferring general rules higher up in the knowledge hierarchy (Elio & Sharf, 1990).

The process in the first stage has been summarized as a process of induction by Holland, Holyoak, Nisbett, and Thagard (1986) and as a process of (scientific) discovery by Qin and Simon (1990) and Klahr and Dunbar (1988). Klahr and Dunbar developed scientific discovery as dual search (SDDS) theory. This theory sees discovery as a search in two "spaces"—hypothesis space and experiment space—and provides the basis for identifying detailed processes of discovery by describing moves within and between these two spaces. Following Klahr and Dunbar's theory, discovery learning is determined by the prior knowledge (the configuration of hypothesis and experiment space) and skills (discovery processes) of an individual. A division into a more general and a more specific component for both knowledge and skills can be made. For knowledge, this concerns knowledge of generic structures of domains (e.g., the existence of asymptotic relations) versus prior knowledge in the domain (e.g., definitions of specific variables); for skills, this concerns intelligence and general metacognitive skills (e.g., a structured working method) versus specific skills of scientific discovery (e.g., knowing when to keep variable values constant).

In our studies, we concentrated on determinants of discovery learning as depicted in Table 10.1. These determinants are all cognitive determinants; in this way, we abstract from other factors such as the characteristics of the domain and the context (e.g., time constraints) in which the discovery takes place. Two other potential (student-related) factors are personality characteristics and students' epistemological views. With only very few examples (e.g., Leutner, 1993, on anxiety), personality factors are hardly ever mentioned in this context. Reiser et al. (2001), for example, discussed the influence of students' understanding of the nature of science at learning, but a specific influence on students' inquiry behavior was not mentioned. The main research topic of our proposed program was to find out the (relative)

TABLE 10.1
A Schematic Overview of Person-Related Factors That Influence Discovery Behavior

Knowledge		Skills	
Specific	Generic	Specific	General
Domain knowledge	Model knowledge	Discovery skills	Metacognitive skills
			Intelligence

influence of the different types of prior knowledge and skills on the inductive learning process. Before presenting our results, in the next section we
give a literature overview.

DETERMINANTS OF DISCOVERY LEARNING

Generic knowledge is the knowledge that is needed to understand qualitative
or quantitative relations and to appreciate structures of models in a very
general sense.

Models are basically constructed from variables, relations, and (possibly)
conditions. Knowledge about a relation can exist at various levels, from
purely qualitative (e.g., "A and B are somehow related"), to purely quantitative (e.g., A = 2B) (see van Joolingen & de Jong, 1997). Mathematical relations can be represented in formulas, graphs, or in general terms (e.g., in
terms of "monotonic decreasing," "exponential," etc.). The idea of the use of
generic knowledge of mathematical relations in discovery learning is related
to Plötzner and Spada's (1992) argument that learners have to utilize in a
learning environment, among others, "mathematical knowledge about
functional relationships and various arithmetical procedures" (p. 107). In
fact, the relations one knows of determines what one can state as a relation
in the domain under inquiry.

Apart from knowledge of relations, students may also have knowledge of
the structure (variable organization) of a domain. As far as we know, no real
literature exist on this issue, but Glaser, Schauble, Raghavan, and Zeitz
(1992), who compared the learning behavior of learners across three different domains, showed different patterns of discovery behavior over the three
environments. The pattern used was clearly influenced by the structure
(e.g., a more correlational or functional structure) and content of the specific environment. This may suggest an influence of domain structure on
discovery behavior.

Conditions, finally, constrain the validity of relations between variables.
Also here, we may expect that generic knowledge of types of conditions

(e.g., time, temperature, etc.) limits what a learner will actually find as conditions.

Specific Knowledge (Domain Knowledge)

The amount of prior knowledge a person has about a domain (i.e., knowledge of the variables that make up the domain and the relations between variables) can have a large influence on learning about that domain. This notion can be extended to include discovery learning. A number of studies have reported differences in discovery learning between students with varying amounts of prior knowledge. Njoo and de Jong (1993), for example, found that students working with a simulation in control theory who had high prior knowledge test scores also gained high test scores after completing a simulation-based computer laboratory. Njoo and de Jong could not find, however, a relation between prior knowledge test scores and discovery learning patterns. Such a relation was found by Glaser et al. (1992) (see also previously) who made a comparison of learning in three different simulation environments and found that for the domain for which the learner's prior knowledge was higher, more alternative hypotheses of all kinds (general and specific, correct and incorrect) were stated. In a similar vein, Lavoie and Good (1988) reported that students with high prior knowledge display better discovery behavior; they were, for example, better able to predict the outcome of experiments. Shute and Glaser (1990) found that students with more domain knowledge found it easier to consider alternative hypotheses. It is not only the amount of prior knowledge but also its specific quality that is important. Schauble, Glaser, Raghavan, and Reiner (1991) measured learners' knowledge before they went into a learning session with Voltaville, a simulation environment on electricity. Schauble et al. (1991) made a careful analysis of the quality of the prior knowledge. Schauble et al. found four levels of prior knowledge of electrical circuits. The first level indicates a simple, superficial understanding of the domain, and the highest (fourth) level represents deeper (objects were interpreted as voltage sources or resistors) and more integrated knowledge. First, Schauble et al. found that learners with a higher level prior knowledge made higher learning gains in Voltaville than learners with a lower level of prior knowledge. The level of prior knowledge also influenced the experimentation behavior of participants. Thinking aloud protocols revealed that students use their prior knowledge for stating predictions and generating explanations. Also, students with higher levels of prior knowledge searched more broadly through all possible experiments and were more persistent in finding out the principles of one circuit before jumping to a next one, whereas poor students even had trouble remembering what they had discovered. Schauble et al. (1991) pointed out that there is an intricate relation between knowledge models and experimentation strategy because both influence each other. Prior knowledge may, however, also have a negative influence on discovery learning. Glaser et al. (1992), for example, emphasized that prior knowledge may help the learner to interpret data but may also cause learners to "distort, ignore, or selectively interpret the evidence that they generate" (p. 360) when the prior knowledge is incorrect. Chinn and Brewer (1993) added that students will not easily adapt their theory on the basis of anomalous data when their prior knowledge is more deeply rooted and when learners have additional (background) knowledge that may help them to reason the anomalous data away.

General Skills (Intelligence and Metacognitive Skills)

In a number of studies, the relation between intelligence and discovery learning performance has been examined but with varying outcomes. For instance, Leutner (1993) obtained correlations ranging from −.32 to .55 between intelligence and participants' achievement in a simulation game. Shute and Glaser (1990) found a correlation of .18 between students' intelligence scores and learning performance in Smithtown (a simulation environment in the domain of economics). Veenman (1993) found, over a number of studies, intellectual ability to be correlated with simulation-based learning outcomes. Using different domains and different types of learning measures, Veenman reported correlations that ranged between .46 and .68 over seven studies. An obvious difference between the studies concerns the assessment of intelligence, as Leutner (1993), Veenman (1993), and Shute and Glaser (1990) used different intelligence tests. Also, the situation presented in the simulation environments was different too. In Leutner's study, participants had to control the simulation, trying to reach a specific value for one of the output variables, whereas in Veenman's studies, participants were free to explore a domain with a specific optimization assignment. This may have resulted in a more transparent environment in Veenman's case, meaning that participants were given a more direct view on systems variables and their relations. Funke (1991) reported that the correlation between intelligence and achievement increases when the simulation environment becomes more transparent. However, in Shute and Glaser's simulation, learners were given a so-called hypothesis menu in which variables were directly presented, thus also leading to transparency. Perhaps the huge number of variables in Smithtown was responsible for the low correlation in that study. According to Elshout (1987) and Raaheim (1988), a curvilinear relation exists between intelligence and performance. Intelligence is assumed to play little part in very familiar (and therefore easy) learning situations. As familiarity with a learning situation declines (and task complexity consequently advances), intelligence is called on increasingly. At a certain point of task complexity, one can optimally profit from one's intellectual resources. This point is called the "threshold of problematicity" (Elshout, 1987) at which verge one is still capable of managing a relatively unfamiliar problem. If, however, task complexity moves beyond the threshold, the impact of intelligence gradually diminishes.

Another relevant predictor of learning performance in discovery environments is metacognitive skillfulness (Wang, Härtel, & Walberg, 1990), that is, the ability to regulate and control one's learning behavior. In a number of studies, Veenman and Elshout (1995) focused on the metacognitive skillfulness of novices in several simulation environments. Metacognitive skillfulness was assessed through the analyses of thinking-aloud protocols on the quality of orientation activities (e.g., distinguishing independent from dependent variables, hypothesizing about relations, and planning experiments), systematical orderliness (e.g., varying one independent variable at the time), accuracy (e.g., accurate note taking), evaluation activities (e.g., monitoring and checking outcomes), and elaboration activities (e.g., recapitulating and drawing conclusions). Veenman and Elshout (1995) more specifically examined the mutual relations between intelligence, metacognitive skillfulness, and learning outcome. Veenman and Elshout (1995) found that high-intelligent novices exhibited a higher level of metacognitive skillfulness relative to low-intelligent ones. However, Veenman and Elshout's (1995) studies also show that although metacognitive skillfulness and intelligence were correlated, metacognitive skillfulness partly had its own contribution to learning outcome on top of intelligence. In fact, intelligence uniquely accounted for 13.2% of variance, and metacognitive skillfulness uniquely accounted for 19.4% of variance, whereas both predictors shared an additional 22.8% of variance in learning outcome (Veenman, 1993). Research by Veenman, Elshout, and Meijer (1997) further revealed that the metacognitive skillfulness of novices is a person-related quality rather than being domain or task specific. Novices passed through three different simulation environments. Their metacognitive skillfulness was independently assessed for each environment and proved to be invariant across environments. For more advanced learners, metacognitive skillfulness in the domain of their expertise was not correlated to intelligence and included more domain-specific characteristics (Veenman, 1993).

Specific Skills (Discovery Skills)

How to perform discovery learning can be seen as a distinct set of skills apart from general metacognitive skills. Shute and Glaser (1990) in their study on Smithtown concluded that general intelligence is certainly a component of discovery learning but that specific scientific behaviors account for considerably more variance (p. 71). Schunn and Anderson (1999) also showed that discovery skills are distinct from general reasoning ability and that they can be learned and transferred from one research area to another.

At a general level, de Jong and van Joolingen (1998) distinguished four main discovery learning processes: hypothesis generation, design of experiments, interpretation of data, and regulation of learning. Apart from regulation of learning, this distinction parallels the SDDS model of Klahr and Dunbar (1988) in which discovery learning is described as a search in a hypothesis space and an experiment space and the coordination between these searches. Kuhn, Garcia-Mila, Zohar, and Andersen (1995) made a similar distinction by describing scientific discovery in terms of a coordination between theory and evidence. Skills specific to discovery learning can be inferred from the main discovery learning processes distinguished by de Jong and van Joolingen (1998).

Hypothesis generation is probably one of the most difficult and most important processes in discovery learning. Shute and Glaser (1990) found that learners who show "hypothesis-driven behavior" have better learning outcomes than other students. de Jong and van Joolingen (1998) distinguished several difficulties that learners generally encounter in hypothesis generation. These difficulties have two aspects. On one hand, learners may have problems with simply forming hypotheses; they may not know what a hypothesis should look like (Njoo & de Jong, 1993). On the other hand, learners may be unable to adapt their hypotheses on the basis of experimental evidence, a result very often found in studies on discovery learning (e.g., Chinn & Brewer, 1993; Klahr & Dunbar, 1988; Kuhn et al., 1995).

There is evidence that suggests that processes pertaining to the design of experiments and interpretation of data, among others, correlate with good discovery learning outcomes. Schauble et al. (1991) compared the discovery behavior of learners who were successful in learning with Voltaville with those who were unsuccessful. Schauble et al. (1991) found that both groups of students were equally active in the simulation but that good learners performed better in

> the class of evidence generation (controlling extraneous variation), evidence interpretation (generating and evaluating alternative hypotheses, inferring regularities in the data, producing sufficient evidence to support a hypothesis), data management (systematic data recording), and planning (developing plans that are goal oriented rather than procedure oriented). (p. 223)

Lavoie and Good (1988) studied the cognitive processes of 14 high school students learning with a simulation on water pollution. One of the comparisons they made in their study concerned the cognitive processes of good and poor "predictors" (students received a "prediction test" after the simulation). The main differences were that good predictors compared to poor ones used abstract reasoning (e.g., introduced qualitative scales for variables), worked in a more systematic way (e.g., changed only one variable at a time, returned variables to baseline conditions, looked for worst and best conditions), made notes during the exploration, were able to find more complex relations (bidirectional and ratio relations), and showed a high interest and motivation (e.g., by persisting to complete the learning sequence). Thus, it seems that successful predictors conduct more informative experiments (e.g., controlling extraneous variation, changing one variable at a time, returning variables to baseline conditions) and are better able in interpreting the data (e.g., inferring regularities in the data, finding more complex relations). In similar vein, Klahr, Fay, and Dunbar (1993) observed the discovery behavior of learners in the BigTrak environment. They identified a number of successful heuristics for hypothesis generation and experiment design such as designing simple experiments to enable monitoring, designing experiments that give characteristic results, focusing on a single dimension of a hypothesis, exploiting surprising results, and choosing a hypothesis-based experimental strategy. At a more detailed level, Gruber, Renkl, Mandl, and Reiter (1993) found that variation in input in a simulation of a jeans factory was correlated with success in a later phase in which profit of the factory had to be maximized. Similar results were reported by de Jong, de Hoog, and de Vries (1993).

THE OPTICS LEARNING ENVIRONMENT

In the research program, a simulation-based learning environment in the physics domain of geometrical optics was created and used.

The Domain

The Optics learning environment represents the domain of geometrical optics. Geometrical optics deals with phenomena concerning light propagation through an optical system and the creation of illumination patterns (Hecht, 1998; Langley, Ronen, & Eylon, 1997). Optics simulates an optical workbench with which the behavior of optical systems can be studied. The focus lies on optical systems that demonstrate light propagation through one or more (thin) lenses.

The Learning Environment

Main Interface. Figure 10.1 shows an example of the interface that is used in Optics. The interface consists of two parts. In the upper part, icons that represent objects that can be added to the simulation and icons that represent operations that can be carried out on objects in the simulation are

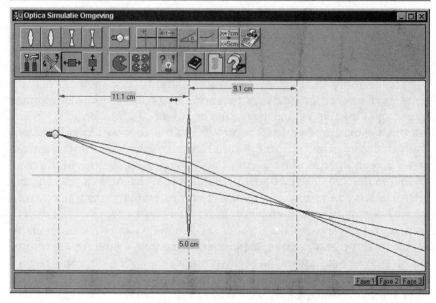

FIG. 10.1.   Example interface of the Optics learning environment.

shown. The lower part of the interface consists of the working area. At first, this area only shows a flat horizontal line on the screen. This is the principal axis on which objects are placed; properties of these objects can subsequently be altered. All objects can also be removed from the working area. Fig. 10.1 shows a lamp shining through a lens, one which has three laser-like light beams, each of which strikes the lens at a different angle. The focal length of the lens is shown underneath it. Students can manipulate the distance and properties of different objects that are shown on the screen. Also, the distances between objects can be measured; while moving an object, the measured distance is dynamically changed in the display. In Fig. 10.1, the distance of the lamp to the lens and the distance between the lens and the point where the light beams converge are shown. By moving the lamp or the lens or by changing the incoming angle of the light beams, regularities in these measures can be explored.

Special Characteristics.   A number of characteristics about the Optics learning environment are worth noting. First, the effect of manipulating objects in the environment is immediate: The simulation updates in real time. Because experimenting with the environment proceeds continuously, there are no clear boundaries between experiments. Second, the simulation creates the possibility of making visible objects and relations between objects that in the real world always remain invisible. The consequence of this is that students get insight into the effects of their actions on the environment even when in reality, these effects would not be visible. Third, any notes that students want to make can be entered in an online notebook. In the notebook, the current situation in the working area is displayed along with text that the learner types.

Research Characteristics. To be able to obtain different measures of student behavior in the environment, it was necessary to add some features. First, objects can only be moved around after a button has been pressed to indicate the direction of movement. Second, when the simulation updates itself, all numerical values that are in the simulation change into question marks and only become available again once a button is pressed. This gives information about the occasions when a student is interested in quantitative measures. Third, in some cases, we used an environment in which the light beams disappeared when a student, for example, moved the light. Students then had to decide themselves when they wanted to see the light beams, which gave us more insight in the data inspection behavior of students.

RESEARCH METHODS

For measuring the knowledge and skills factors as distinguished earlier, several measuring procedures have been used throughout the different studies that we conducted. The ways we measured knowledge and skills covered paper-and-pencil, verbal, and computer techniques. Measures were applied before, during, and after participants were in a learning session with the Optics learning environment. In following sections, we summarize the measuring procedures used.

Generic Knowledge

In the studies we conducted, generic prior knowledge was measured as general mathematical knowledge. What was tested primarily was the ability of participants to interpret data, as they could come from experiments like the ones performed in the Optics environment. The items of the test for general mathematical knowledge that was used (for a complete overview, see Hulshof, 2001) covered several topics about mathematical relations and a number of ways of depicting these. None of the relations that were used in the test was more complex than relations from the Optics learning environment. The tests used were paper-and-pencil tests. The items were four- answer, multiple-choice questions or required a short answer such as a formula. Examples are items that require the learner to infer a relation (sometimes quantitative, sometimes qualitative) from a series of data or items that require the recognition of the nature of a relation as depicted in a graph.

Domain Knowledge

For the assessment of domain knowledge, two types of tests were used, namely a what-if test and a more traditional test. In a what-if test item, a situation of the system is displayed in a drawing or graph, and a change of one of the independent variables is described in text (Swaak & de Jong, 1996). Three or four predictions presented in text, number, or graph give possible results of the change. The learners were asked to choose the correct one. Swaak and de Jong used the what-if test format to assess *intuitive knowledge*, described as a "quick perception of meaningful situations" and "hard to verbalize." Therefore, a speed instruction was added to the what-if test format. It was hypothesized by Swaak and de Jong that particularly intuitive knowledge is acquired during discovery learning in a rich computer-based learning environment. In our studies, (versions of) the what-if test format was used to assess qualitative conceptual knowledge (see Fig. 10.2). Quantitative knowledge was assessed by a more traditional test format. In Hulshof (2001) and Prins (2002) full versions of the tests used can be found.

Metacognitive Skills and Intelligence

In the project, general metacognitive skills were measured by using thinking-aloud techniques. When using the think-aloud method, it is important

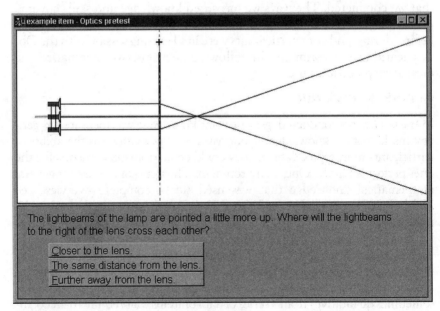

FIG. 10.2.   Example of a what-if item for the Optics learning environment.

not to challenge participants to theorize about their behavior but just encourage them to keep thinking aloud. In that case, the learning process is only slowing down and not changing (Veenman, Elshout, & Groen, 1993).

The quality of metacognitive skillfulness of participants was scored on four subscales: orientation activities, systematic orderliness, evaluation, and elaboration activities according to the criteria of Veenman and Elshout (e.g., Veenman, 1993; Veenman & Elshout, 1995; Veenman et al., 1997). *Orientation* activities concern the preparation for the task. These activities were judged on indications of analyzing the problem statement, determining the independent and dependent variables, building a mental model of the task, and generating hypotheses and predictions. Judgments of *systematical orderliness* were based on the quality of planning activities, the systematical execution of plans, completing an orderly sequence of actions, and the avoidance of unsystematic events (such as varying two variables at the same time). *Evaluation* activities concern the regulation and control of the learning process. They were judged on monitoring and checking, both on the local level (e.g., detecting errors and checking calculations) as well as on the global level of keeping track of progress being made (e.g., verifying whether the obtained results provide an answer to the problem statement). Finally, judgments of *elaboration* concern the intention of storing of findings and concepts in memory. They were based on indications of recapitulating, drawing conclusions, relating these conclusions to the subject matter, and generating explanations. Elaboration itself may be conceived as a cognitive activity, but it is assumed that the occurrence of such cognitive activity at an appropriate point of time results from metacognitive activity.

The four subscales of metacognitive skillfulness were rated on a 5-point scale ranging from 0 to 4. Aspects of metacognitive skillfulness were judged on the quality of performing regulatory activities, not on the correctness of the information these activities resulted in. For instance, extensive, although incorrect predictions or conclusions, may still result in high scores on orientation or elaboration. A sum score over the four subscales for each participant was computed to obtain a total score for metacognitive skillfulness.

The intellectual ability of the participants was assessed in a series of tests including five primary intelligence factors: inductive reasoning, quantitative reasoning, verbal ability, closure flexibility, and sequential reasoning (Carroll, 1993). The test battery included tests for vocabulary, verbal analogies, linear syllogisms, number series, number speed, and embedded figures. The unweighted mean of the scores on these six tests can be regarded as an IQ-equivalent (Veenman & Elshout, 1999). Those students whose intellectual ability score deviated at least 1 SD from the mean were denominated as either high- or relatively low-intelligent.

Discovery Skills

In the program, we used three ways to measure the students discovery skills. The first one was a specifically designed computer task called flexible inductive learning environment ("FILE"; Hulshof, Wilhelm, Beishuizen, & Van Rijn, in press; Wilhelm, 2001; Wilhelm, Beishuizen, & Van Rijn, in press), the second one was a simulation environment on a nonexisting topic (called "Bubbles"; see Hulshof, 2001), and the third one consisted of log files of learners who had learned with the Optics environment.

FILE. FILE provides learners with the task to find out particular relations in a domain by varying values of input variables and observing the effect on an output variable. The content of FILE is adaptable in terms of the topic covered and the relations in the model. In our studies, we used a problem domain (as shown in Fig. 10.3) about arranging the duties of breakfast and driving to arrive at school in time. In the example case, a boy has to make several choices about how he bikes to school. These choices determine his arrival time at school. The learner can interact with the FILE environment using the mouse. The learner selects a level for each of the independent variables to conduct an experiment and is presented with the outcome on one dependent variable. The independent variables are shown in Fig. 10.3 on the left side of the screen (Region A). Each variable is shown in its own row as an array consisting of small pictures for each level of the

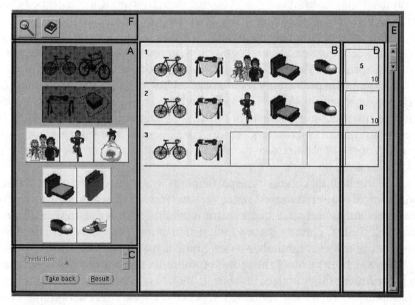

FIG. 10.3.   The flexible inductive learning environment.

variable. For example, in the first row, a racing bike and a normal bike are presented, which represent the two levels of the first variable "type of bicycle." After selecting a level of a particular variable, a picture referring to the chosen level is added to the experiment window in the middle part of the screen (Region B). FILE disables the row, making it impossible to select another picture from that row, and gives visual feedback by graying out the row. After the learner has selected a level for all five variables, the "Result" button is enabled (Region C). After pressing this button, the outcome of the newly constructed experiment is shown. This outcome is presented on the right side of the screen (Region D). After the Result button is pressed, the rows of variables are enabled again, and the learner can construct the next experiment. Besides the Result button, there are two additional interface elements in Region C. First, the learner has to give a prediction before the outcome is shown. Second, if the learner selects a level and later on decides that the selection of that level was incorrect, this selection can be taken back by pressing the "Take back" button. This button removes the last selection made from the experiment and reenables the variable to which it belongs. Completed experiments stay fixed and cannot be changed by the learner.

If the learner conducts more experiments than the number of experiments that fit on the screen, the earlier experiments scroll off the screen. By using the scroll bar (Region E), the learner can scroll back to previous experiments. Another way to examine previous experiments or to compare different sets of experiments is to select a set of experiments and to display these in a separate window. Selecting an experiment is done by clicking on one of the experiments shown. The background color of this experiment changes to indicate that the experiment has been selected. If the learner presses the magnifying glass (Region F), a window is shown with all selected experiments. If the learner has selected more experiments than can be shown at once, a scroll bar can be used to scroll the other experiments into view. Finally, if a learner presses the button depicting the book in Region F, a window with task instructions pops up. A learner can reread the instructions at all times during task performance.

Bubbles.   The topic of the computer simulation that forms the Bubbles test is a special fictitious chemical reaction that takes place when two or more liquid materials are put together and the resulting mix is heated. The names of liquids as well as the rules underlying the chemical reaction are artificial. Students are introduced to the simulation by means of a background story that puts them in the role of a scientist aboard a spaceship on a newly discovered planet. The planet resembles Earth except for the presence of four unknown liquids: Magnum, Kryton, Sybar, and Guernic. Heating a mixture of these liquids results in the appearance of bubbles, the number of which changes over time. The task for students is to find out how different mixtures and quantities of the liquids influence the resulting reaction. The number of bubbles that appear is plotted in a graph. Students have to specify points in time where they want to make measurements in the graph (the maximum number of simultaneous points is four). An example of the Bubbles task is shown in Fig. 10.4.

Because Bubbles uses a fictional domain, it is not possible for students to possess prior knowledge with respect to the underlying model of the simulation. This creates the possibility of manipulating (prior) domain-specific knowledge. While experimenting with the simulation, students can make notes on their findings using a notebook feature. The notebook shows the current situation in the simulation, which makes it possible to compare different settings and their outcome. Similar to the other computer tasks that are used in this program, all operations that students perform in the simulation are registered by the computer and are available for analysis.

Logfile Analysis.   In all studies performed, students' interactions were fully logged including a time stamp. Analysis of registered operations is, however, not straightforward and can only shed light on specific aspects of discovery behavior. A useful way to consider meaningful operations at an appropriate scale is to consider the actions that are carried out. An *action* can be defined as a (short) sequence of one or more operations in a simulation. In the case of the Optics computer simulation, it was chosen to analyze registered operations by counting the frequency of different actions. In Optics, a number of different actions can be distinguished. There are actions that concern manipulation of objects (e.g., adding a light beam to the work-

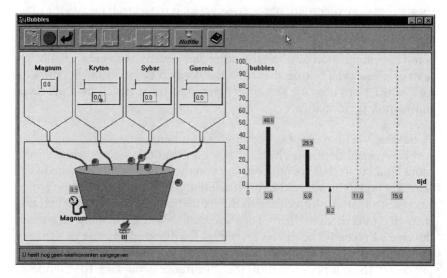

FIG. 10.4.   The Bubbles computer simulation.

ing area) and actions that are more peripheral (e.g., making a note in the notebook). Also, sequences of operations can be distinguished that mark either qualitative actions (i.e., actions that provide qualitative information) or quantitative actions (i.e., actions that provide precise numerical information). When a learning session with Optics is divided into different time periods (e.g., periods of 1 min each), an analysis of learning behavior can be made as it evolves over time. The overall frequency of actions and the way the type of actions that are performed changes over time are both indicators of the discovery skill of students.

OVERVIEW OF RESULTS

The projects conducted in our research program each focused on one or two of the influencing factors that we distinguished in Table 10.1. The first project concentrated on generic and domain-specific knowledge (see Hulshof, 2001), the second on metacognitive skills and intelligence (see Prins, 2002), and the third one of scientific discovery skills (Wilhelm, 2001). We report the main setup and results of each of these three projects in the following sections. In the fourth and final project in the program, we tried to take results from each of the three more experimental projects to create a computer model of scientific discovery learning. We incorporate results from this last project in the discussion section of this chapter.

Generic and Domain-Specific Knowledge

In three experiments that made use of the Optics computer simulation, the influence of two different types of prior knowledge on the discovery learning process was explored. A distinction was made between domain-specific knowledge (i.e., knowledge about the physical laws that govern the behavior of light that passes through a lens) and generic knowledge (i.e., knowledge of and aptitude to work with mathematical relations of varying complexity).

The first experiment examined the influence of generic knowledge and domain-specific knowledge on scientific discovery learning processes. Domain-specific knowledge was measured in the case of the Optics simulation and manipulated in the case of the Bubbles simulation (by training one group of students; see earlier for an explanation of Bubbles). One expectation was that more proficient students would show more hypothesis oriented discovery learning behavior. No influence of domain-specific prior knowledge on discovery learning processes in the Bubbles and Optics simulations was found and only a limited effect for generic knowledge. However, activity (number of changes and observations made) in Bubbles (that can be regarded as an indication of level of discovery skill) was found to be positively correlated with performance on a domain-specific knowledge test.

The second experiment also focused on more and less proficient students on generic and domain-specific knowledge. In addition to using revised tests for generic and domain-specific knowledge, this study used a test for discovery skills (the "Peter" test), which made use of the FILE task (see earlier for an explanation of this task). Discovery learning behavior was studied in four situations (ranging from simple to complex) in the Optics simulation. This study showed a consistent effect of prior generic knowledge on the discovery learning process: students with high generic knowledge were more active in the Optics simulation than students with poor generic knowledge. Discovery skills were related to discovery learning behavior in the first two (simple) situations in the Optics simulation. Students with high discovery skills were more active in these situations than students with poor discovery skills. For domain-specific prior knowledge, it was shown that students with high domain-specific knowledge were less active than students with poor domain-specific knowledge in one situation in the Optics simulation.

The third experiment focused on a situation in the Optics simulation for which a difference between groups of high and poor prior domain-specific knowledge had been found in the previous experiment. This experiment again explored prior generic knowledge, domain-specific knowledge, and discovery skills in relation to discovery learning in the Optics simulation. However, one group of students had a set of "knowledge tips" at its disposal. These hints comprised both domain specific and general discovery aspects. By letting students have access to knowledge tips, knowledge about optics was manipulated in this experiment. It was found that students who had the tips available to them showed a learning gain from pretest to posttest as opposed to a group who worked in a similar way in the Optics simulation but without knowledge tips.

Metacognitive Skills and Intelligence

A series of studies was carried out with Optics to explore the relation between metacognitive skills, intellectual ability, learning behavior, and learning performance during discovery learning. In the first study, high- and relative low-intelligent novices worked with a complex configuration of the Optics learning environment. In a second study, high- or relative low-intelligent novice and advanced learners passed through an Optics learning environment that was made less complex because this time only the independent variable of the model had to be identified, the dependent variable of the relation that had to be discovered was given in the assignment. In a third study, an aptitude treatment interaction perspective was taken. A structured learning environment may be helpful to novice learners who lack sufficient metacognitive control. However, such a structured learning environment may be detrimental to low-intelligent novices with a relatively high level of metacognitive skillfulness (Veenman & Elshout, 1995). In this study, participants' quality of metacognitive skillfulness was assessed independently from their learning actions in the Optics learning environment. Participants were then matched on their level of metacognitive skillfulness and assigned to either a structured or unstructured condition.

Results showed that during initial discovery learning in a complex configuration of the Optics learning environment, novice learners drew heavily on their metacognitive skillfulness, which results mainly in qualitative knowledge (Veenman, Prins, & Elshout, 2002). Metacognitive skillfulness happened to be positively related with learning behavior and with scores on the qualitative tests (see earlier for a description of the qualitative and quantitative knowledge tests). High-intelligent students scored better on the quantitative tests than low-intelligent students. Metacognitive skillfulness and intellectual ability appeared to be unrelated. Earlier studies of Veenman (1993; Veenman & Elshout, 1995) have shown substantial correlations between metacognitive skillfulness and intellectual ability, but in these studies, less complex learning environments were used. To conclude, when novice learners are asked to acquire knowledge in a complex computer learning environment, they either should have sufficient metacognitive skills or receive instructional support aimed at the regulation of their initial learning behavior. In the second study, the theory of the threshold of problematicity (Elshout, 1987) was supported. The pattern of correlations between metacognitive skillfulness, intellectual ability, and learning outcome of novices in the relatively easy version of Optics resembled the pattern of correlations of advanced learners in the more complex phase. Metacognitive skillfulness appeared to be the main determinant for learning, whereas intellectual ability only had a moderate impact. Moreover, intellectual ability was related with the number of rules formulated during completion of the posttest (students were thinking aloud during the posttest and mentioned rules they had discovered) and thus especially important for data interpretation. In the third study, we found that intellectual ability was the main determinant for learning in the group of learners that received the support, whereas metacognitive skillfulness appeared to be the main determinant for learning in the group that received no support. Apparently, supporting the regulation of the discovery process is especially suitable for learners with weak metacognitive skillfulness and high intellectual ability.

Discovery Skills

Using different configurations of FILE in combination with log file and protocol analysis, several predictors for successful discovery learning were identified. These predictors seemed to be indicative of a working method typical of the scientific method (empirical cycle; see de Groot, 1969), stating a hypothesis, making a research plan (especially plans to identify a previously unknown effect and plans to test a specific hypothesis), conducting a sound experiment (usage of the control of variables strategy [CVS]; Chen & Klahr, 1999), and stating a conclusion. The number of research plans and conclusions stated was highly correlated. This set of behaviors was interpreted as the coordination of intent and inference (Kuhn et al., 1995). Therefore, a more explicit kind of coordination of intent and inference evidenced by more hypotheses, better research plans, better experiments, and more conclusive statements resulted in better learning outcomes. From the log files of FILE, it was inferred whether learners inspected their data set. To do this, they could use the scrolling and selection function. These data management activities also appeared to be related to learning outcome. The extent to which these predictors related to learning outcomes was dependent on type of domain or topic covered in the learning task. In abstract configurations of FILE in which variables were represented by geometric shapes in different colors, the predictors accounted for significantly more variance in learning outcome than in configurations in which a familiar, everyday-life topic was covered. Obviously, domain-specific knowledge attributes to learning outcomes in familiar domains. However, when one cannot rely on domain-specific knowledge, then careful coordination of intent and inference becomes crucial for discovery learning. In a training study, sixth-grade children received a training in discovery skills. The training focused on inferring and testing the effects of independent variables. Usage of the CVS (changing one variable at a time and keeping other variables constant) was stressed, and the children were explained how main effects, irrelevant effects, and interaction effects could be inferred and tested. It appeared that both training and practice improved learning outcome but that the improvement was also dependent on the topic covered in the learning task. The question remained whether discovery skills are distinct from general intellectual skills. In our studies, tests of intellectual skills were also administered. It appeared that although intellectual skills and discovery skills showed significant correlations, they did not entirely coincide. Especially, usage of the CVS had a separate contribution to the variance accounted for in learning outcome.

Findings from this project underscore the importance of skills in hypothesis generation, the coordination of intent and inference, systematic experimentation, and data management for successful discovery learning. Type of topic covered in the learning task and intellectual skills also play a major role, but it is suggested that discovery skills are a distinct set of skills that need to be taught in an explicit way.

CONCLUSION AND DISCUSSION

In this discussion, we review the results of the different studies and place them in the context of creating a simulation model of discovery learning as was the goal of the fourth project in our research program. We also draw conclusions for the use of discovery environments in educational settings.

THE ROLE OF DETERMINANTS AND THE CREATION OF A SIMULATION MODEL OF DISCOVERY LEARNING

In the foregoing sections, several phenomena were described that were observed in the context of inductive discovery learning. One of the purposes of this discussion section is to provide a framework for more detailed explanation of some of these effects in the form of detailed process models. When a model becomes complex, it is useful to use computer simulations to construct the implications of the model. Although we did construct several such models, the most important characteristics of the models can be seen without details of the implemented systems. Here, we review some of the principles that underlie the models (for details of models, see van Rijn, 2003; van Rijn, van Someren, & van der Maas, 2000).

In general, we take discovery learning as a task in which a person is presented with an environment in which experiments can be performed by manipulating certain aspects of the environment (independent variables) and can observe other variables (measurable, dependent variables). The variables can be discrete or continuous, and the experiments can be static or dynamic. In dynamic environments, an experiment may cause a series of events that happen over time. The goal is to find the actual relation between independent and dependent variables that exists in the environment. This process of discovery learning can be split into three subtasks: constructing hypotheses, generating experiments, and interpreting data (see Klahr & Dunbar, 1988). A (runnable) model of discovery learning consists of a model of the cognitive architecture and of the acquired knowledge and skills for performing these three subtasks. Here, we concentrate on the effects of prior knowledge and discovery skills.

Discovery Learning and Prior Knowledge

For a person who has no prior knowledge about possible relations in a domain and who is set in a discovery situation, the only option is to perform as many experiments as possible given practical conditions and try to narrow down the set of possibilities. However, a little analysis shows that this can be difficult.

Consider the FILE discovery task. This task involved five discrete independent variables with a total of 48 possible combinations of values. The (single) dependent variable is continuous. Without any assumptions at all, in the worst case, an arbitrary value could be assigned to each combination of values. Remembering these combinations would create a memory problem and the resulting hypothesis would feel very unsatisfactory. Many participants assume (implicitly or explicitly) that each value of a variable contributes a certain number of minutes to the arrival time. This simplifies the problem and reduces memory load. This assumption is not correct, however, and prevented participants from finding the actual relation.

In the Optics task, the variables were not given: The simulation shows many changes if the position or orientation of the lamp is changed, and also, many changes are symmetric. Key domain specific prior knowledge is therefore (a) a good set of (dependent and independent) variables and (b) knowledge of possible hypotheses in terms of these variables (e.g., that light beams can be broken to and from the central axis). Without these two, it is hard to design and interpret experiments. It is difficult to imagine that someone acquires prior knowledge of (a) and (b) outside the context of optics education. The experiments reported earlier showed, however, little effect of domain specific prior knowledge on what was learned in the Optics and Bubbles tasks.

This analysis shows that without assumptions based on prior knowledge, these tasks are virtually impossible to perform perfectly. The human cognitive architecture neither allows us to effectively maintain the large number of possible hypotheses (or the current best hypothesis) nor to complete experiments and the necessary reasoning in time. Assumptions reduce the number of experiments and the memory load for traversing the hypothesis space. Discovery methods similarly should reduce the number of experiments and reduce the memory load of reasoning about possible hypotheses. It is clear that without assumptions, it is impossible to reduce the number of experiments, but defining a structure on the possible hypotheses may enable more efficient reasoning. At the same time, the assumptions must be correct and not prevent the learner from discovering the actual underlying pattern.

Domain specific prior knowledge means that the learner knows in advance which hypotheses are possible (or impossible) for a domain or in case of uncertainty, which hypotheses are a priori more likely. Generic prior knowledge helps to reduce the number of options by suggestions patterns from the structure of the domain or from potential relations between variables.

For example, in the FILE task, many participants assumed that the generic structure of the domain was that the effect of one variable is independent of the value of other variables. This reduces the number of experiments needed to discover the pattern from 48 to 9 and reduces managing the possible hypotheses to adding a single variable statement after each experiment, which has a very positive effect on both the number of experiments and the memory load. The assumption loses the complete correct hypothesis, leaving only parts to be discovered.

Consider the experiments reported earlier from this perspective. In the Bubbles task, there was no domain specific prior knowledge. Generic prior knowledge was the class of possible relations. The actual relation in Bubbles involved thresholds and complex nonlinear effects. Knowledge of a class of relations that includes this is obviously necessary. Other knowledge about possible relations were, for this particular task, not useful. In fact, it was harmful because it complicated reasoning about possible hypotheses and also led to more experiments. For the optics domain, an overall effect of generic knowledge could be found.

Overall, studies that we performed underlined the importance of generic knowledge for discovery learning and gave less indications that domain specific knowledge plays a major role. This seems to be not in line with recently reported results elsewhere (e.g., Baker & Dunbar, 2000) and our own analysis of the potential influence of domain specific prior knowledge. However, in the case of optics, we should keep in mind that our students, despite varying in level of prior knowledge, had overall little prior knowledge when they entered the experiment and (possibly as a result) also learned little. Furthermore, the optics task and domain are characterized by problems that are less prominent in other discovery tasks. In particular, it is not obvious what the variables are. For example, when a light beam passes through a lens, the distance between light and lens or the angle between light beam and horizontal axis can be taken as variable, but another reasonable choice is the angle under which the light enters the lens. Unlike many other discovery tasks, it is not obvious from either the task setting or the instruction which of these (or both) should be used. This adds an extra dimension to the discovery task that is absent in many other tasks: identifying suitable variables.

Discovery Skills

Knowing a wide range of possible hypotheses in principle enables the learner to discover a wide range of regularities. However, at the same time, it leads to a very large number of experiments that need to be done to find the right hypothesis, and it also complicates reasoning about hypotheses. Prior knowledge can reduce the number of experiments and the load of managing the hypothesis space, but to really benefit from knowledge of possible hypotheses, a learner needs additional skills to reduce the cognitive load. Specific discovery skills are needed to generate informative experiments and to update the possible hypotheses. As pointed out by Schauble et al. (1991) and others, the CVS (Chen & Klahr, 1999) is a strategy that could perform an excellent job here. It gives a very simple way to systematically generate experiments (vary one variable with respect to an earlier experiment) and use the outcomes to locally construct and modify the hypotheses. However, simple CVS no longer works when the environment contains more complex patterns. For example, in the FILE domain, simple CVS would not be effective, and more complex methods are needed. This means that discovery skills are not specific for domains but for classes of possible hypotheses. For example, the CVS method is effective for domains in which most or all variables are relevant and effects are independent. If there are many irrelevant variables, it is more effective to vary half of the variables to find those that have an effect, and if effects are not independent, then a simple CVS strategy will miss the actual relation.

The results of our experiments show an effect of discovery and metacognitive skills on discovery behavior and learning outcome but also interactions with characteristics of the domain were found. We previously reported that metacognitive skills especially have an effect in complex domains (as Optics is) and earlier, it was concluded that in abstract, nonspecific domain related tasks, discovery skills have a larger impact than in situations in which domain specific prior knowledge might play a role. These results underline what was already highlighted in the previous section, namely, that domain specific and generic prior knowledge and discovery skills might compensate for each other in certain situations.

Implications for Instruction

The implication of the preceding is that for discovery learning to be fruitful, it is most useful to teach about the area in which discovery is to take place, general mathematical concepts for formulating hypotheses (e.g., the general linear model, categorical models, classes of numerical functions, and calculus), and methods for generating and interpreting data. In our work, several methods for support were tested out. When students were provided with simple hints (containing a combination of domain specific background information and experimentation activities) together with the optics environment, this improved the results of the students (Hulshof & de Jong, 2004). Also, giving students a more structured learning environment, helping the students in setting the right steps at the right moment, and helping them to keep track of their action helped students to get better results, especially the high-intelligent students. Both these measures concerned support that was integrated in the learning environment and provided the students with support the moment they needed it. As such, it fits in a line of instructional design efforts in which complete integrated environments are being developed and evaluated (see, for an overview, de Jong & van Joolingen, 1998). However, studies like the one we presented in this chapter also show that in the area of discovery learning in simulation environments, there is an intricate relation between characteristics of the learner, the domain, and the instructional support offered.

ACKNOWLEDGMENTS

We thank Bob Wielinga (University of Amsterdam), Wouter van Joolingen (University of Twente/University of Amsterdam), and Bert Bredeweg (University of Amsterdam) for their contribution to this research program. The Optics and Peter learning environments were designed and created by Jan Wielemaker (University of Amsterdam) using SWI-Prolog. Frans Prins is currently at the Open University of the Netherlands; Pascal Wilhelm is now at the University of Twente, Hedderik van Rijn is now at the University of Groningen.

REFERENCES

Anderson, J. R. (1993). *Rules of the mind.* London: Lawrence Erlbaum Associates.

Baker, L. M., & Dunbar, K. (2000). Experimental design heuristics for scientific discovery: The use of "baseline" and "known standards" controls. *International Journal Human–Computer Studies, 52,* 335–349.

Carroll, J. B. (1993). *Human cognitive abilities. A survey of factor-analytic studies.* Cambridge, England: Cambridge University Press.

Chen, Z., & Klahr, D. (1999). All other things being equal: Acquisition and transfer of the control of variables strategy. *Child Development, 70,* 1098–1120.

Chinn, C. A., & Brewer, W. F. (1993). The role of anomalous data in knowledge acquisition: A theoretical framework and implications for science instruction. *Review of Educational Research, 63,* 1–51.

de Jong, T., de Hoog, R., & de Vries, F. (1993). Coping with complex environments: The effects of overviews and a transparent interface on learning with a computer simulation. *International Journal of Man–Machine Studies, 39,* 621–639.

de Jong, T., & van Joolingen, W. R. (1998). Scientific discovery learning with computer simulations of conceptual domains. *Review of Educational Research, 68,* 179–201.

Elio, R., & Sharf, P. B. (1990). Modeling novice-to-expert shifts in problem-solving and knowledge organization, *Cognitive Science, 14,* 579–639.

Elshout, J. J. (1987). Problem solving and education. In E. de Corte, H. Lodewijks, R. Parmentier, & P. Span (Eds.), *Learning and instruction* (pp. 259–273). Leuven: University Press.

Funke, J. (1991). Solving complex problems: Exploration and control of complex systems. In R. J. Sternberg & P. A. Frensch (Eds.), *Complex problem solving: Principles and mechanisms* (pp. 185–223). Hillsdale, NJ: Lawrence Erlbaum Associates.

Glaser, R., & Bassok, M. (1989). Learning theory and the study of instruction. *Annual Review of Psychology, 40,* 631–666.

Glaser, R., Schauble, L., Raghavan, K., & Zeitz, C. (1992). Scientific reasoning across different domains. In E. de Corte, M. C. Linn, H. Mandl, & L. Verschaffel (Eds.), *Computer-based learning environments and problem solving* (pp. 345–371). Heidelberg, Germany: Springer-Verlag.

de Groot, A. D. (1969). *Methodology, foundations of inference and research in behavioral sciences*. The Hague, Netherlands: Mouton.

Gruber, H., Renkl, A., Mandl, H., & Reiter, W. (1993). *Exploration strategies in an economics simulation game* (Forschungsbericht Nr. 21). München, Germany: Ludwig-Maximilians-Universität, Lehrstuhl für Empirische Pädagogik und Pädagogische Psychologie.

Hecht, E. (1998). *Optics* (3rd ed.). Reading, MA: Addison-Wesley.

Holland, J. H., Holyoak, K. J., Nisbett, R. E., & Thagard, P. R. (1986). *Induction: Processes of inference, learning and discovery*. Cambridge, MA: MIT Press.

Hulshof, C. D. (2001). *Discovery of ideas and ideas about discovery: The influence of prior knowledge on scientific discovery learning in computer-based simulations*. Unpublished doctoral dissertation, University of Twente, The Netherlands.

Hulshof, C. D., & de Jong, T. (2004). *Using domain-specific and generic knowledge to support discovery learning about geometrical optics in a computer-based simulation*.

Hulshof, C. D., Wilhelm, P., Beishuizen, J. J., & van Rijn, H. (in press). FILE: A tool for the study of inquiry learning. *Computers in Human Behavior*.

Klahr, D., & Dunbar, K. (1988). Dual space search during scientific reasoning. *Cognitive Science, 12*, 1–48.

Klahr, D., Fay, A. L., & Dunbar, K. (1993). Heuristics for scientific experimentation: a developmental study. *Cognitive Psychology, 25*, 11–146.

Kuhn, D., Garcia-Mila, M., Zohar, A., & Andersen, C. (1995). Strategies of knowledge acquisition. *Monographs of the Society for Research in Child Development, 60*(4, Serial No. 245).

Langley, D., Ronen, M., & Eylon, B. (1997). Light propagation and visual patterns: Preinstruction learners' conceptions. *Journal of Research in Science Teaching, 34*, 399–424.

Lavoie, D. R., & Good, R. (1988). The nature and use of prediction skills in a biological computer simulation. *Journal of Research in Science Teaching, 25*, 335–360.

Leutner, D. (1993). Guided discover learning with computer-based simulation games: Effects of adaptive and non-adaptive instructional support. *Learning and Instruction, 3*, 113–132.

Njoo, M., & de Jong, T. (1993). Exploratory learning with a computer simulation for control theory: Learning processes and instructional support. *Journal of Research in Science Teaching, 30*, 821–844.

Plötzner, R., & Spada, H. (1992). Analysis-based learning on multiple levels of mental domain representation. In E. de Corte, M. Linn, H. Mandl, & L. Verschaffel (Eds.), *Computer-based learning environments and problem solving* (pp. 103–129). Berlin, Germany: Springer-Verlag.

Prins, F. J. (2002). *Search and see: The changing roles of metacognitive skillfulness and intellectual ability during novice inductive learning in a complex computer simulated environment*. Unpublished doctoral dissertation, Leiden University, The Netherlands.

Qin, Y., & Simon, H. A. (1990). Laboratory replication of scientific discovery processes. *Cognitive Science, 14*, 281–312.

Raaheim, K. (1988). Intelligence and task novelty. In R. J. Sternberg (Ed.), *Advances in the psychology of human intelligence* (pp. 73–97). Hillsdale, NJ: Lawrence Erlbaum Associates.

Reiser, B. J., Tabak, I., Sandoval, W. A., Smith, B., Steinmuller, F., & Leone, T. J. (2001). BGuILE: Stategic and conceptual scaffolds for scientific inquiry in biology classrooms. In S. M. Carver & D. Klahr (Eds.), *Cognition and instruction: Twenty five years of progress* (pp. 236–305). Mahwah, NJ: Lawrence Erlbaum Associates.

Schauble, L., Glaser, R., Raghavan, K., & Reiner, M. (1991). Causal models and experimentation strategies in scientific reasoning. *The Journal of the Learning Sciences, 1*, 201–239.

Schunn, C. D., & Anderson, J. R. (1999). The generality/specificity of expertise in scientific reasoning. *Cognitive Science, 23*, 337–370.

Shute, V. J., & Glaser, R. (1990). A large-scale evaluation of an intelligent discovery world: Smithtown. *Interactive Learning Environments, 1*, 51–77.

Swaak, J., & de Jong, T. (1996). Measuring intuitive knowledge in science: The development of the what-if test. *Studies in Educational Evaluation, 22*, 341–362.

van Joolingen, W. R., & de Jong, T. (1997). An extended dual search space model of learning with computer simulations. *Instructional Science, 25*, 307–346.

van Rijn, H. (2003). *Exploring the limited effect of inductive discovery learning: Computational models and model-based analyses.* Unpublished doctoral dissertation, University of Amsterdam, The Netherlands.

van Rijn, H., van Someren, M., & van der Maas, H. (2003). Modeling developmental transitions. *Cognitive Science, 27*(2), 227–257.

Veenman, M. V. J. (1993). *Intellectual ability and Metacognitive skill: Determinants of discovery learning in computerized learning environments.* Unpublished doctoral dissertation, Amsterdam: University of Amsterdam.

Veenman, M. V. J., & Elshout, J. J. (1995). Differential effects of instructional support on learning in simulation environments. *Instructional Science, 22*, 363–383.

Veenman, M. V. J., & Elshout, J. J. (1999). Changes in the relation between cognitive and metacognitive skills during the acquisition of expertise. *European Journal of Psychology of Education, 14*, 509–523.

Veenman, M. V. J., Elshout, J. J., & Groen, M. G. M. (1993). Thinking aloud: Does it affect regulatory processes in learning. *Tijdschrift voor Onderwijsresearch, 18*, 322–330.

Veenman, M. V. J., Elshout, J. J., & Meijer, J. (1997). The generality vs. domain-specificity of metacognitive skills in novice learning across domains. *Learning and Instruction, 7*, 187–209.

Veenman, M. V. J., Prins, F. J., & Elshout, J. J. (2002). Initial learning in a complex computer simulated environment: The role of metacognitive skills and intellectual ability. *Computers in Human Behavior, 18*, 327–342.

Wang, M. C., Härtel, G. D., & Walberg, H. J. (1990). What influences learning? A content analysis of review literature. *Journal of Educational Research, 84*, 30–44.

Wilhelm, P. (2001). *Knowledge, skills and strategies in self-directed inductive learning.* Unpublished doctoral dissertation, Leiden University, The Netherlands.

Wilhelm, P., Beishuizen, J. J., & van Rijn, H. (in press). Studying inquiry learning with FILE. *Computers in Human Behavior.*

Author Index

Note: A page number followed by an 'n' indicates a footnote.

Subject Index